Leadership
Volume III

Leadership
Volume III

Sterling W. Sill

Bookcraft, Inc.
Salt Lake City, Utah

Library of Congress Catalog Card Number: 78-52932
ISBN 0-88494-336-4

First Printing, 1978

Lithographed in the United States of America
PUBLISHERS PRESS
Salt Lake City, Utah

Contents

Part Eight

Part Nine

Part Ten

Part One

Leadership and Success

Getting the Spirit
Priesthood Leadership
The Agenda
The Do Family
My Serving Men
The Great Success Books
Put Yourself on the Team

Chapter 1

Getting the Spirit

I like to read the thrilling story of the Creation. As the scene opens upon the universe, the earth is without form and void and darkness is upon the face of the deep. We may try to imagine what it might have been like when that brooding, unbroken darkness covered our planet. The record says that the Spirit of God moved upon the face of the waters. It also moved upon the face of the land, and we may picture what it might have been like in that thrilling moment when God first said, "Let there be light." (Genesis 1:3.) God then looked out upon his creation and called it very good. And to that statement we might respond with a strong amen.

The scriptures also tell of another important development when they say that God fashioned the human spirit in his own image and endowed it with a full set of his own attributes and potentialities. God also created the fantastic physical body of man out of the dust of the ground and gave it life and animation by putting into it the miraculous spirit of man. God gave the human soul dominion over everything upon the earth; and man's greatest dominion was to be that exercised over himself, for we get the most out of ourselves only when we develop a vigorous control over ourselves.

Referring to the Creation, God said, "Nevertheless, all things were before created; but spiritually were they created and made according to my word." (Moses 3:7.) The earth itself has a spirit. In his heavenly workshop, God gave the plants and animals, as well as his children, spirits before they were given temporal bodies. But we, the children of God, can do something which his other creations cannot do; we have been given the ability to give spirits to our own ideas and ambitions. We talk about the spirit of America, the spirit of truth, and the spirit of understanding. To what extent are we able to endow with spirit the meaningful parts of our lives?

Former President Hadley of Yale University once said that the most important thing any student ever gets out of college is the college spirit. That is when he begins to play for the school. That is when his classmates become as his brothers and their success becomes as important to him as his own.

When Columbus arrived in America, some Indians told him that there was an herb growing here which would take away fatigue. In a sense there is an herb with a similar effect growing in our own spirit. When a person has the spirit of what he is doing, he becomes invulnerable to fatigue. One seldom feels tired while winning nor quits while ahead. When we are on top of our job, we love it. When it is on top of us, we hate it. When we have an absorbing love for what we are doing, our ability to do it is multiplied. It is the spirit of accomplishment that makes the difference. Shakespeare was on the right track when he said, "Care I for the limb, the thews, the stature, bulk, and big assemblance of a man! Give me the spirit!" (King Henry IV, Part II, act 3, scene 2, line 276-8.)

Having the spirit of our endeavors is a goal worthy of continual prayer and work. The Lord said, "This is my work and my glory—to bring to pass the immortality and eternal life of man." (Moses 1:39.) He has invited us into his family enterprise, and hence it is also *our work* and *our glory* to bring to pass the immortality and eternal life of man, and to magnify that calling in us in which he himself is totally engaged. We may therefore echo Shakespeare in our prayer to God: "Give us the spirit. Give us the spirit of leadership. Give us the spirit of success. Give us the spirit of enthusiasm. Give us the spirit of industry. Give us the Spirit of the Lord."

We may pray that the Spirit of God will move upon the

face of our leadership as it once did upon the face of the waters, that we will develop the spiritual guarantees necessary for the important work we have been given to do. Certainly our leadership efforts must not be without form, and void, and covered with darkness.

A young man came to me seeking help to discover why he wasn't more profitable to himself and to the firm where he was employed. His problem was that he lacked the spirit of success. He had few convictions. He lacked the spirit of dedication and the spirit of joy in his work. There was no work that appealed to him sufficiently to merit his devotion for the rest of his life. I suggested that he read some good occupational books to give him the spirit of the particular success which he most desired. I urged him to try feeling a little more excited about what his share of the work of the world was going to be.

In contrast, I was reminded of a young man who, some time ago, became a salesman. He read the life stories of men who had done well in this field, and he became enthusiastic about their successes and about the corresponding opportunities that were now available to him. He fed his hungry mind on the spirit of the other men's accomplishments. Now no effort seemed too much for the advantages he contemplated, and in his new business he performed like a well-oiled machine with a perfect and pleasant operation set in high gear. He loved to think about and plan his work. He made me think of Sir Isaac Newton, who was once asked how he happened to discover the law of gravity and who replied, "By thinking about it all of the time." Isaac Newton's response can serve as a model for us as we prepare to do our best in the work of the Lord. We ought to ponder our projected plans and procedures a great deal more than most of us do. We need to think about them continually, or we may lose the spirit of our work.

As an example of arousing the spirit, consider Jesus. When he was twelve years old he was already found in the temple enthusiastically teaching the wise men. Luke follows up with an interesting progress report for him which says, "And Jesus increased in wisdom and stature, and in favour with God and man." (Luke 2:52.) Thus, when the time for his ministry arrived he was already in emotional and spiritual high gear and completely ready for the finest success.

The Prophet Joseph Smith received from the Lord a revelation for his father in which the qualifications for the labors of the ministry are set forth. The Lord said: "Therefore, O ye that embark in the service of God, see that ye serve him with all your heart, might, mind and strength, that ye may stand blameless before God at the last day. Therefore, if ye have desires to serve God ye are called to the work." (D&C 4:2, 3.)

This scripture indicates the spirit needed for success in leadership. We should undertake a comparable preparation in seeking to develop the necessary ambition. Certainly we need the Spirit of the Lord to impart maximum drive to our enthusiasm. The Lord has said, "And if ye receive not the Spirit ye shall not teach." (D&C 42:14.) And without the spirit, ye shall not undertake to lead. But with the proper spirit of leadership every success is placed within our easy reach. Not only does a strong desire help us to get that spirit, but it is a part of the call to serve and an important source of the industry with which to carry out our tasks.

We live in an age when the Lord is trying to prepare the world for the glorious second coming of Christ and the inauguration of the millennial reign upon the earth. We are the ones he must depend on for excellence and leadership. We not only need the know-how, we need the know-what and the know-why and the know-when. We need the right attitudes, skills, habits, and personality traits, in addition to our faith and works.

Thus we might again pray unto the Lord and say: "Give us the spirit. Give us the spirit of success. Give us the spirit of enthusiasm. Give us the spirit of dependability. Give us the spirit of accomplishment. Give us the spirit of faith. Give us the spirit of industry. Give us the spirit of righteousness. And give us the Spirit of the Lord."

Chapter 2

Priesthood Leadership

In the Church we say that the priesthood is the *authority* to act in the name of the Lord. But the leadership is the *ability* to act in the name of the Lord. I suppose one isn't of very great consequence without the other. That is to say, what good is it if a missionary has the authority to make converts if he doesn't have the ability to make converts? A home teacher may have the authority of an apostle, but if he lacks the skills and dedication of leadership the authority may be wasted. The Lord gives us the authority, but he asks us to develop the ability. In the division of our responsibilities he furnishes the capital, but we must supply the labor to make it effective.

That is the reason why we hold priesthood leadership meetings. They are somewhat like business or scientific conventions. One of the biggest businesses in the world is that of holding conventions. Every week throughout this country and every other progressive country, men and women in every field are meeting together to discuss their problems, exchange ideas, and try to find more effective means to accomplishment.

We think of our world as having many problems, but a lot of them boil down to just one. I believe that it doesn't matter very much whether the desired accomplishment is to do church work, build a business, or run an empire; the problem is usually leadership.

Those who are the leaders in their stakes and wards are serving at the intake of the Church. More than any other consideration, it is they who will determine the quality of the membership of the Church in their stakes for time and in eternity. The scripture says we reap what we sow, but that is only a part of the fact. Mostly we reap as somebody else sows for us. We reap as our parents have sown, we reap as our teachers have sown, and one of the most exciting ideas is that all the people in a given stake, whether members or nonmembers, will reap as its leaders sow. The people will not get to the celestial kingdom merely by what *they* do alone, on their own initiative, but in large measure because of what the leaders do and they can get the people to do.

Over the years, I took some liberties with President Joseph Fielding Smith. I was his bishop for ten years, and one time I said to him, "President Smith, while I was reading in your book the other night I found some false doctrine." Of course, he was interested in knowing just where he had made his mistake. I said to him, "You say in your book that to become a son of perdition is the worst sin. And I think I can prove to you that there is a sin 770 times worse than that." He had never heard of such a serious sin, so I told him about having been out in a stake the week before. In one ward, 87 percent of the Aaronic Priesthood young men received an individual award. In another, with the same kind of boys but with different kind of leaders, 10 percent received an award. That is, in one ward the accomplishment rose to 87 percent and in another it rested at 10 percent.

Now, here is an interesting experiment to try. If you change the leaders, you substantially change the scores. That is, if you put the 87 percent leaders with the boys having a 10 percent accomplishment, the score will immediately begin to rise until it rests at 87 percent; whereas, if you put the poor leaders with the great accomplishment, the accomplishment will soon begin to fall. We usually rise to the level of our leadership. Now, suppose that these scores were typical of all of the other people in these two wards, and suppose each of these wards had a membership of one thousand. In one ward 870 people are going to get their blessings and in the other ward only 100 people will get their blessings. That means that in the ward with the poor leaders 770 people are going to lose their blessings, not for anything particularly that they did, but because of what the leaders did (or did not) do.

I suggested to President Smith that if I became a son of perdition only one person would lose his blessings as a consequence; but that if I became a poor bishop, 770 people could lose their blessings. Therefore, it might be argued (stretching things a little for the sake of the argument, it is true) that, at least from one point of view, to be a poor bishop might be a sin 770 times as bad as being a son of perdition. President Smith didn't say what he thought of my theology. I don't know what you may think of it. I am not quite sure even what I myself may think about it. But one thing is clear—it is pretty difficult to rise above our leadership.

What a wonderful advantage it gives us when we have good parents and good teachers and good leaders! I would like to pay my tribute to the possibilities of such leaders in the words that were once used by Thomas Carlyle as he appraised the influences that had made the English-speaking nations great. England and her offshoot nations are the only nations that have made the idea of democracy and free enterprise work on a large scale over a long period. Carlyle gave credit to the system of government that obtained in England from the time of the Norman conquest down to the time of Charles I, when England was ruled by peers. According to Carlyle, the king had nominated each of these men by saying, "Come you to me, sir, come out of the common level of the people, come here and take this district of country and make it into your own image, more or less. Be a king under me, and understand that this is your function."

Then Carlyle said: "I say that this is the most divine thing that a human being can do to another human being. And no other kind of thing whatever has so much of the character of God Almighty's divine government as this thing we see that went on all over England. And that is the grand soul of England's history."

It seems to me that in almost exactly the same way the Lord has said to us, "You come out of this common level of the people and take this little section of the Church and make it into your own image, more or less." That is, you take this quorum or this Sunday School class or this ward or this function of the high council and develop in it the same excellence and godliness that you have in yourself, and by this process you develop others into your accomplishment image. And isn't that exactly what always happens?

Example is a great power. We tend to do what we see and hear others do. That is the way we learn to walk, to talk, and to do every other thing. We also reform others more easily when we walk uprightly. Example is also one of the important ways that we get our enthusiasm, our faith, and our leadership effectiveness. That is, we absorb them readymade from someone else; and then, around their newly acquired resolutions and ideas, the good leader builds in his followers success habits. A good habit is closely associated with the effectiveness of example and is another of the world's great powers. What the rails are to the streamliner, habit is to success. As the rails support and guide the streamliner, so habit supports and guides our success.

An important business of life is to succeed. God did not give us our miraculous potentialities and then expect us to waste our lives in failure. He did not give us these potentially magnificent minds, these miraculous personalities, and these fantastic physical powers without expecting the greatest kind of accomplishment in us and in those for whom we have responsibility. And unless we build up our own dedication and success, the accomplishment will be distorted in the lives of those who follow us.

Man is primarily a thinking being. A great psychologist once asked the question, "How would you like to create your own mind?" But isn't that exactly what we all do? It has been said that the mind is made up by what it feeds upon. The mind, like the dyer's hand, is colored by what it holds. If I hold in my hand a sponge filled with purple dye, my hand becomes purple, and if I hold in my mind and heart great ideas of righteousness and faith in God, my whole personality is colored accordingly. We need to get great ambitions, great enthusiasms for righteousness, and great initiative into the lives of those who make up the membership in the Church of Jesus Christ.

Herbert Spencer once said that the ability to organize is the ability to bring all available energy to bear upon the particular problems at hand at the precise time when needed. This involves a high order of discipline in ourselves and a substantial ability to transfer the effects of that discipline to others.

Frequently we think of ourselves as having great faith. We bear fervent testimony, but we do not always carry through on the actual performance. With no one to effectively keep our score, it becomes pretty easy to allow our leadership to degenerate into a kind of mere verbal Christianity.

You may be interested to know that I know as much about *how* to be a great baseball pitcher as Vernon Law does. You remember that Vernon Law was the Pittsburgh pitcher who won the baseball World Series from the New York Yankees some years back. I was in Pittsburgh just after this happened, and I said to him: "Vernon, I would like to be a great baseball pitcher. Would you teach me how to be a great baseball pitcher?"

"I would be very glad to," he replied. Then he explained, "You hold the ball like this, then you do the windup like this, and then you throw the ball like this."

"Is that all there is to it?" I asked.

"That is all that I ever do," he responded.

I asked him, "Will you go through it again with me so that I will be sure not to miss anything?" Again he showed me exactly how to hold the ball and exactly how to do the windup and exactly how to deliver the ball. At that minute he was the greatest authority on that idea that there was in the world. I now did it under his direction in exactly the way he told me to do it—except that, when I threw the ball, it didn't even get down to where the catcher was.

Now, what is the difference between Sterling Sill and Vernon Law, so far as being a great baseball pitcher is concerned? There may be several other differences, but one is that Vernon Law has thrown the ball a few million times.

That is, he has practiced and drilled and persisted in throwing the ball in exactly the right way over a long period, until he does it most effectively almost automatically.

I once asked a group of missionaries if they knew why Vernon Law was so much better as a baseball pitcher than Sterling Sill, and they didn't know. I told them that Vernon Law had a big, wonderful, powerful pitching arm, and that it just looked as if you couldn't fail to be a great pitcher with the power and control of such an arm. Then I showed them the little, puny arm that the Lord had given me. I have as much muscle on the back of my arm as on the front. They could all immediately see why I was not a great baseball pitcher. And yet *my* arm was probably just as good as Vernon Law's arm when the Lord first gave them to us. But it is what we have done (or not done) with them since that time that has made the difference.

There is no excellence without labor, there is no championship without skill, and there is no skill either in athletics or Church work without constant, expert study, drill and practice. The great athletes all develop skill in their muscles as well as know-how in their brains. There are a lot of potentially great leaders who have knowledge, but no dexterity; they have testimony, but no competence; they have brains, but no skill; they own a kit of tools, but don't know how to use them. In most of those places where we fall down, the problem comes because we don't know how to succeed.

For example, some time ago my sister came to see me, and as we sat and reminisced she was talking about those days when she was being courted by the young man who became her husband. She started out by entertaining him in our little family living room, which was probably 10 feet by 12 feet in size, and our father was usually sitting reading in one corner. She soon decided against this arrangement, because she said our father was not very friendly to her boyfriend. Now, I think I knew our father a little better than she did, and I don't think there was anything in the world that our father wanted more than to be friendly. But he just didn't know how. He certainly hadn't practiced being friendly as hard or as long or as expertly as Vernon Law had practiced throwing a baseball.

Suppose someone should ask you to teach them how to be friendly, how would you go about it? It is an interesting fact that virtually everybody wants to be a warm, friendly, pleasant, helpful person, even though we do not all have the reputations of being that kind of person. We all know how to do it in our brains, but we may never have been able to get that skill transferred over into our personalities by practice. This example of learning to be friendly may be a little too difficult, so suppose we take the easier and related job of learning to shake hands.

Some time ago, I was talking with a group of missionaries about shaking hands. It might seem a little ridiculous to talk to anybody about how to shake hands. Everybody knows how to do that from the time he is two years old. You just shake hands. But think how many different ways there are to do it. When you shake hands with some people, you feel as if you have a dead fish by the tail. Others make you think you have put your hand into a bone crusher. When you shake with some people, you think they are trying to pull your arm out of its socket. There are still other methods—like the man who shook hands with ten people, one of whom was me. He proceeded at about a mile a minute while he was talking with somebody over his left shoulder at the same time. I don't think he had any idea who he had shaken hands with, nor did he seem to care very much. And for some reason I did not get any great thrill or uplift out of his handshake.

Many years ago, a prominent businessman from New York was in Salt Lake, and he and I were up at the Church Office Building when President David O. McKay invited us to come into his office. I am going to tell you everything that happened. President McKay took this man by the hand with a fine, firm, friendly pressure. He wasn't in a hurry. He held on while he looked this man in the eye and told him a joke and asked him a few things about himself, and then he told him a little bit about the Church. Then he put an arm around him and hugged him a little. Nothing very profound was said, but when we got out of there, this man said, "That is one of the greatest experiences I have ever had in my lifetime."

Now, President McKay did not just shake with his hand; he shook with that light in his eye and the warmth that came out of his heart and the radioactivity by which you could feel his spirit. Every time I ever shook hands with President McKay it seemed to me that he thought I was one of the greatest persons in the world. And this is how other people felt when they shook hands with President McKay, because that is how President McKay felt about people. President McKay knew how to shake hands and how to inspire other people with faith. In other words, President McKay put excellence into his handshake. If some have difficulty in getting excellence into their handshake, they may have even more trouble in getting it into their home teaching or their family home evenings or their missionary discussions. We can learn to do better in a great many areas. Merely having the authority to do Church work does not mean that we have the ability to do Church work. The tragedy of this situation is that when we fall down, we are creating others in our own image who have this same disability, and the work of the Lord suffers as a consequence.

Winston Churchill once said that he was not appointed Her Majesty's Prime Minister to liquidate the British Empire. Yet sometimes the welfare of those we lead goes down at such a pace that it is necessary for changes in office to be made so that our share of the work of the Lord is not liquidated. We each need to learn how to do things better and then to motivate ourselves to actually *do* better.

This all means that we develop the knowledge, the attitudes, the skills, the habits and the personality traits of true leadership effectiveness, which includes doing in addition to knowing or talking or promising. To be able to get the ship into port is an ability that carries a high value tag in every field.

A commercial company may have a group of salesmen who altogether make two hundred thousand dollars in commissions in a year under one sales manager. But get them a more skillful sales manager and the same group of men may soon be making eight hundred thousand dollars a year. That is, the actual workers are worth two hundred thousand dollars, but the leadership may be worth six hundred thousand dollars. The Lord has said that the worth of a soul is very great in his sight. If a missionary or a home teacher labors all of his days and brings but one soul to the Lord, how great his reward shall be. But under a different kind of mission president or a different kind of stake leader, that same worker, because of greater leadership, may bring many souls to the Lord. One great mission president or one great bishop may multiply by ten the effectiveness of those who serve under his direction.

If you were going to fight a national war against a strong, relentless enemy, you would want to get your forces organized with some generals, colonels, majors, captains, sergeants, corporals, and privates. You would want to get them all well trained so that, like a championship football team, each man would expertly know his job and be able to carry it off with great skill. But the most important thing you would want to have would be a commanding general who could guarantee victories for his army. As has been said, "All wars are either lost or won in the tents of the generals." And all leaders must bear the responsibility that goes with their authority. We who are endowed with the authority of the Lord must not fail to develop the leadership to make the authority effective.

President John Taylor once said, "If you do not magnify your calling, God will hold you responsible for those you might have saved, had you done your duty." How many of us actually believe that? If you or I do not magnify our callings, do you really think that God will debit our accounts with the losses that result? President Taylor seemed to think that he will.

It is the job of the home teacher not merely to make visits but to make converts. To say our prayers is not enough. To bear our testimony is not enough. To do the best we can is not enough. We must know the laws governing each particular success, and we must actually get each job done.

So we come back again to where we began. The basic problem which encompasses many other problems is leadership. Through our leadership we create others in our own image, more or less. May God bless us that in both the qualitative and quantitative aspects our leadership may be more and not less.

Chapter 3

The Agenda

One of the most effective means of leadership accomplishment is the habitual use of a well-planned agenda. An agenda is usually thought of as a list of items to be discussed at a meeting, arranged in a logical sequence.

The dictionary describes an agenda as a memorandum of responsibilities to be performed. It is a list of important duties that should be taken care of. Of course, before it can be prepared, the matters to be discussed have to be chosen so that they can be set down in writing. When the agenda has been thoughtfully prepared, the problems will already have been partly solved.

The dictionary points out an interesting relationship between the words *agenda* and *credenda*. An agenda is a list of duties that should be taken care of and a credenda is a list of doctrines that should be believed in. In these two words we might see something of the traditional conflict that has always existed between our deeds and our creeds. To insure that important matters are discussed in a meeting, good business practice usually indicates that a letter be sent to those who will attend, outlining the matters to be considered.

A written explanation of what will be on the agenda will motivate those involved to think through the matters that will be considered, and will encourage them to have all supplementary material available. This procedure will also enable those attending to make all necessary preparation to protect their interests and those of the organization they serve.

If those conducting an important meeting do not have a well-planned agenda in writing, the meeting usually will not be nearly as productive. Those present may have to guess at the pertinent facts and depend upon memory, a faculty which is not always reliable.

A good agenda has several additional uses. I know a very successful salesman who makes up a written agenda for himself before he undertakes any important sale. He usually has a fact-finding interview with the prospective buyer. Then, in a kind of sales rehearsal, he makes a written outline of the specific points he wants to make. Every good salesman needs an agenda of facts, thoughts and reasons as to why and how the sale can best be made.

In addition to making an agenda for every sale, a good salesman may also make an agenda for each of those days, weeks, months and years that are soon to become part of his career. A good agenda, prepared and written down well in advance of its date of use, will help to mature his thinking and keep him on course so that his program will not be disrupted by unscheduled distractions.

I know a man who does a great deal of personal interviewing. He has an agenda of questions to use that have been worked out in advance. In this way he makes certain that he will get all the necessary information; and while he is filling in the answers to his questions, he is also getting a written account of the interview. As well as recording the person's answers, he notes his attitudes and ambitions.

There is at large a conflicting philosophy to that of using the agenda, under which many people hold their meetings and conduct their business and make their sales on a kind of hit-and-miss basis. Because these people do things only as the thoughts occur to them, they never put much real planning or forethought into their work. Rather, they act on their impulses with whatever may come into their hands or minds. This lesser philosophy, featuring a *lack* of planning, is expressed in the recurring theme of the song which says,

"Doing what comes naturally." Such people allow themselves to be governed largely by conditions, or by whichever wind may be blowing at the moment.

Dr. Leon Tucker, a great teacher of the Bible, used to tell a story of a lady who had poor health. As her friend's would ask her how she was, she would reply, "I am feeling as well as could be expected under the circumstances." In making a comparison with another kind of poor health, Dr. Tucker said, "Far too many people, including a lot of Christians, allow themselves to live most of their lives 'under the circumstances' "; whereas everyone is far more successful when he lives above and ahead of and beyond the circumstances. Someone once asked Napoleon, "How are conditions?" The great emperor replied, "I make conditions." When we live at our best, so do we.

At one point, as Julius Caesar was in the process of conquering the world, he was crossing a rough sea during a severe storm. The captain of the ship expressed his serious concern for the safety of those aboard. "Fear not," said his famous guest, "thy boat carries Caesar." A great part of Caesar's success was his confidence of controlling conditions. When we fail to do this, our conditions will control us. When we succumb to our temptations or allow ourselves to be overpowered by our weaknesses, we are living under the circumstances.

In excusing his mediocrity, a salesman said to his sales manager, "I think I did pretty well under the circumstances." His manager responded, "What in the world were you doing way down there?" And that is a good question for many of us to ask ourselves. When we have no agenda we let all kinds of unauthorized activities get into our programs, and dilute our effectiveness. On the other hand, if we had a good agenda, planned well in advance, thoughtfully considered, and completely followed, we would always be the master of our circumstances.

Frequently we imitate the weathercock who waits to see which breeze is going to blow before he decides what his own direction will be. We may resemble the chameleon that doesn't know what his color will be until he enters his next environment—we wait to see what our circumstances will be before we make up our minds about what kind of people we are going to be. Thus we wait on luck, chance, conditions, and the devil.

When a person associates with those who drink or smoke or take dope or tell lies, he is likely to feel that under the circumstances it might be well for him to do those things also, no matter how unprofitable they may be. We tend to excuse our lack of judgment by saying, "When in Rome, do as the Romans do." Hence when we breathe the air of dishonesty, atheism or immorality, we have a strong inclination to take up the habit. We reason that if others are doing it, it must be all right. The philosophy of "everybody's doing it," however, is a doctrine of weakness and evil.

We must not compromise our excellence, either in the work of the Lord, in the work of the world, or in our personal affairs, as all weakness is contagious and harmful. The story is told of a woman running a boardinghouse who was showing a certain room to a prospective tenant. The tenant was critical of several defects. The woman admitted that the place was not very clean and there were other things wrong with it. The woman said, "But, as a *whole*, don't you think it is quite satisfactory?" The prospective tenant replied: "Yes, as a *hole*, it does very well. However, as a place to live, I don't think I could be very happy here."

This situation is related to that of the man who said to his friend, "For a jerk, don't you think I have come quite a long way?" Jerks, poor managers and sinners don't have a strong, well-planned agenda to which they have made a wholehearted commitment. A good agenda also greatly reduces the chances for errors and the necessity for making snap judgments. Our agenda tells us what should be on the program and what should be left off. Under formal rules of order it can be unconstitutional and unfair to take action on any matter that is not listed on an agenda. But it may also be unprofitable and unwise.

Somebody has figured out that there are at least two ways to pack a trunk. One way is to have a place prepared for everything and then see that everything goes into its place.

One compartment may be reserved for your shoes, one for your shirts, and these and all the other items are exactly fitted in those places where they belong. In that way all available space is utilized to the best possible advantage. The other way to pack a trunk is to dump everything into it helter-skelter, with no order and no priorities—that is, the trunk has no agenda.

I know of a doctor who packs his office by loading it helter-skelter with patients who are required to wait for hours before their turn comes. I don't know how successful he is in his efforts to preserve their health, but he is certainly very successful in wasting their time. This doctor would do well to learn more about how to organize his day. Similarly a lot of us would do well to learn how better to organize our lives.

Now, what are we going to do about organizing an agenda for ourselves? Certainly there isn't time for us to make all the possible mistakes personally. That is a luxury we can't afford. And when we rationalize our mistakes by saying that everybody's doing it we are just kidding ourselves. Some people are doing some wrong things and some are doing other wrong things, but no one does all of them. Likewise it is impossible to take advantage of all of the good experiences, and this makes it even more necessary to have some system of priorities. We must work out what we want on our own life's agenda.

Someone has said that the four most important dates in anyone's life are these: The day he is born; that is when a new life comes into being. The date he is married; that is when a new family is organized. The day he selects his life's work; that will determine the amount of his service and his own self-development. The date on which he dies; that is the day he graduates from life with either honors or dishonors.

Henry Thoreau said that we should thank God every day of our lives for the privilege of having been born. He went on to speculate on what it might have been like if we had never been born. He pointed out some of the excitement and accomplishments we would have missed in that case. What Mr. Thoreau may not have known was that one-third of all of the children of God never *were* born and never can be born because they didn't comply with God's agenda prepared for their first estate. When Lucifer rebelled against God, someone in the propaganda field may have said "Everybody's doing it," in which case all who fell for that line failed to graduate into their second estate.

Every spirit child of God hungers for a body. Those unembodied spirits who appeared to Jesus in his day preferred to inhabit the bodies of swine rather than to have no bodies at all. With our present battery of birth-control pills and our high abortion rate, however, we are making it pretty rough for even those who passed the requirements of their first estate to be born. We ought to remove all immorality and disobedience from the agenda. Nothing destroys our leadership more than our fundamental internal conflicts.

We ought to have a good education placed high on our life's agenda. We should follow the instruction of Jesus and be born again so that we can become devoted members of his kingdom. We should put a godly character and a temple marriage on the agenda. We ought to make sure that the quality of our faith and our works will entitle us, upon graduation from this life, to enter the celestial kingdom.

We need to understand that every principle and ordinance of the gospel has to do with the celestial kingdom. For example, if we are only interested in the lower kingdoms it is not necessary to keep our minds healthy and our bodies clean. But if we plan to qualify for the presence of God in celestial glory, we had better put each of the Ten Commandments and the other gospel principles on the agenda to be lived under the strictest discipline. And we had better be sure to leave off the agenda the practice of all those things about which God has given us stern warnings by saying, "Thou shalt not." If the enticements of atheism and immorality were forbidden by God when he appeared on the top of Mount Sinai, we had better not include them now in any program for our own lives.

We should never make a decision in anger or fear or undue haste. A great businessman once said that one of the best aids to his success was to make a list before undertaking a task, a list of those things he would not do under any circumstances. The Lord thundered one such list from the top of Mount Sinai some thirty-four hundred years ago. If we make up our minds about those things that we must not do, we will have all of our time free for those things that we should do.

Every one of God's commands comes to us with a blessing of righteousness, prosperity and happiness attached. It has been said that the scriptures are in effect a large collection of promissory notes. It is our privilege and opportunity to put ourselves in the position of collecting on these notes, and the best way of establishing the priorities that will help us to qualify is to get them into our life's agenda.

Chapter 4

The
Do Family

If you were trying to identify the most important message given by the Savior of the world while he was here upon earth, what would it be? If we could effectively learn that lesson and govern our lives accordingly, we would almost automatically become wise and successful. Jesus was not only the Son of God, but he was the wisest of God's spirit children. He was the first begotten in the spirit and the Only Begotten in the flesh. Because he was the most capable of all the intelligences of heaven, he was the one that could help us most. He announced the purpose of his own mission by saying, "I am come that they might have life and that they might have it more abundantly." (John 10:10.) That abundance can only be brought about in our lives if we follow his directions.

If I were going to try to identify his most important message, it would be the one in which one of his servants said, "Be ye doers of the word. . . ." (James 1:22.) One of the greatest thoughts in the world is that even the finest ideas or programs have no value unless we do something about them. That is, nothing ever works unless we work. The religion of Christ is much more than a set of great ideas; it is a set of great activities. The principles of the gospel are not only things to think about; they are things to do and ideals to live by. When Jesus came among us saying "Follow me," he knew where he was going and what we would have to do to obey that command.

The Lord still has this message in mind. In our own day he has said, "Now let every man learn his duty, and to act in the office in which he is appointed, in all diligence. He that is slothful shall not be counted worthy to stand, and he that learns not his duty and shows himself not approved shall not be counted worthy to stand." (D&C 107:99-100.)

As God's greatest institution he has given us the family. The family is the basis of most of our education, success, and happiness. God said that it is not good for man to be alone. But it is not good for woman to be alone either, and it is not good for a child to be alone. Each by himself is incomplete. It is a part of our good fortune that we are all members of the greatest of all families—the family of God.

The benefits that have come through great families are inspiring. There are royal families, families of inventors, and families of wealth. There is the family of Adam and the family of Abraham. The Lord said to Abraham, "And in thy seed shall all the nations of the earth be blessed." (Genesis 26:4.) It is interesting that ideas, activities, convictions, and beliefs also come in families. And one of the most profitable families for us to get acquainted with is the "DO" family.

In a rural section of southern California a Mexican mother died, leaving eight children. The oldest girl, not yet seventeen, was a small child upon whose frail shoulders fell the burden of caring for her brothers and sisters. The neighbors watched her as she took up the task with courage and ability. She kept all of her family members clean, well fed, and in school. She did every part of her task with unusual competence and good cheer.

One day, a neighbor woman complimented her on her great achievement. The girl replied, "I can take no credit for something that I have to do."

"But, my dear," said the friend, "you don't *have to*. No one can require this labor of you."

The girl thought for a moment and said, "That may be true, but what about the 'have to' I have inside of me?"

This unschooled little Mexican girl gave utterance to one

of the most important phases of leadership success. "Have to" consists of that "internal pressure of responsibility." It is an impelling sense of urgency to do right. It was this same inside "have to" that made Socrates say, "Whatever duty thou assignest me, sooner will I die a thousand times than to forsake it." This important leadership quality is more than initiative. It is a combination of enterprise, conscience, and a godly pressure to do right that always distinguishes human beings at their best.

During World War I the captain of a gunboat gave the order for his ship to try to rescue a stricken comrade vessel. The mate pointed out to the captain the many hazards of their projected undertaking. Their return would surely be cut off, leaving little chance for them to get back to port. The captain said to the mate, "We *have to* go out, we *don't have to* come back."

Young Abraham Lincoln had a lot of "have to" which was building up in his heart from his earliest years. He spent his evenings lying before the open fire reading the Bible and *The Life of Washington*. He said, "I will prepare myself now and take my chances when the opportunity arrives." And when the chance came, Abe was ready. His great "have to" never left him. Later he said: "I am not bound to win, but I am bound to be true. I am not bound to succeed, but I am bound to live by the best light that I have. I will stand with anybody that stands right, and I will part from anybody when he goes wrong." It is this "have to" that keeps great men going against great odds until the cause is won.

Many years ago, Elbert Hubbard wrote a famous story entitled, *A Message to Garcia*. It told of an impossible mission which succeeded because the one who carried the message had enough "have to" to work his way through the jungles against insurmountable odds, swim dangerous rivers, find his man, and deliver his message.

But it is not good for "have to" to be alone, so some other helpful members of the "DO" family are necessary. One of them is "can do."

A story from *The Arabian Nights* is about a young man named Aladdin who had an unusual lamp. By rubbing this lamp he summoned a giant genie to do his bidding. Nothing was impossible to Aladdin's genie. This helpful servant built a beautiful palace for Aladdin and gave him wealth, power, and luxury. The genie made it possible for Aladdin to marry the princess and live happily ever after.

Actually, every one of us has a potential genie sleeping inside him with a miraculous power to be aroused. Someone has appropriately named our genie "Can Do." It took Aladdin quite a while to find out how to handle his giant's strength, and it also takes a bit of doing for us to develop our "can do." But with enough "can do," nothing is impossible. When we do intelligent planning and make good decisions about things, our "can do" often becomes about ten feet tall.

We can help our "can do" by reading some good books about accomplishment. We need to get the spirit of success. And we learn to do by doing. Thinkers, hearers, and talkers are a dime a dozen. Doers are more rare. Let us emphasize the statement previously quoted: "Be ye doers of the word, and not hearers only, deceiving your own selves." (James 1:22.) Mere talkers deceive themselves. As someone has said,"When all is said and done, there is usually a lot more said than done." This apt and anonymous sentence comes to mind: "What miracles we could accomplish if our hands moved as fast as our tongues!"

We have another great member of the "DO" family to meet named "Ought To Do."

Emerson once said, "What I need more than anything else is someone or something to get me to do the things that I already know for sure that I ought to do." That is the primary need of every seeker after success. Edward Everett Hale once said: "I am only one, but I am one. I can't do everything, but I can do something. What I can do, that I ought to do. And what I ought to do, by the grace of God, I will do."

"Ought to do" has a twin named "Want To Do."

One of the great secrets of success is to learn to WANT in capital letters. No one would be very happy without a "want to" in his family. Shakespeare said, "Desire is the pilot of the soul." A great American prophet explains that God grants unto every man according to his desires. (See Alma 41:5.) "Want to," then, is another genie of giant power.

There is another brilliant member of this "DO" family called, "Plan To."

A government survey indicated that most people could actually do the work involved in the assignments they were given, but that 14 percent worked their way to the top because they not only could do the work effectively but were also capable of the "follow-through" on their own initiative. Of this group, 2 percent became the real leaders because they could not only do the work and supply their own supervision, but they could also plan.

Then there is "Expect To."

Someone has said that our lives are dyed the color of our imaginations. One of our best allies as we seek success is high expectations. One of the devil's beatitudes says, "Expect nothing and you will never be disappointed." This is a principle of weakness and failure. When we have strong expectations for the very best, assisted by other giants such as "plan to," "want to," and "have to," making our way easier, then, with "can do," and "will do," some wonderful victories are assured.

"Will" is one of the most powerful members of the "DO" family:

> You *will* be what you will *to* be;
> Let failure find its false content
> In the poor word *environment*,
> But spirit scorns it, and is free.
>
> Will masters time, it conquers space,
> It cows that boastful trickster Chance
> And bids the tyrant Circumstance
> Uncrown, and fill a servant's place.
>
> The human will, that force unseen,
> The offspring of the deathless soul
> Can hew the way to any goal,
> Though walls of granite intervene.

> Be not impatient in delay,
> But wait as one who understands;
> When spirit rises and commands
> The gods are ready to obey.

"Will" is the one who makes up his mind and gives the orders for the job to be done.

The prophet Nephi had a great "will do," whereas his brothers, Laman and Lemuel, were afraid and ran away. They sided with their lesser selves. They cultivated weakness whereas Nephi lived at his best. He said, "I will go and *do* the things which the Lord hath commanded, for I know that the Lord giveth no commandments unto the children of men, save he shall prepare a way for them that they may accomplish the thing which he commandeth them." (1 Nephi 3:7.) The big difference between Nephi and his older brothers is that Nephi had will power, whereas Laman and Lemuel had won't power.

What an exciting experience to have "will do" as a member of our own success family! Our "have to" and our "can do" and our "want to" and our "ought to" and our "expect to" and our "plan to" and our "will do" give us membership in another fine family—the "DONE" family.

Two of the members of this family are "have done" and "well done." Everything we gain, including our eternal exaltation, will be determined by what we have done. Jesus gave us a great idea when he said, "If ye know these things, happy are ye if ye do them." (John 13:17.) Carl Erskine, the famous Brooklyn baseball pitcher, said, "I never pray to win; I just pray to be in my best form." There are no better prayers than those which seek to put us in our best form. Our best form is the form that God intended us always to maintain.

In the Garden of Gethsemane, Jesus said: ". . . . I have finished the work which thou gavest me to do. And now, O Father, glorify thou me with thine own self with the glory which I had with thee before the world was." (John 17:4-5.) Later, upon the cross, he said, "It is finished." (John 19:30.) That is, he had done the job.

In any race, as in the race of life, people congregate at the finish line. No one is very interested in how many starts we made, but everyone likes to know how well we finish. The apostle Paul was a great finisher. As a prisoner in Rome, he wrote to his young friend Timothy and said: "For I am now ready to be offered, and the time of my departure is at hand. I have fought a good fight, I have finished my course, I have kept the faith." (2 Timothy 4:6-7.)

May the Lord help us to be doers of his work, to do it well, to do it enthusiastically, and to do it now. If we perform in this way, the Lord will say to us, as did the lord in the parable of the talents, "Well done, thou good and faithful servant."

Chapter 5

My
Serving Men

One of the important factors determining our accomplishments is the amount and quality of the help we receive along life's way. In the past some people have commanded great armies or owned large numbers of slaves or have employed many servants to assist them. In earlier days most of the work of the world was done by the puny muscle power of men and animals, and for thousands of years very little progress was made. Then came giant knowledge explosions to start us on our way. This change came gradually at first as we invented the iron horse, the horseless carriage, and the wireless telephone and made them our servants.

We used to dream of having powerful genies, seven-league boots, and magic carpets. In our imaginations these were our slaves to help us build our mansions, provide our food, perform our labors, and carry us to our destinations with great speed. But in recent years we have far surpassed the wildest of our earlier dreams. We now fly through the stratosphere faster than sound. We may live in the depths of the ocean and sail under the polar icecap.

With modern farm machinery, one man can now raise more food than an army of slaves could have a few years ago. The most ordinary man in most western nations may now command the services of a telephone, air conditioning, a vacuum sweeper, an automobile, a refrigerator, and a color television. He may summon food from every corner of the world. He has servants located around the earth collecting news to be printed on paper and laid on his front porch, sometimes on the very day that the events take place.

By flipping a switch, he can flood his domain with light, and by turning a knob, he can summon any number of entertainers, musicians, lecturers, news analysts, or financial experts to entertain, advise, or enrich him. Using his telephone, he can send his voice to any part of the world and receive answers to his questions in the same minute they are asked. Through his television set he can see and hear what is taking place in any foreign land almost as if he were there in person. On occasions he can even travel to the moon.

Instead of the lowly, uneducated servants of former days, who had to be maintained at great expense, we may now staff our homes with the wisest college professors, the greatest statesmen, the most successful financial advisors, and the greatest athletes with virtually no cost or obligation to us. But there is a catch. If we are to make the most of these outside situations, we must have some inside keys to make the benefits meaningful. Success is never in New York, or London, or Chicago, or Moscow; it is in us. If we do not find peace and plenty in ourselves, we will never find them anywhere else.

The scriptures say that no gift is profitable which we are unable to receive. (See D&C 88:33.) Television would have been possible in the Dark Ages; but the people were not able to produce or receive it. Cain and Abel were offered equal opportunities; but because of a difference in their abilities to receive the proffered blessings, Cain brought the most severe punishments upon himself. How we respond to the miracles and wonders of our day will determine whether we receive good or evil from them.

The following is attributed to Francis Bacon:

It is not what we eat but what we digest that makes us strong.
It is not what we earn but what we save that makes us rich.
It is not what we read but what we remember that makes us learned.

It is not what we think but what we do that makes us
  successful.
It is not what we preach but what we practice that makes us
  Christians.

Thus, we might ask ourselves how we can make the most
of our own situation.

Rudyard Kipling gave us some interesting keys to
accomplishment when he wrote:

> I keep six honest serving men
> (They taught me all I knew);
> Their names are What and Why and When
> And How and Where and Who.

Each of us can also have these six serving men who will
act as the powerful genies of our leadership success. We must
not make the mistake of hiding them within the dark recesses
of ourselves. Suppose we get a little better acquainted with
these interesting serving men and arrange to have these
servants help us more effectively.

First, here is Mr. What. The whats of our lives are
important. Our way is sometimes complicated because we
have a seemingly infinite variety of good and bad from which
to choose.

The word *infinite* refers to something that is endless,
inexhaustible, immeasurable, without limit or limitation, and
capable of endless division. In introducing us to some of the
whats of success, someone pointed to the three infinities.
These infinities not only encompass endless possibilities but
they are attended by endless satisfactions and followed by
endless rewards. The three infinities may also serve us as the
three general headings under which our Whats may be
classified.

1. *What to know.* Francis Bacon said, "Knowledge is
power." After our first parents had eaten the fruit from the
tree of knowledge of good and evil, the Lord said, "The man
is now become as one of us to know good and evil." And I
would like to point out that the right kind of knowledge still
tends to have that effect upon people. To know still tends to

make men and women become like God. In fact, Jesus himself said, "And this is life eternal, that they might know thee the only true God, and Jesus Christ, whom thou hast sent." (John 17:3.)

2. *What to do.* The Lord has said that we will be judged according to our works. Jesus came asking for doers. Everything depends upon what we do.

3. *What to be.* It was said that Washington won the independence of the American states not so much by what he *did* as by what he *was*. Wealth is not so much what we *have* as what we *are*. We work not merely to acquire; we work to become. Success in life is not so much what we can get out of it, but what we can become by it.

God is God because of what he *knows*, what he *does*, and, primarily, what he *is*. What an exciting idea that if we properly direct the whats of our lives, we may order for ourselves the highest ideals, the greatest accomplishments, and the most valuable characters!

One of the most important of our serving men is number two, Mr. Why. Work and life become much easier and much more pleasant when we know the reason for things. Husbands, wives, children, employees, always accomplish more when we know why we are doing a particular thing. In religious situations, we frequently hear of "blind obedience," but our society is now beset with a great plague of "blind disobedience." There are rebellious spirits who have set themselves against the establishment without knowing what it stands for. They are opposed to the government. They are anti-parents. They are filled with religious contrariness and rebellion.

There are many things we know are right without knowing the reason why they are right. Blind obedience to God is certainly much better than blind disobedience. The scriptures tell of an experience God had with our first parents:

"And he gave unto them commandments, that they should worship the Lord their God, and should offer the firstlings of their flocks, for an offering unto the Lord. And Adam was obedient unto the commandments of the Lord.

"And after many days an angel of the Lord appeared unto Adam saying: Why dost thou offer sacrifices unto the Lord? And Adam said unto him: I know not, save the Lord commanded me." (Moses 5:5-6.)

The angel explained to Adam that this was a similitude of the sacrifice of the Only Begotten of the Father. (Moses 5:7.) When Adam knew the whys of what he did, his worship became much more meaningful; likewise, with an intelligent, comprehensive understanding of the whys of religion, our chances for exaltation are greatly increased. It was a very wise man who said that he not only obeyed God but he also agreed with him. We always feel better about our lives, our work, and our religion when we understand the important reasons behind the things we do.

What an exciting thing to know the purpose of life! We should also know a great deal about our eternal destiny. The whys include the reasons for things we do, the purposes of our existence, and the consequences of our actions. It is of the utmost importance to understand why good is better than evil, why success is better than failure. We are stronger, more enthusiastic and more joyful when we know what the end of life will be if we obey God. And intelligent Mr. Why can be very helpful as one of our serving men.

Number three is Mr. When. The whens have the greatest possible importance. Timing determines a great many things in our lives. There are voices all around us reminding us that there is no time like the present. A great American prophet once said, "For behold, this life is the time for men to prepare to meet God." (Alma 34:32.) The present is also the time to do a lot of other wonderful things. We ought to sit down occasionally and make a list of our whens. We can feel ourselves grow as we come to understand the whats and the whys and the whens. The greatest time to begin is now. We can't do our great deeds yesterday, and tomorrow never comes. That leaves us only today. Procrastination is not only the thief of time; it is also the thief of opportunity and of every other part of success.

Next we come to number four of our magic serving men: Mr. How. Everyone wants to succeed in life. Everyone wants fulfillment and happiness. The primary reason we don't get what we want is that we don't know how to go about it. We don't know how to succeed in our businesses, in our families, or in our personal lives. For the most part we have never even learned how to resist temptation, which is an elementary "how-to" for any successful life endeavor.

Frank Bettger wrote a book entitled *How I Raised Myself From Failure to Success in Selling.* Dale Carnegie authored a book, *How To Win Friends and Influence People.* There are books entitled *How To Take Off Weight.* The holy scriptures are written for the purpose of telling us how to get into the celestial kingdom. We ought to spend more time thinking about our hows and reading some great how books. When we solve the whats, whys and whens of life, we need to find out about the hows.

Number five is Mr. Where. The greatest good fortunes and successes of life have been brought about because the right man was in the right place at the right time. As timing is important, so place is also important. When opportunity knocks at our doors, many of us are down in the basement of life where we can't hear the knock. It is even more disastrous when we are at the pool hall or in the tavern. How fortunate we are to have Mr. Where to help us be in the right location at the right time!

During the famous Dark Day in Connecticut the state legislature was in session when suddenly a strange, unexplainable darkness settled over everything. People started to panic, and someone shouted, "It is the end of the world!" One of the fine, faithful old legislators calmly arose and said, "If it is the end of the world, I wish to be found in my place when it arrives, doing the work that I have been called to do." Then he made a motion that candles be brought, and the legislature proceeded with the work at hand.

The last, and one of the most important, of our honest servants is Mr. Who. We ought to know who we are and how we can become the kind of person we should be. Someone said to a friend, "Who do you think you are?" The friend whispered quietly to himself, "I wish I knew." Some day we are going to discover the profound implications of the fact that we are the children of God and that we have been created in his image and are destined to become like him. Then, I suppose, the earth itself will not be able to contain our enthusiasm. The two most important people in the universe are God, and you. If you have used your Mr. Who in the right way, you will know who God is and that you are literally his son or daughter.

There is a book entitled *Who's Who in America*. There is another book that could be entitled *Who's Who to God*. Each of us who uses the six serving men will find that his name appears high on God's list. We do this by recognizing that we are God's serving men, and that to be successful in that capacity we must know and act upon the whats and the whys and the whens as well as the hows, the wheres, and the whos of God's service.

Chapter 6

The Great Success Books

The central fact of the universe is God. He is our Eternal Heavenly Father. He is the designer of our lives and the architect of our success. One of the most certain facts of our existence is that he wants us to be successful. In programming our future, he has made it possible for us to become even as he is. He has called us to work in the great enterprise in which he himself is engaged.

When God said "Be ye therefore perfect, even as your Father which is in heaven is perfect" (Matthew 5:48), and "Ye are gods; and all of you are children of the most High" (Psalm 82:6), he was not trying to mock us. It has been said that God did not build the stairway of human life to lead nowhere. We must not live below the standards of excellence he has established.

One of the means he has provided to help us bring about our eternal destiny is the process of reading. Through reading we may transfer the great ideas and procedures from the lives of others to help us achieve our own success. God has fashioned a system of economics which is referred to as the United Order. Under this system, people may arrange to have their material things in common. God has also established a kind of United Order in books. The standard works of the Church may belong as much to the prospective elder as to the President of the Church, and may yield one as much value as the other if properly used. It is a wasteful process for each child of God, or each would-be leader, to disregard the learning of others and start from the beginning to learn everything for himself. It is much more economical to build on those sure foundations that have already been developed and are laid out for us in books. Hence the use of great books can be a great aid to leadership.

Someone has pointed out that books are among life's most precious possessions. They are the most remarkable creation of man. Nothing else that man builds lasts. Monuments fall, civilizations perish, but books continue. The perusal of great books is like an interview with the noble men and women of past ages who have written them.

Charles Kingsley wrote:

"There is nothing more wonderful than a book. It may be a message to us from the dead, from human souls we never saw, who lived perhaps thousands of miles away, and yet these little sheets of paper speak to us, arouse us, teach us, open our hearts and in turn open their hearts to us like brothers. Without books God is silent, justice dormant, philosophy lame."

John Milton said: "Books are not dead things, but contain a certain potency of life in them as active as the soul whose progeny they are. They preserve as in a vial the purest efficacy of the living intellect that bred them."

Great men in every field have written their ideas and they are available to us almost for the taking. Some time ago I discovered an interesting word: *bibliotherapy*. This word is compounded from two Greek words meaning *books* and *treatment*. It refers to the particular kind of self-improvement that comes from reading. It means a kind of literary remedy for problems, and it denotes a cure brought about by the effective use of good ideas.

I have always felt very sorry for those who lived in periods of time when there was no great literature. As an example, if Cain had read the right kind of good books in his spare time, as did Abraham Lincoln, he may not have started the first crime wave by killing his brother Abel.

A prominent ward leader said that during the previous

five years he had not read a single book. His kind of life might have been a tragedy even in the Dark Ages. But how unfortunate it is that such a condition can exist in the age of wonders and enlightenment that we know as the dispensation of the fulness of times. So much depends on what and how we read. It is very likely that the greatest invention of all time is the printing press.

Books have the advantage of preserving great ideas and events in their original form, thus allowing us to relive those circumstances again and again at our own pleasure. Through books and our imaginations we may again attend the council in heaven or stand with the hosts of ancient Israel at the foot of Mount Sinai to absorb the inspiration as well as the letter of the law associated with the Ten Commandments. We can learn to live and relive the tremendous lessons of the Sermon on the Mount. We become the beneficiaries of what great educators, successful captains of industry, and powerful motivators have put down in print. Among other things, their writings may contain ideas on such important leadership subjects as selection, recruiting, induction, training, supervision and motivation. Out of their own successful experience, these leaders discuss such helpful procedures as the delegation of authority, personal counseling, salesmanship, building prestige, and public relations. There are some wonderful books on problem solving as well as on effective communication and the use of persuasion.

So we ought to get out the great success books and pump their lessons into our bloodstreams. Daniel Starck wrote a little book worth more than its weight in gold called *How to Develop Your Executive Ability.* James F. Lincoln wrote a book on motivation called *Incentive Management.* Out of a Harvard Graduate School of Business seminar came a wonderful little book called *The Management Team.* John Gardner wrote a how-to-do-it book called *Excellence.* If anyone needs to know these things, it is Church leaders. These, and many other books, ought to be a part of the working success library of every Church leader.

If I were going to advise someone about how to be a great salesman, I would suggest that he digest some great books on salesmanship and thereby immerse himself in the spirit of leadership success.

The holy scriptures are the greatest success books. The Bible was written long before the Dark Ages began, when the camel was the fastest means of land transportation and, next to the sun, the candle furnished the brightest illumination. Yet the Bible is more up-to-date, in some ways, than tomorrow's newspaper, and it points out many things that are on the agenda for our future. A book on science that was written even fifteen years ago may now be completely outdated, but the Bible for many centuries has been the world's finest book on religion. It is the world's first book of philosophy. It is the world's first book of history. It is the world's first book of knowledge. It is the world's first book of literature. It is the world's first book of salesmanship. In the Church, however, in addition we have three great volumes of new scripture outlining in detail the simple principles of the gospel of Christ, and with every doctrine there is a "thus saith the Lord" attached.

We live in the day of the greatest expansion of knowledge and prosperity ever known in the world. Ideas that have taken generations to develop stand ready to serve us through the writings of men who have achieved success in various fields of endeavor.

The Lord himself laid the foundations of our lives and occupations upon the earth. He established our science and encourages our invention. He has said that to him all things are spiritual. God is the greatest planner, organizer, and inventor. He is the greatest example of industry and practical thinking. His abilities and intelligence are manifest in his creations. It is through him that we gain knowledge of our universe, and a great deal of this very helpful information has been made available to us in books.

It was not his intention that all our problems would be solved merely because we are nice people. We must be able to pay our way by giving useful service. The man who tore down his barns to build larger ones may have been a good man but he was foolish. And the scriptural concordances make about as many references to fools as to sinners.

God is not only the greatest businessman but is also all-wise. He knows his business and ours backwards and forwards. To us he is the inventor of planning, the designer of preparation, and the creator of personal work. He is the personification of persistence and the finest example of creative thinking, self-discipline, and character development. As the master of all knowledge, he is supremely skilled in teaching and inspiring his children.

To help us develop our own mental capacities, God has led men of achievement in all walks of life to record and preserve their ideas. Our literature contains the most workable ideas that have been developed during the six thousand years of recorded history.

In these last days God has entrusted us with the greatest work of the world. We live in the dispensation of the fulness of times. It is our job to see that the gospel is effectively preached to every person upon the earth—and a good place to start is the house next door. It is our job to prepare the earth for the second coming of Christ. Yet it is difficult to get many of our own people to come to sacrament meetings.

Certainly we will solve our problems more easily if we have the spirit of success and can learn from what has been written by great leaders. But we should remember that if we don't have the spirit of leadership, the know-how of leadership, and the skill of leadership, we cannot lead.

Chapter 7

Put Yourself on the Team

When I was a freshman in high school many years ago an enterprising music teacher taught us a song, a part of which has remained with me through the years. It makes reference to Shakespeare's schoolboy who went "creeping like snail, unwillingly to school." While the one who wrote this song must have been a very wise person, I did not appreciate it at that time as much as I do now. The words of the song said:

> Will Shakespeare tells a tale of woe
> About a boy who whined,
> And then when schooltime came, you know,
> Would always lag behind.

> He'd rather stay at home and play
> Or mope around and dream.
> But then, you see, in William's day
> They had no football team.

> Things at best in Shakespeare's day
> Were murky, as a rule.
> They didn't have much fun or play
> When William went to school.

> But things have changed since William died;
> Our school is just a dream.
> For almost everyone who's tried
> Thinks he will make the team.

The writer of these lyrics, and Shakespeare himself, was trying to tell us that we ought to get more personally involved with life and success; we ought to get more pleasure from what we do; we ought to develop our God-given competitive instincts. Winning gives us great personal pleasure and stimulates us to have a better self-image.

Not only should we get on the team, but we also ought to learn how to carry the ball and bring about victories. I remember in my own football days the students used to chant, "We want a touchdown, we want a touchdown." That is what everybody wants. The students not only wanted touchdowns, they wanted players who could win victories for the school. They wanted color and courage and stamina and resourcefulness in those who represented them on the field. Some of these qualities apply also to other departments of life.

A man once complained that he had been a member of a certain religious congregation for ten years and during that entire period had never been called upon to speak or teach a class or take any active part in the group's affairs. He felt that he had substantial abilities but that these had gone unrecognized by his associates and leaders. He seemed like a potentially capable football player who was never invited to play. Yet whether in football, or religion, or civic affairs, school, or any other part of life, we sometimes need to develop and practice our abilities on our own initiative with such effect that we will be invited or even begged to play. Certainly we should not sit endlessly on the sidelines waiting for someone to discover the abilities we have not yet developed.

Anyone who can demonstrate that he is able to win for the school can usually get on the team. For example, as a young man Heber J. Grant wanted to be a great baseball pitcher. But the others wouldn't let him even practice with the team, since he was physically unimpressive and appeared to be weak. The other boys called him "skinny Grant." But he didn't sit down and mope while others won the honors. Instead he went to work developing himself. He got a baseball and went out behind his mother's barn, where hour after hour and day after day he threw the ball against the barn door. Eventually, as a result of his persistence, Heber J. Grant was the pitcher on the baseball team that won the championship of the Territory of Utah.

In effect no one appointed Heber J. Grant as the team's pitcher. He appointed himself. Because only he could win for them, the team could not possibly choose any pitcher except Heber J. Grant. He put himself on the team as its leader in spite of the original poor opinion and opposition of the other boys. Neither did he put himself in some minor role. He put himself on the pitcher's mound, where most of the action takes place.

It is quite likely that in many instances the presidents of the United States, the leaders of great corporations, and even the heads of religious organizations are primarily responsible for their own appointment. When Heber J. Grant started to think baseball and to develop his desire to play and his ability to throw, he was appointing himself pitcher even though the actual announcement didn't come until later. In somewhat the same way Heber J. Grant began doing other things which were responsible for his being selected as the youngest stake president in the Church, then as an apostle at age twenty-six, and finally as the President of the Church.

Similarly George Gipp appointed himself to be one of the most spectacular football players of all time. At Notre Dame George Gipp came under the influence of the immortal coach, Knute Rockne. Gipp absorbed the spirit of this great man to a point where he breathed Rockne's rhythm and lived his enthusiasm. It was only natural that effective play execution came in turn. Gipp learned to do everything well. He blocked and kicked and passed and ran and schemed and tackled. He was at his best when playing against the hardest competition. In fact, someone has said that if Notre Dame had been playing a mediocre schedule with easy opponents, the world might never have heard of George Gipp.

He wasn't interested in easy games. During those games, he looked like an average player. But, like many great men, he was set on fire by a challenge. He fought the hardest when his back was against the wall. Then he was six jumps ahead of his opponent. He had his campaign mapped out before the crisis arose. Unlike many athletes, Gipp was not temperamental. He didn't have to be humored or pampered or aroused or appointed by someone else. Gipp worked on his own initiative and was at his best when Notre Dame was up against it. Then he was magnificent. When quick thinking and smart strategy was required to pull the team out of a hole, he played like Superman. He never allowed himself to lose control of his emotions, he let his calculating mind rule his every move. Even when he was outwardly inspired, inwardly he was calm.

Gipp had no bad days. He was constant like a fixed star. He was always in good physical condition, yet he came out of the game drained of every ounce of energy and exhausted from having given everything he had. This was the way Gipp did things. He was in the game all the way, and he fought for the glory of Notre Dame rather than for personal applause. He was indifferent to publicity. The only satisfaction he asked was to know he was accomplishing something. Rockne learned to trust Gipp, to place confidence in Gipp's confidence, and to rely on him to pull the team through tough spots with his own ingenuity.

In the latter part of the 1920 season, Gipp fell sick. Rockne later said: "In our final game against Northwestern at Evanston, Gipp got out of the sick bed to make the trip. I used him very little that day. We were winning. The final score was thirty-three to seven. But in the last quarter the stands chanted Gipp's name so loud and long that I finally sent him in for a few plays on the ice-covered field with the wind off Lake Michigan cutting us all to the bone. He played brilliantly. After the fans had been appeased, I got him out as soon as I could. But he returned to school with a raging fever. Gipp went back to his sick bed, from which he never got up. Pneumonia had him backed up against his own goal line. He lived barely two weeks."

Rockne sat at his bedside as Gipp lay dying. Someone said, "It's pretty tough to go." "What's tough about it?" Gipp smiled feebly. "I have no complaints." "Rock," he said, "I know I'm going. It's all right, I'm not afraid." His eyes brightened in their frames of pallor. "But," he added, "I would like to make one last request. Sometime, Rock, when

the going isn't so easy—sometime when the team's up against
it and things are going wrong, when the odds are against the
team and the breaks are beating the boys, then tell them,
Rock, tell them for me to go in there with all they've got and
win one for me. Just tell them to win one for the Gipper. I
don't know where I'll be then, Rock, but I will know about it
and I will be happy." A moment later Gipp was gone.

In the 1928 game, Army and Notre Dame played to an
overflow crowd. At the half, the score was zero to zero. The
members of the Notre Dame team were badly battered and
bruised, being hardly able to drag themselves to the dressing
room at the end of the half. It was then that Rockne granted
Gipp's wish, and for the first time told the boys what Gipp
had said. The rest is history. A sobbing band of Fighting Irish
raced out onto the field to meet Army at the last half.
Grantland Rice later said: "When Notre Dame lined up for
the kickoff, I knew they were playing with a twelfth man,
George Gipp. Then I watched that inspired team as they went
smashing, clawing, passing, driving, eighty yards to victory.
And somewhere the great heart of George Gipp must have
been happy."

At Gipp's last game there were more than fifty thousand
people in the stadium. The one person they wanted to see
play was George Gipp. Every Notre Dame fan was glad that
he was on their team. The spirit of George Gipp, like the
spirit of every other champion, is a long way from
Shakespeare's schoolboy who, each morning, drags a reluctant
spirit to school. We all need to be eagerly involved in the
bigger game of life.

Heber J. Grant and George Gipp prepared themselves.
Being part of the team and learning how to win championships came later on. In contrast, the member of the religious
congregation I spoke of wanted to be put on the team before
he started his training. If he had been appointed to teach the
most important class, he would have been unprepared, just as
Heber J. Grant would have been unprepared to pitch a
championship game before throwing the ball up against his
mother's barn for days and months. This man who wanted to
be a religious leader and teacher could have imitated

Demosthenes in shouting his oratory to the waves first, then the honors would have come later; or he could have learned all the skills of teaching and the logic of wisdom, and soon the people would have been begging him to teach their class so that they could share in his wisdom.

Too many people blame all their weaknesses and mistakes on Satan or chance or circumstance, and too many of these same people wait for the Lord to make them successful or accomplished or famous before they put the effort into what they would like to do. This tendency was indicated in a group of missionaries. One missionary pair stood up and said, "Last week the Lord blessed us with four convert baptisms." The next pair stood up and said, "Last week the Lord didn't bless us with any convert baptisms." In their subconscious minds, apparently, they were waiting for the Lord to do their work for them. But the Lord can do much better work if he has missionaries who have a fighting heart and an uphill spirit, and who have practiced endlessly and tirelessly. Someone wrote some lines about this idea, in which he said:

Listen to one who's lived clear through from soup to nuts—
The Lord don't send no derricks 'round to hoist folks out of
    ruts.

We need to get personally involved. We need to remember the great decree of God in that early morning of creation when he gave us our initiative and our free agency, saying, "Thou mayest choose for thyself." It has always seemed to me to be a little bit unsportsmanlike to ask an all-powerful God to help us win the victory over our opponents. That is, we are asking him to intervene in our behalf because without his help we may lose the game. There is a much better way to win. The prayer of industry and thoughtfulness as we prepare for the game will surely be answered on the day of the championship contest. God has given us an unlimited ability to develop our godly potentialities in brain and muscle and spirit and enthusiasm. He has given us the ability to train and to develop extra power. When the other team has done this better than we have, to ask the Lord to intervene seems to me not to be very sporting.

I imagine that under these circumstances the great God of the universe, who said, "If ye are prepared ye shall not fear," would like to see us get a good trouncing just to impress us with the idea that if we want to win we ought to follow those important God-given laws of success which usually bring victory.

In a leadership discussion, one member of the group told of writing a doctoral thesis as part of the requirement for obtaining his advanced university degree. In this experience he had discoverd an important key to learning. Since that time, whenever he has wanted to do some intensive creative work, he has proceeded as though he were actually making an investigation for a doctoral dissertation. He recommended this leadership procedure to all.

It seems illogical that so many people achieve prominence in the world with little or no formal schooling. Yet the reason is possibly found in the fact that such people have done their own investigation and thinking instead of merely reading and accepting the conclusions of someone else.

Thus we come back again to the idea that we ought to put ourselves on the leadership team. If we will master the process of initiative, original investigation, and enthusiastic thinking, and work at developing the great, God-given capabilities within ourselves, we may join the team as captain.

Part Two

Orientation to Excellence

Our Success Orientation
The Quest for Excellence
A Going Concern
Getting the Most out of Ourselves

Chapter 8

Our Success Orientation

One of our greatest books is the dictionary. It has many excellent ideas which can help us increase our capacity for success and happiness. I consulted the dictionary about the word *orientation*. This rather formidable word is an enlargement of the word *orient*, which originally referred to the region of the sky where the sun rises, the east. Later, this word was applied to the countries east of the Mediterranean Sea. Japan is specifically referred to as "The Land of the Rising Sun."

The word *orient* is also used to describe certain lustrous eastern pearls, because their brightness resembles the sun. Then someone figured out that to *orient* oneself would be to look toward the east so as to face the source of many blessings. A properly *oriented* church or temple was thought of as one constructed with the most sacred areas in its eastern end—that is, the right place for the chancel containing the altar, toward which the congregation faces in worship, was thought to be in the east. We not only get sunlight, lustrous pearls, and oriental rugs from the east, but much of civilization itself has come from that direction. For example, all six of the major religions began in Asia—Christianity, Mohammedanism, Hinduism, Confucianism, Buddhism, and Shintoism.

We even orient our graves with the feet toward the east. Legend has it that this custom was established so that when the angel of the resurrection blows his horn we can all stand up and face the sunrise together. This idea is closely related to that which, five times each day, prompts the Mohammedans to point their prayer rugs toward their capital city of Mecca, the source of their religious light and direction.

But this interesting symbolism has other valuable applications. Educational institutions and business organizations conduct *orientation* courses. These are designed to give participants a kind of "preview" or "overview" of the experiences they can expect to have within the school or organization. We *orient* our lives by developing a dependable sense of spiritual direction and by putting our conduct in harmony with the principles of eternal success.

By this means we not only develop a sense of our own position but we can also create a more harmonious relationship with our environment and focus better on our personal objectives. Certainly each of our projected achievements must be oriented to success; and, when any program is finished, the amount of success attained should be measurable. Someone has expressed this success orientation in verse. He said:

> Night swoops on me with blackest wings,
> But I'll succeed.
> I see the stars that darkness brings
> And I'll succeed.
> No force on earth can make me cower,
> Because each moment and each hour
> I still affirm with strength and power,
> I shall succeed.

This should apply a hundredfold to our religious success.

In preparing for the new interests and greater responsibilities of marriage, one should orient himself to successfully and permanently fit into his new life. This will render him better able to make the adjustments that will ensure his future domestic prosperity and happiness. One of the most serious needs of our lives is for a more sound religious orientation.

Jesus held up before each one of us the inspiring objective of qualifying for eternal life in the celestial kingdom. No one can go higher than that, and we should conform to those divine gospel principles that have this end in view. The scriptures themselves refer to the sun, which comes out of the east, as the symbol of this highest glory of God.

It is a real, honest-to-goodness spiritual and success orientation that will help us to point our lives and the lives of those who follow us toward the eternal goal which Paul describes as the "glory of the sun." (1 Corinthians 15:41.) Jesus referred to himself as "the bright and morning star." (Revelation 22:16.) The morning star is actually a giant, distant sun which, to us, heralds the dawn of each new day. The Redeemer proclaims our day of gospel light, and when our lives are oriented toward him we are like those mariners who guide their vessels by the undeviating light of a solitary, fixed star. John the apostle points out that "sin is the transgression of the law." (1 John 3:4.) That could perhaps include transgression of the laws of success. We might also think of sin as some serious error in our orientation.

As the ancients looked to the sun for health, food, and life itself, so we receive our orientation toward honor, righteousness, and eternal life from the word of God. God is our Father and our Creator; he is also the source of every blessing. He is the greatest authority on success in the universe. He is the greatest teacher. He is the greatest physician: he can heal our bodies because he created them in the first place.

In one of his finest orientation courses, he has said that we should live by every word that proceedeth forth from the mouth of God. We do not always do this. Frequently we commit those tragic sins involving fractional devotion and marginal morals. Our actions often seem to be on a minimum performance basis. The Lord has given us an important set of success laws through which every blessing may be brought about. But we often fail in our orientation and, instead of looking toward success, we allow ourselves to drift into failure.

During the United States' Constitutional Convention,

George Washington sat in the president's chair with the picture of a half sun on its back. As the delegates were signing their names, Benjamin Franklin arose and addressed the convention. Referring to the picture before them, he said, "Painters find it difficult in their art to show the difference between a rising and a setting sun." He went on: "Often during these sessions and the vicissitudes that have attended our hopes and fears, I have looked at the painting behind the president without being able to tell whether our sun was rising or setting. But now I know that it is a rising sun."

In 1831 the Lord gave a special revelation to the members of the Church about what they should do to lift the Church out of obscurity and out of darkness. He said that this was the only church upon the face of the earth with which he was well pleased. But then he added that he was "speaking collectively and not individually." It is a stimulating thought that if we do as we should, God may someday be able to say of each of us individually and personally, as he did of his First Begotten in the spirit, "This is my beloved son (or daughter) in whom I am well pleased." We may be sure this will not happen if we are accurately classified as "setting sons," or idle sons, or unthinking sons, so far as his work is concerned.

The Lord has decreed that the Church itself shall ultimately be successful; but he has given no guarantee of success to us as individuals or to the wards and stakes in which we live. We ourselves must assume that responsibility. There are some individuals who have been outstanding missionaries and some who have not. Some stakes and wards have done very well, others have not done so well. As individuals we sometimes have fits and starts of faithfulness but fall down badly over a longer period of time. Probably our biggest problem is that of orienting ourselves to the greatest accomplishments, squaring our lives with the laws of success.

Since individuals are different, they need different training and supervision. A prominent sales manager once said that when he addressed his salesmen to inform or motivate them, he always had the top 10 percent in mind in determining what he would say. This procedure, however, does not always solve the needs of the bottom 10 percent. If the sales manager talks honestly and frankly to the bottom 10 percent, someone could get the impression that he is discrediting the whole program or staff. If he addresses the needs of only the top 10 percent, those in the bottom group may be seriously misled. They may be lulled into a false security as they fall into the legendary trap of the destroyer: "All is well in Zion; yea, Zion prospereth, all is well—and thus the devil cheateth their souls, and leadeth them away carefully down to hell." (2 Nephi 28:21.)

Because all of us have blind spots and don't see ourselves clearly, we need someone who will counsel with us frankly about our own situation. Sooner or later even the top men may find themselves in a lower group.

When we are considering any project, it is a good idea to walk all around the idea so that we see it from all sides. We learn by understanding opposites. Jesus talked a great deal about failure, not how to produce it but how to eliminate it. He described the unjust judge, the prodigal son, the older brother who was angry. He was severe with the Pharisees and Sadducees as well as with the publicans and sinners. He exposed the evil of the priests and leaders so that the people could see their own sins. If we could all learn to look through our blind spots and recognize our own weaknesses, we would greatly enlarge our strengths. While we should frequently use as a model the performance of those who do their work well, we occasionally should be very critical of our own poor work. There aren't many people in the world who will be frank enough to give us the personal help we may need in order to qualify for the statement of praise we would someday like to receive from God, whose work we are doing.

G. K. Chesterton once wrote: "It is wrong to say Christianity has been tried and failed. Christianity has been found difficult and has not been tried." Similarly, some magnificent programs given by the Lord have not been fairly tried by us, with the result that we have allowed our part of the work, as well as ourselves, to remain in obscurity and darkness. To prevent this, we need to learn how to recognize our weaknesses and orient our lives to success.

One of the greatest opportunities of our lives is to go back to this important word *orientation* that comes from our great book, the dictionary, and see that our own lives are looking toward the sunrise, that we are headed into the dawn. If we will orient ourselves to the greatest success described by the Lord himself, we can be effective instruments in lifting the Church and ourselves out of obscurity and out of darkness. There are several hundred sectarian churches whose members claim to believe in Christ, but the important question is, What kind of lives do they live? How successful are they in their families? How many of the numerous truths taught by the Savior do they accept and live?

God is the God of law and order. He is the God of beauty and success. He is the God of truth. He cannot lie. Neither is he a lawbreaker. The holy scriptures and the living prophet of the Lord provide our greatest orientation course, as they give us the most helpful overview of our work. We must be judged by what we do. We have a great correlation program, and we should also have some great coordination and orientation programs. The holy scriptures and the living prophet point out the disciplines that must be acquired and the things that must be done if we are to reach God's highest kingdom. If a good orientation course is essential for chemistry and medicine, it is a thousand times more essential for the greatest of all enterprises—life.

Successful orientation is that process by which we turn our faces toward our objectives. With an improper religious orientation, we may find ourselves standing up on resurrection morning facing in the wrong direction. That could be disastrous, for, as someone has said, "We may not always look where we are going, but it is pretty certain that we will all go where we are looking."

Chapter 9

The Quest
for Excellence

A number of years ago, the Chesapeake and Potomac Telephone Companies ran a series of ads under the general title "The Quest for Excellence." Because of what appears to be a lowering of standards in so many areas of present-day activity, these four ordinary words could also serve as the heading under which some of the values in our own lives may be analyzed and upgraded. If it is profitable to develop excellence in a telephone company, it is many times more profitable to develop it in the government and the Church and our personal lives.

Whatever the field of our endeavor, success always shines its spotlight on quality. An increase in the excellence of a person's life goes far beyond increases that may be brought about in his finances. Excellence not only improves and beautifies, it motivates individuals who are concerned with it, and helps to bring about greater accomplishment.

The idea of excellence comes very near to being the purpose of life itself, and for that reason it runs through everything we do. Every business and every professional group and every worthwhile social unit is conducting a constant search for quality. Quality is what we are attracted to and what we are inspired by. It is what we want in an automobile, in a home, and in a family. It is what we look for in everything we do, in everything we are, and in everything we ever hope to become.

Probably no other theme has gripped the American imagination so intensely as the discovery of outstanding character qualities or genuine talent in unexpected places. We are thrilled when someone from the slums becomes a scientific genius. We are delighted to hear of frail youngsters developing great athletic skills or to see poor boys become captains of industry. One history of excellence tells of a group of humble, unlearned fishermen and tax collectors who became saints and apostles.

Important points about the quest for excellence are that everyone is involved and that each person may direct his compass toward the goal of his greatest interest. It is a revered tradition in America that "anybody can become somebody." Our literature is filled with heroes and heroines. Every one of us has been given a divine gift in the form of a strong inclination to lift himself upward by following an ideal. It is a profitable undertaking to hold in our minds the images of great thinkers, great doers, and great prophets. As we pay homage to the honesty of Abraham Lincoln and to the devotion of Paul the apostle, we become the beneficiaries of both. No one can hold a good idea in his mind or cherish a noble ambition in his heart without gaining from it. No one can do a good deed or discover a more effective way to render a service without himself being lifted up and made better.

A hundred years ago, Horatio Alger stimulated the ambitions of many young Americans with his "rags to riches" success stories. But excellence does not merely mean going from rags to riches. Its course also runs from "log cabin to president," from "plowboy to prophet," from "darkness to light," from "depression to happiness," and from "bad to good." The quest for excellence encourages self-discovery, awakens ambition, arouses industry, inspires emulation, and improves every accomplishment. Everyone has within himself a vein of greatness, and, more often than not, it is a touch of excellence that leads to its discovery. It is not unusual for one who has won outstanding success to say, "I never dreamed that it could happen to me," or, "I didn't think I had it in me." But excellence has the power to create success or bring it to the surface. It also teaches us how to engineer the shaft so that we may draw out the gold.

While speaking on the campus of Stanford University in 1906, William James said, "The world is only beginning to see that more than about anything else the wealth of nations consists in the number of superior men it harbors." When God created man in his own image and endowed him with miraculous faculties, it was his desire to fill the earth with superior men. God does not want us to become trapped in treacherous downdrafts that thrust so many people into a state of mediocrity and depression. The purpose for the organization of the Church upon the earth was to build excellence in the Lord's children for both here and hereafter.

Of course, the first step in producing excellence is to believe in it. Frequently people are ashamed to be out-standing. It seems so much more comfortable to be mediocre. There is constant pressure pushing people toward being average. And when one has average goals and average ambitions, excellence becomes very difficult to achieve. Satan is the inventor of an unprofitable state of satisfaction that makes peoples content in just getting by. This is the way in which myriads of people are prevented from finding life's proper meaning. Too often we join some "cult of easiness" or attempt to find happiness in apathy, aimlessness, and the pursuit of lesser things and lower goals. As a result we contract that widespread disease which surely is some variety of the inferiority complex.

John W. Gardner wrote a great book entitled *Excellence.* Its purpose is to help us orient our lives toward living at our best. He points out that while we have always paid the most pious lip service to the idea of excellence, we have really trifled with it in actual practice. There can be no real success or happiness without excellence, however, and there can be no excellence without intelligent effort.

Because every worthwhile thing in life is at stake, we should prepare our minds, our muscles, our hearts, our attitudes, and our spirits themselves for the promotion of excellence. Exceptions should not be tolerated. If anything is worth doing it is worth doing well, and we cannot personally afford to practice any degree of mediocrity. Godhood is the ultimate result of excellence. We must not send back to God a life that has only been half used. The greatest waste in the world is not the devastation of war; it is not the cost of crime; it is not the erosion of our soils; nor is it the depletion of our raw materials, nor the loss of our gold supply. The greatest waste in the world is that human beings, you and I, live so far below the level of our possibilities. Compared with what we might be, we are just partly alive.

Excellence is a curiously powerful word. It can overcome all of life's downdrafts. As we absorb the spirit of excellence, we can perform almost any miracle. When we develop a strong, deep feeling about it the most vigorous work becomes easy, and greater ambitions and more worthwhile interests follow in due course.

Excellence means different things to different people. To some it means to become a great scholar or a fine athlete, or to develop a noble character. To some, *excellence* may symbolize the golden age of Greece, or it may make us more aware of the problems of our own day and help us to weave into our own aspirations those specific activities necessary to create the better world we ourselves expect to help build.

The power drawing us upward is the pattern of excellence in him who was ordained to be our example. The mission of the Son of God was to redeem us from death and to help us live so that God's will could be done on earth as it is done in heaven. When this kind of quest is accompanied by the proper amount of searching, aspiring, and longing, it produces an affinity for good that can bring us back to God. For this purpose the Creator has placed within us an upward reach, an improvement instinct, a divine urge for superiority that should have our constant encouragement.

When enough strength is given to this ambition to do our best, it gives dignity and character to our work, pleasure to our hearts, happiness to our families, and eternal glory to our souls. Whether one works as a janitor, a judge, a surgeon, a technician, or whatever work he may do, his life, to be complete, must have excellence. When anyone does a slovenly, dishonest, or halfhearted job in anything, he lowers the general level of his society and to that extent becomes a burden upon it.

Excellence not only involves competence, of course. It implies also the highest standards and the greatest devotion. Only when we cherish what Whitehead calls the "habitual vision of greatness" do our lives find their most satisfying fulfillment. As we make greater demands upon ourselves, we entitle ourselves to look forward to more vitality and greater happiness. Any individual who lives at less than his best cheats himself, and no society that is passive, inert, and preoccupied with its own comforts will long endure.

The idea of quality should never be ignored or forgotten, whether in the most humble activities or in the most exalted places. One of the biggest problems of our present world is that we do not pay enough attention to excellence. For some reason people are crowding toward the bottom levels of life where only the lower prizes are available. Jesus pointed out, and history has proven, that it is the broad road leading toward death that is the most heavily traveled. Many serious problems arise in our lives when our ambitions are aimed below our best.

The ten plagues were sent upon the people of Egypt because their lives lacked quality. The history of our planet, from Cain to the present day, is largely made up of a long series of plagues, famines, pestilence, earthquakes, wars, and diseases. We have attracted these to ourselves because we have not lived up to the standards required by the Lord. The people who will live upon the earth during the Millennium will be those who have made the greatest progress in the quest for excellence. Even in heaven, people will be happy and compatible according to the measure of their success in that quest.

Paul the apostle described the three degrees of glory in which immortal beings will live after the resurrection and the final judgment. They are called the *celestial*, the *terrestrial*, and the *telestial* glories. Paul compares them in brightness respectively to the sun, the moon, and the stars. Then he says: "For one star differeth from another star in glory. So also is the resurrection of the dead." (1 Corinthians 15:41-42.) The

Lord intended this comparison to stimulate our ambition and to help us provide ourselves with the abilities and motivations that will bring about our highest glory.

Thomas Jefferson once pointed out that while life is trying to educate us it is also sorting us. He said, "The geniuses will be raked from the rubbish." Jesus expressed this idea in his parables: the goats being separated from the sheep, the tares being sorted out so that they could be tied in bundles and burned.

The causes for our happiness or unhappiness can be found inside ourselves. To help us develop excellence and achieve eternal exaltation a divine program has been given to all men. After the dropouts have been eliminated, the rest will be classified according to their degree of excellence. Some of us are like the indolent student whom the professor described by saying that he had received great gifts but he had never unwrapped them. What a tragedy when we fail to unwrap the divine gifts of faith, courage, and industry, of which excellence is composed! In developing these traits we must *want* in capital letters.

Jesus said, "Ask, and it shall be given you; seek, and ye shall find; knock, and it shall be opened unto you." (Matthew 7:7.) We must ask loudly enough, and seek sincerely enough, and knock long enough to get the right answer.

If our desires are weak, our industry will fail and our achievement will be small. There is an old saying that you can't keep a good man down, but that is just not true. Some of the potentially best men are presently being kept down by habits of mediocrity, ignorance, sin, sloth, and other natural enemies of excellence. We must turn on enough faith and develop enough ambition to carry us above our present questionable level. We need more excellence in our precepts, more excellence in our motivations, more excellence in our drive, more excellence in our preparation for life, and more excellence in our ambition to live life at its best.

Captain Cook shows us the spirit of excellence when he says about his early-day voyages of discovery, "I had an ambition, not only to go farther than any man had ever been before, but I wanted to go as far as it was possible for any man to go." Suppose that in the journey of our lives we set our goals to go as far as it is possible for anyone to go. Then we would be within reach of the goal of perfection set for us by the Master. We learn perfection by practicing perfection. No excellence is ever developed in a vacuum, and the Lord always fits the back to the burden. If we want a strong back, we should seek out a heavy load. What a thrilling opportunity to dedicate our lives in a quest for the excellence of God's celestial kingdom!

Chapter 10

A
Going Concern

Traveling on an airplane once, I had a very interesting conversation with my seat companion who was the chief investment counselor for his company. He had the primary responsibility for buying the securities that made up his company's financial portfolio. I was impressed with his knowledge of investments and the conditions that make men and companies successful or unsuccessful.

It seemed to me that he was almost completely familiar with most of those stocks being traded on the leading financial exchanges. He had made it his business to know as much as could be known about the men who ran the companies issuing stock to be sold to the general public, and to get an accurate opinion about the growth and income possibilities of those particular investments that would give the investor the greatest safety and the largest return. He was also fully abreast of the research of other experts in these fields.

There was one company whose stock he liked particularly well. It manufactured a product that was absolutely necessary to our way of life. This company did 40 percent of all of the business in that particular field. The thing that he was most enthusiastic about was the integrity, resourcefulness, and industry of the men who ran the company. He felt that this company had the most capable researchers, the finest administrators, and the most stimulating esprit de corps running throughout the organization. The company had a profit-sharing program which made every employee personally and financially interested in the company's success.

My friend felt there was no other company in the field that even came close to competing with this one. In product, technical expertise, reputation, finances, integrity, and management, this company was so far ahead of any competitors that even if the trends should be reversed it would take many years for anyone to catch up with it. The company was a "going concern" with a capital G.

There was only one thing about the situation that bothered my friend, and that was that the government was becoming concerned that this company, being so far ahead, would probably gain a practical monopoly. Though several other companies in this field were larger in size and resources, they could not compete, largely because of the greater human resources of the company which my friend liked so much.

I thought what an interesting employment this man had. He lived and breathed and thought and investigated success. It was his job to study the accomplishment of the greatest corporations and be able to recognize those elements which cause the most substantial progress. He had to be familiar with the most successful companies and products which, through intense competition with each other, help make up the strong nation that we know as America with the highest standard of living ever known in the world in any age. His personality, food, and drink consisted of being familiar with new inventions being made each year which would give the company producing them an advantage. He had an intimate familiarity with the kind of initiative and procedures of management that would guarantee the future growth of a company against the strongest competition under all conditions.

The records of the past indicate that while many companies are going out of business, others are emerging as the world's great automobile companies, merchandising institutions, airplane manufacturers, and banking institutions.

As a result of the planning, industry, and resourcefulness of inventors, scientists, and businessmen, we have giant grocery chains, educational institutions, medical research laboratories, all competing with each other to produce more effective goods and more efficient services at less cost with a greater profit to those who finance and promote the companies and use their products.

We live in the greatest age of wonders and miracles ever known in the world. In the parable of the sower, Jesus lets us listen to the heartbeat of a previous age. He tells of a farmer who sowed his wheat a handful at a time in a poorly prepared seed bed where some of the seeds fell among the thorns and thistles. Others fell on stony ground or upon the hard places and were lost. This was the way planting had been done since the beginning of time. When I was young, however, I saw my father plant his wheat by the same method.

In many areas of human activity our world has continued with little or no progress since time began. In the past, many people believed that they lived on a flat, stationary earth. They plowed their ground with a wooden stick and did many other things on a comparably low economic level. But that spirit is now out of date. The mood of our world has changed to one of atomic power and jet propulsion, with all of the miracles of manufacturing and merchandising extended to their highest limits. The gospel of Jesus Christ has been restored to the earth in a fullness never before known, and we must not let our share of the work of the Lord be done in the spirit of antiquated ineffectiveness.

Important changes have taken place also in the men and women who are responsible for carrying on our modern-day work. In the great invention and business interests of this country we have seen men like Thomas A. Edison, Henry Ford, and Albert Einstein, who, with short periods taken out for sleep, have worked around the clock at a terrific pace to make wonders of accomplishment available for the people who live on our earth. We may own stock or have our employment in the most efficient and useful of worldly organizations. Meanwhile the people's spiritual welfare is in the hands of those who make up their religious leadership.

In pondering the miracles and wonders of our age, I thought of the organization which we represent, The Church of Jesus Christ of Latter-day Saints. I wondered how some expert, like my friend of the airplane ride, would appraise the effectiveness of my work. I was made aware of the fact that, while American business is one of the modern wonders of the world, not all business people share in that success. Some represent those organizations that are going out of business, with great losses to everyone concerned. Some are identified with undertakings which could never be classified as a "going concern." Some sell shoddy merchandise and put themselves in a class with the unprofitable servant mentioned by Jesus. It is much better to be possessed of those virtues that bring success than those weaknesses and vices that cause failure. The Bible points out one of our greatest opportunities when it says: "Seest thou a man diligent in his business. He shall stand before kings, he shall not stand before mean men." (Proverbs 22:29.) We must not abandon the goal of excellence for mediocrity.

Many have lost fortunes for themselves and their stockholders by bad judgment and lack of industry, whereas investments of a thousand dollars made in any one of dozens of leading American corporations a few years ago have grown into fabulous fortunes.

We find the same situation in spiritual affairs, so far as good and bad performance is concerned. Everyone is not successful, even in that most important of all enterprises having to do with our own souls. Again the difference can be found in the know-how, attitudes, skills, and industry of individual human beings. We should keep our eyes open to the things we may be doing wrong as well as to the things that we are doing right. One prominent spiritual leader said that as a general rule, in his opinion, if we conducted our businesses the way we do our Church work they would be bankrupt in thirty days.

It seems to me that it would be a good thing for us occasionally to make an inventory of our own personal assets and liabilities in order to determine the effectiveness of our accomplishment in Church work and in life. The consequences of these things are much more important than the business and scientific projects in which as a nation we have recently made such great progress. We could list the areas in which we progress as well as the areas where we are falling down. Then we could improve on the things that are lifting us up, and eliminate the attitudes and procedures that are drawing us down. The following are some considerations which should make for our success:

1. We labor in the interests of The Church of Jesus Christ of Latter-day Saints, and the Master himself is its backer. He is tremendously interested in its success and will greatly prosper the life of anyone who advances its interest.

2. Our Father's business has the most important product. Better computers and typewriters, more effective airplanes, and more luxurious automobiles are fine in their way. But the product being promoted by the Church is eternal life, eternal success, and eternal happiness for everyone who will follow the direction of this divine organization. There is no product that can compare or compete with this in importance.

3. One of the things that influences the success of every business is how well it meets its competition. I have a list of some 2,460 makes of automobiles that have been manufactured in the United States in the last seventy-five years. With the exception of some five or six companies, all of these have now gone out of business and their make of automobile has been discontinued. A company may have a good product, but if its competition has a better one even a good company may fall.

While in my Father's business there is a great deal of competition, so far as other churches and doctrines are concerned, they all have a vastly inferior product. None of them offers marriages for time and for all eternity. None of them maintains the organization set up by the Savior of the world. None of them has divine authority to carry on their work. None of them is established upon the rock of revelation. All of them claim that the canon of scripture is full and that God will never again speak to his people upon the earth, whereas the Church of Jesus Christ has three great volumes of modern scripture outlining in every detail the simple principles of the gospel of Christ so that no one need get off that straight and narrow way except by his own choice. The Church teaches that there is much additional information that God will yet reveal to his people on the earth. None of the other religious organizations is built upon the foundation of apostles and prophets. In none of them are ministers called according to the direction given by the Lord.

There are many other contrasts. Some religious groups espouse the "new morality" instead of the stern "thou shalt nots" of the Ten Commandments. They settle for pleasures on the Sabbath day instead of the spiritual development, growth, and rest for which the Sabbath was intended. They do not have the organization that Christ said should be in his church. They do not do temple work or make any attempt to bind their families together eternally. For all this, in some cases they may be far outdistancing us in promoting their poor products over those which have been designed by God himself.

Clearly we must not fall down in our important assignments. We must not be unprofitable servants. We must not indicate to others that our part of the Lord's business is not a going concern. Success in the work of the Lord is everything. If we fail, many of those we are responsible for will lose their eternal blessings. The company with the best product would be acting foolishly if they employed mediocre salesmen or a weak, lethargic management. A good salesman working for a poor company will usually do a lot more business than a poor salesman working for a good company, and an effective leader of a church with man-made doctrines will, in many cases, have a larger following than a weak leader in The Church of Jesus Christ of Latter-day Saints. For all practical purposes we ought to be able to develop a near monopoly for the Lord, for he desires that none of his children should lose their blessings. We have a divine organization. We have the doctrines of truth. If we are the most reverent people and develop the finest leadership we cannot fail.

If any one of the present automobile companies should be given a monopoly to manufacture and sell all of the automobiles in the United States, with no foreign competition, just think how their business would soar. In our relationships with the people we are trying to help, we can point to the temples, to the greatest theology that has ever been known in the world, to divinely commissioned officers and leaders inspired by God, in a work which he himself has commanded, and a thousand other benefits and advantages. By permitting weaknesses in our leadership we may throw away many of our advantages. If the city that we set upon the hill is one that is not capable of the highest admiration and attraction, or if we ourselves sit down or lie down or fall down on the job, our Father's business cannot help but suffer tremendous losses.

We must never make the mistake of depending upon even good products to sell themselves. Emerson once said that if a person builds a better mousetrap than anyone else, though he lives in the woods, the world will beat a path to his door. But that is not always so. Even superior goods must be publicized and their virtues pointed out. The prospective purchasers must be informed and motivated, or they will not accept many things that are in their own best interests. Many people will not even seek an education or medical care or religious instruction without someone doing the promotion work. A business organization, even though it has a great product, needs to have a well-trained sales force, impressive company prestige, a good advertising program, and a wise, hard-working management. When we leave the promotion among the prospective elders, neglect our home teaching privileges, or conduct a family home evening without understanding or enthusiasm, we can easily foretell that the result will be some degree of failure. When we let down in our public relations, when we fail in the quality of our teachings, even the work of the Lord will suffer. We must see to it as leaders that we are conducting a "going concern." We must pay constant attention to those things in which we are not doing as well as we should.

Suppose we make a list of things we could do better. When a person wants to make a choice between automobiles, he usually likes to see the products. He wants to ride in them and find out about their gasoline mileage, trade-in value, and durability. Frequently, people come to Salt Lake City and to other Church centers where they can actually see the Church in operation. We talk to people that we would like to see as members of the Church, and they say, "Let me go and spend the day in seeing the Church and its people in actual operation."

As we showed them around, they might ask, "If the Church is all you say it is, why doesn't everyone join?" That is a good question. (Actually, many more would join if we members set the right example. As Emerson once said, "What you are thunders so loudly in my ears that I cannot hear what you say.")

Suppose we told our investigators about our weaknesses. Suppose we told them about our statistics on member inactivity, our large percentage of prospective elders, and our Word of Wisdom violations. Suppose we talked about our divorces and the disorder frequently existing in our sacred meetings. Their enthusiasm might be seriously reduced.

Recently I attended a priesthood meeting where almost every member of the priesthood was late. Planning for the meeting had not been well done. Many seats were empty. Many of the young people were poorly groomed, and wearing clothing unsuitable for the Sabbath day and the house of the Lord. And the attitudes of reverence and accomplishment were on a very low level. I thought what a disheartening assignment it would be to recruit nonmembers into this kind of situation. Many evidences testified that this ward just didn't give the impression of being a "going concern" in the best meaning of that term.

I tried to imagine the shock that an ambitious, forward-looking convert might feel after having gone through an inspired presentation of the restoration of the gospel in the greatest and final of all the dispensations, with the specific mission to prepare the world for the second coming of Christ, and then, after his conversion, to find himself a member of a ward filled with this kind of lethargy, disorder, negativism, inactivity and absenteeism.

As an important aspect of leadership we must learn to be

successful. We must not give the impression to anyone that The Church of Jesus Christ of Latter-day Saints cannot compete successfully in all-around attractiveness with man-made churches.

Chapter 11

Getting the Most out of Ourselves

I once read a stimulating magazine article entitled, "How to Get More Out of a Book Than There Is in It." That could turn out to be one of our most useful skills.

If a person could get out of a book everything there was in it, that would mark him as a superior person. Much of the information available for our lives comes from books, and reading with comprehension has always been an important skill. In recent years, however, with the progress made in radio and television, many people have lost much of their ability to read for themselves, with the result that the printed page tells some people much less than it does other people. We develop a great power in ourselves when we can transfer to our own minds, personalities, and characters, those things that are available to us on the printed page. But the article I mention above pointed out that even if we could transfer 100 percent of the good from the book to us, we would still be able to do even better. That is, we could get out of the book all that there is in the book and then, in addition, we could get all the things the book makes us think about.

Everyone has had the experience while reading, of the mind striking an idea which causes it to ricochet out into space. This magazine article suggested that we not be too quick to draw it back, but let it follow its impulse; and that then, as the mind climbs the chain of its own thought, it will produce some of its most constructive ideas.

Suppose you make notes of the various ideas your own mind generates while on these mental excursions. Then, when it has exhausted itself, draw it back into the book again and let it proceed to the next point where it may again eject itself. The human mind is equipped with a great power not only to create ideas but to improve on those that have already been created. Sometimes, when I hear myself "quoted," what I am given credit for is not what I said, or even what I thought. What happened was that I said something, and a listener thought about it. Then he told people what *he* thought, and he said that I had said it. He probably thought that I had said it because this thought was in his mind while I was speaking. The ideas that I am given credit for are usually better than what I actually said. To be agreeable, I frequently nod my head in acceptance even when actually I did not say or even think it quite as the listener expressed it.

By this process of association and addition we can get more out of a book than there is in it. By the same processes, we may get more out of an activity or a meeting or an association than there is in it. We may also get more out of a virtue or ambition than we thought was there when the virtue or ambition first presented itself. The best way to get leadership ideas is by doing. As Jesus pointed out in a parable, some of our good works pay us back thirtyfold, some sixtyfold, and some a hundredfold. If we go about it in the right way, we can get more out of life than we were able to recognize in it when we started out on life's journey. There are people who succeed in life to a far greater extent than they imagined to be possible when they first surveyed the landscape of the area they intended to traverse.

We ought to continually remember that we are the children of God with the potentiality and the capability of becoming like him. His projection of our destiny goes far beyond our own vision of our possibilities. God should be a partner with us in all of our righteous enterprises, and to keep up with our destiny we must not only "lengthen our stride" but we should also enlarge our vision, elevate our enthusiasm, strengthen our ambition, and quicken our heartbeat. Robert Browning said, "A man's reach should exceed his grasp, or what's a heaven for?" If we attempt a righteous undertaking in the right spirit, we may hope that our accomplishments outdistance our expectations. In this direction we may be stimulated by Horace Walpole's story of the three princes of Serendip who, in their excursions into life, were always finding wonderful things which they did not expect and for which they were not looking.

Certainly there will be wonderful things in heaven that we are unable to contemplate while we are here. The apostle Paul projected this idea when he said, "Eye hath not seen, nor ear heard, neither have entered into the heart of man, the things which God hath prepared for them that love him." (1 Corinthians 2:9.)

The poet was trying to help us when he wrote:

> Trust in thine own untried capacity
> As thou wouldst trust in God himself.
> Thy soul is but an emanation from the whole.
> Thou dost not dream what forces lie in thee,
> Vast and unfathomed as the grandest sea.
> No man can place a limit in thy strength;
> Such triumphs as no mortal ever dreamed
> May yet be thine if thou will but believe
> In thy creator and thyself.
> At length some feet shall stand
> On heights yet unattained.
> Why not thine own?
> Press on, achieve, achieve.

Because we cannot see the end from the beginning, because we cannot understand the power of our maturity from the weakness of our infancy, our accomplishment should always be greater than our original expectation. Our success is like a transcontinental locomotive as it begins its journey of three thousand miles. It has only enough power in its headlights to see what lies down the track for one mile, but before the engine's wheels outrun its headlights its light is extended for another mile, and thus the train proceeds down the rails a mile at a time.

When I stood at the beginning of my second estate, I would have sold out my success prospects pretty cheaply in every one of my life's departments. I have not done as well as I might have done, yet, in my opinion, in every good way my life has far excelled my wildest dreams, imaginations, and hopes. Even now, in company with many other people I know, I am still placing too mean an appraisal on the productivity prospects of my own life. My personal expectations do not come very close to the inference Jesus made when he compared the worth of my soul and your soul to the wealth of all of the earth.

It is a good thing never to underestimate life, neither the kind that God has nor the kind he has prepared for us. Neither should we underestimate what we can get out of it or what we can become by it. And we may be sure of one thing, that the more we put into it the more we will get out, and that result may represent a large multiplication factor. Life well lived is the most profitable enterprise in the universe, and the results or the rewards to be gained will indicate what its value really is.

It may be stimulating to our general leadership success to develop our reading skills far beyond their present level. A UPI report published in San Diego, under the date of June 23, 1977, indicates one of our biggest general success problems:

"Illiteracy among young Americans has become so widespread that the Navy is having trouble finding recruits who can read well enough to function, according to the chief of Naval personnel, Vice Admiral James D. Watkins.

"One illiterate sailor did $250,000 worth of damage to an engine because he couldn't read the instructions, and the Navy is increasingly obliged to teach recruits to read—sometimes up to a sixth grade level, so they can read urgent warnings.

"A recent study of 23,000 recruits at the Naval base here showed that thirty-seven percent of them could not read at the tenth grade level, Watkins told the Chamber of Commerce. Of those, 70 percent could not read well enough to complete boot camp, he said."

This modern-day inability to read has infiltrated all segments of our lives, including our religion. Church members need to learn to read and understand the scriptures. On the desks of many Church leaders can be found instructional and developmental mail which not only is unread but unopened. Much of that which has been read is not understood, and much of that which is understood has not been acted upon. It seems that these defects should be discussed and corrected, because reading disability among our Church leadership can cause some serious malfunctions in the purposes of the Church and in the eternal welfare of the membership.

Part Three

Management

Chapter 12

The Management Function of Leadership

In most businesses, job titles also serve as a description of the job to be done. For example, in a grocery store, one person may be pointed out as the manager, another as the janitor. There may be check-out people, bag carriers, buyers, and shelf-stockers.

In our Church assignments, the situation may be a little more complicated. To say that one is a high priest or a stake president, or a high councilor, may not, in itself, have much educational or motivational value in getting the job done.

If a businessman were to rename the leadership assignments of the ward with business titles, he might call the bishop the ward manager. The elders quorum president would also function as a manager of the lives of a large group of people, including prospective elders. These men, who are missing some of the important blessings of their lives, under an expert management may be brought to full fellowship. To manage effectively is one of the most valuable abilities that anyone could hope to develop. Suppose we take some examples from other fields. How fortunate are those engaged in business affairs who work under the direction of someone who is effective in his public relations and has his production and earning skills fully developed!

No ambitious football player would like to have his future tied up with a coach who did not know his business or how to manage the lives and efforts of his players. What a thrilling idea in any field to work under the direction of someone who knows how to teach and train and supervise and inspire and motivate! When Vince Lombardi took over the job of coaching the Green Bay Packers, his team was right on the bottom. They had lost almost every game for two seasons. In the seven years that Lombardi coached the Packers, however, they won five national championships.

It was said that Lombardi never coached a losing team. And it is quite likely that, so long as he kept to his standards, he never would. When any player played for Lombardi, that in itself would be almost a guarantee that he would be a champion, because Lombardi would see to it that he did the things that would make him a winner. Lombardi placed great emphasis on the character qualities as well as the attitudes of the players. It is costly in esprit de corps when we are not highly enthusiastic about our leaders and our associates. No organization is going to succeed which is made up of personal losers or those who lack high morale.

Certainly Lombardi would not permit one of his players to go into the game to throw passes until he was sure that this man not only knew how to throw passes but actually could and would throw passes effectively. If each end and each tackle and each guard and each of the backs and the center and the waterboy were sufficiently expert in all the parts of their jobs individually, the future of the team could be easily predicted. If a player could not be induced to do the things necessary for his own success, the problem could be easily and quickly solved. He just would not be on the team any more, and the coach would replace him with someone who would do all of the things that were necessary.

A number of years ago I read a thrilling book which was written by Harry Stuhldreher, entitled *Knute Rockne, Man Builder*. It describes in great detail the management attitudes and skills of the famous Notre Dame football coach as he went about the job of making athletic champions out of ordinary human beings. Knute Rockne believed as Vince Lombardi believed, that winning is not just the most important thing in athletics, it is everything. Winning is also everything in the great game of life. No organization of any kind and no individual can afford to allow too many exceptions to his success, as a few "little" leaks can sink the greatest ship or destroy the finest religious leadership.

Now, suppose we apply some of these principles to the management functions of the bishop. He is the one who carries the management responsibility for the welfare of everyone in the ward. He must not fall down in any detail, and while he may delegate some of this responsibility to auxiliary heads or quorum leaders or others, he never loses the slightest bit of his original jurisdiction. It is his job to see that a high morale is maintained throughout the ward, that his counselors and all other workers are enthusiastic, well-informed, well-trained, and performing at their maximum. He should make certain, as far as possible, that no one fails in his righteousness or in his relations with other people, or in his accomplishment. Certainly the Lord would not be pleased if the organization that bears his name (The Church of Jesus Christ) and ours (of Latter-day Saints) should turn out a group of delinquents, weaklings, hippies, or other unprofitable servants. The bishop who desires to magnify his calling as ward manager should see to it that the Lord, as well as every member, makes a profit on the bishop's stewardship.

The dictionary says that management is the act or art of managing and directing. I like to think of it as the ability to put all the available power right on the piston head, rather than have an explosion take place in the gas tank or the fuel line. The good manager organizes his forces, and then he is able to release all the power at the right spot at the exact time when needed.

A good manager is a thinker, an organizer, a strategist, a salesman, a motivator. He is the one who draws the blueprint and builds the roadway on which any who desire success may travel. We have a pretty miserable leadership situation any time we have a manager who does not manage effectively and who deals in failures rather than successes.

When I was a boy in high school, I used to work for a farmer during the summer who was always thinking about something else except farming. He had two pieces of land located a few miles apart. He would hook up his horses to the wagon and then, instead of driving the horses, he used to do something comparable to herding them. That is, he would sit in the wagon and flap the horses on the backs with the reins while he read a book on philosophy or on another subject equally irrelevant to the job at hand. It would be a difficult thing for these horses to win a race or a pulling contest with a driver who didn't drive. It is a lot easier for a football team to win games with a coach who knows his players' skills down to the last detail; likewise, it would be easier for a horse to become a champion if he had an expert driver to hold the reins and to effectively apply the whip of motivation or the brakes of caution when necessary.

Someone said that in order to understand any success situation it is a good idea to walk completely around it so as to see it on both its positive and its negative sides. Suppose we consider some cases where Church leaders have proven or may prove to be poor managers. If this cannot be done without the fear of being thought critical, then we could take some hypothetical cases. We learn fastest by opposites, and we need the power of contrast to give effectiveness to our management skills. We must understand weakness if we are going to develop strength.

For example, ward A has a large number of young people between the ages of nine and twenty-one who have not yet been baptized. This fact indicates that the bishop is either not capable of getting these people baptized when they are eight years old, or that he hasn't really accepted his responsibility for getting them baptized. There are people who feel that problems ought to solve themselves, or, in some cases, the leader may be so unenthusiastic that he doesn't think about his responsibility sufficiently one way or the other. The unpleasant fact is that the job is not getting done.

Ward B has a very low percentage of people attending sacrament meeting. Ask the bishop why it is that his people don't come to sacrament meeting, and he may tell you that he does not know. Yet, every responsible leader must know, for how are we going to prescribe a remedy if we do not understand the problem?

To find the right answers to these questions is the job of the management. Thomas A. Edison gave us an important key to success. He said, "There is always a better way of doing a thing than we are presently using." No one else in Thomas Edison's day seemed to be interested in lighting the world, but Thomas Edison was. Because he continued to think about the problem, and because he felt there must be better ways to illuminate the world at night than with a tallow candle, he began coming up with some answers.

Not all of Thomas Edison's experiments were successful, but he learned by cataloging and studying each failure to determine why it failed. In devising our own success experiments, we need to discover why some of our procedures do not work well. Someone has said that a plan is no plan at all unless it is on paper. When we write our mistakes down and find out why our programs are failing, we may discover a better way.

Ward C has a large number of families who pay no ward maintenance. To an industrious, sales-minded, resourceful ward manager there are several good and easy ways of solving this problem. He could write down the possible solutions and have them critiqued by the stake president. Then he could make a graph to show attendance and other success factors as the plan decided upon is put in operation. In this way, the value of the plan will be apparent. A plan has no value if it does not work.

Ward D has a large number of families who do not have family home evenings.

Ward E does very little in the way of genealogical work.

Ward F has a large group of prospective elders. These men may be in danger of losing some of their greatest blessings, and they are in desperate need of the kind of coaches who can make them champions.

Ward G has many of its young people indulging in the kind of marriage which says, "Until death do us part." Neither the bishop nor the stake president knows why this is so. They have made no surveys, no private investigations. They are like doctors trying to treat patients without knowing what diseases are causing the difficulties.

Ward H has only a small percentage of members who have filled missions, and the bishop does not know how to increase this particular activity.

Some wards have a combination of all of these defects. The problems vary in individual wards because of the degree of industry and enthusiasm of the people involved.

No bishop is ever appointed to be the ward manager with the hope that he will allow the work of the Lord to fail in those areas where he holds jurisdiction. And it is likely he will fail or succeed according to his ability to produce success in each area of the ward.

If a great football coach were planning a championship team, he would arrange his training and motivation so as to have some good passers, some excellent pass receivers, some accurate long-distance kickers, and some fast runners. He would want a quarterback with a head full of strategy and a brain capable of quick thinking. He would also want team members who wanted to win and were willing to train for effectiveness and to drill until their skills were developed to a championship level.

This is also what a good bishop should do. If a bishop waits until Sunday School time before selecting and training his Sunday School leaders, he will probably not win the game for that day. If he waits until his young people are ready to get married before he begins to develop their character and morality and their attitude about marriage and success, he can be pretty sure that he will have a lot of marriage failures and unhappiness. If he waits until a young man is nineteen years old to teach him grooming standards and effective lesson presentation, he can be certain that he is passing a real headache on to the mission president, who will be in about the same situation as a football coach would be who had to stop during the game to train his players.

I know of a bishop who starts his people towards baptism on the day they are born, even though it is not proper for them to be baptized until they are eight years old. This bishop knows that if they are going to be enthusiastic about being baptized when they are eight, they need to have good parents and a good Primary organization to teach them. So the bishop sees to it that the parents, the Primary, the Sunday School and all the others involved, effectively do their jobs long before age eight arrives. Someone has said that if you want to make a good man out of someone, you should start with his grandparents. When these children are between seven and eight, an even more intensive preparation is made for their baptism. On their seventh birthday, the bishop writes their parents a letter which says, "Today John is seven years old, and in one year he will be old enough to be baptized." Then he outlines a program for the year. At all times, the bishop knows what the child's position is and knows that he is on schedule for baptism.

Two weeks before his eighth birthday, the bishop goes to see his prospective ward member. He might say to him, "John, what important day is March 31?"

John would say, "That is my birthday."

"Which birthday?"

John would answer, "I will be eight years old."

Bishop: "What is important about that?"

John: "That's the time I'm supposed to be baptized."

Bishop: "Are you ready to be baptized? Is it important to be baptized? Do you want to be baptized?"

The bishop can then stress the importance and significance of baptism in such a way that this young man or woman will always remember it.

Suppose the bishop lets the baptismal day go by unnoticed, even for a day or a week? A good husband knows what a favorable effect can be produced by talking to his wife about their wedding anniversary or other important dates in advance so that she knows this day is important to him and he has made elaborate plans for its happy celebration. But suppose the husband forgets to talk to his wife about the wedding anniversary until three days after the date has passed. The effect produced might be as different as a winter blizzard is to a warm spring day. Much of effective leadership is found in timeliness. It does not take nearly as much time or as much effort or as much intelligence to do a job when it should be done than to try to overcome one's bungling by apologies and lessened prestige after the right psychological moment has passed.

Many a leader does not understand the advantages of

timeliness. He does not know that both children and adults can feel hurt and disappointed if he, the leader, is not properly prepared and organized in his job. There are some people who have never been invited to be baptized even by the time they are twenty-five years of age. Some people have never been invited to prepare for a mission or had the bishop point out to them the thrilling advantages of building excellence into their personal lives. Such a bishop is a very poor manager and may be held personally accountable.

President John Taylor says in substance, "We can get anybody into effective spiritual activity if we go about it in the right way and at the right time." On the other hand, any parent or Church leader can just about ruin someone's chances if he goes about his assignment in the wrong way. Good judgment, punctuality, and good management ability make the difference.

Some time ago, I attended a ward Aaronic Priesthood meeting where the leaders kept referring to four of their boys as "impossible boys." I asked them what they meant, and they said these boys were just impossible—they were disinterested, they had bad habits, and their parents set them a bad example.

I said, "Are you sure you can't get any of them?"

They said they were positive.

I said, "Just suppose that I am a very wealthy man, and that I will pay you ten thousand dollars apiece for each of these boys you can get to church by ten o'clock in the morning. Now, how many can you get?"

They replied, "Oh, if you will pay us ten thousand dollars apiece, we can get them all!"

It was not the boys who made the job impossible, it was the attitude of the leaders. The Lord did not say he would pay us merely ten thousand dollars apiece to get these boys in the celestial kingdom. He said, "Therefore all that my Father hath shall be given unto him." (D&C 84:38.)

I was once consulted by a stake president who wanted to know if I had any suggestions to overcome the tendency in his stake for almost all of the young people to get married outside the temple. I asked him what the reason was for this failure, and he seemed not to have any well-developed idea. I asked him if he had talked to any of them personally about it and he said no. In some ways this stake president was a very good man, but he was a very poor manager of the religious interests of this particular group of his people.

One bishop couldn't understand why his people did not attend sacrament meeting, but anyone of ordinary judgment who attended one of this bishop's meetings could soon find the answer. The bishop took the attitude that the Lord had commanded everyone to attend sacrament meeting, and that should take care of everything, and there was nothing that he could do about it. Apparently he did not understand that a good choir had something to do with sacrament meeting attendance. He did not understand that a high degree of order and reverence would attract many people who were now being repelled. He did not seem to understand that a friendly group of well-trained ushers and greeters could help induce more people to attend sacrament meeting.

I attended a sacrament meeting conducted in the name of the Lord which was almost unbelievable. It was poorly attended. Most of the people came in late. The physical environment was as unattractive as the spirit in which the meeting was conducted. There was an intolerable amount of disorder and confusion. There were many people walking in and out of the room during the service. The meeting was conducted without much planning and in a very unprofessional way. I think the bishop of the ward would have received a very low score in management. He seemed to know very little about the power of attraction, the virtue of reverence, the excellence of order or friendliness, or how beauty can be put into a sacred service where the work of the Lord is being done. Of course, all good management must be based on careful and wise planning.

It is hard to think of any success trait more necessary than good planning, with the possible exception of those qualities found in an enthusiastic, hard-driving human being who is able to supply the industry and motivation to make the planning effective and to win for himself the high title of a good manager.

Chapter 13

Supervision

One of the things that has always given me a lot of satisfaction is the contemplation of a great human being at his best. Like everything else, we can think of people as being made up of their individual qualities. Everyone has some personality traits and character qualities, as well as knowledge, attitudes, skills and habits, in which he may be expected to excel. And anyone can constitute his life in the way that he desires by putting these qualities and abilities together in himself in the right combinations and proportions.

We might think of life as maintaining for our benefit a great personality store where we may go and fit ourselves out with those abilities, skills, and attitudes that would bring out our greatest potential as human beings. Someone wrote some lines in which he said: "I love you, not only for what you are, but for what I am when I am with you. I love you not only for what you have made of yourself, but for what you are making of me. You have made out of the lumber of your life not a tavern but a temple, and you have made of my every day not a reproach, but a song." So it is that we not only fashion greatness in ourselves, but we can transfer the best of our virtues and abilities to others.

If we gave someone the gift of an automobile or a house or a piece of valuable real estate, he would think of us as his good friend. But suppose we help him to develop a high measure of success, good judgment, a love of life, and an enthusiasm for righteousness, then what is our relationship to him?

There is one leadership quality that sets us apart from others which we might call supervision. This is a trait which not only improves us, but when we use it, it can make the lives of everyone around us more worthwhile. In trying to understand some of the aspects of this trait, suppose we divide the subject of leadership into six parts: number one, the *selection* of the leader; number two, *recruiting* him to an enthusiastic acceptance of his leadership office; number three, *induction*—he needs to put on the uniform, so to speak; number four, *training*—a well-trained man is always more effective than an untrained man, whether he be a doctor, teacher, salesman or a leader; number five, *supervision*; number six, *motivation*—there are no failures in life, there are merely people who lack sufficient motivation.

One of the brightest and most helpful of these leadership qualities is supervision. Many of these great words lose their value, however, because we do not understand them or what our relationship should be with them. We sometimes hold ourselves apart from great ideas that would multiply our usefulness by many times.

The dictionary says that to supervise means to oversee, to give direction. It means to superintend, or to inspect with authority. Frequently, in those situations where we need supervision most, there is no one around with authority over us who feels free to give us the kind of direction that we ought to have. Even when we are working under the authority of an employer, he may not feel free to give us the kind of direction that we may need most in those things not directly connected with our work.

Some recent surveys conducted at Stanford University indicated that 94 percent of all people who lost their jobs did so because of some trait not even remotely related to any actual job competence. That is, most people can learn to do the actual work involved, but they fall down because of some personality or moral defect. We may use bad judgment, have poor timing, or be held down by a bad attitude. Someone has said that the best way to judge a person is by what he does when he is away from his job. It seems to me that we can get a great deal out of this word *supervision* by subtracting the authority aspect and breaking the idea down into its parts of *super* and *vision*. Taken separately these words may mean excellence in our ability to see ideas in their right relationships to other things and other people. With this kind of vision and the willingness to make suggestions, someone might help us to see ourselves as others see us. Then we could conduct our lives in a way that would please God and make us more fully acceptable to other people as well as to ourselves.

We think of supervision primarily in relation to our occupation and to someone having some particular authority over us. That, of course, is a very important place where it does belong. But this supervisory responsibility also belongs to a lot of other people. We remember Cain's inquiry to the Lord, "Am I my brother's keeper?" That question might have a great many constructive answers. Supervision belongs to parents; it belongs to friends; it belongs to religious officers. Supervision doesn't work very well in the presence of too many blind spots. I know a religious congregation which has been under the same leadership for several years. In my opinion, the biggest single disadvantage these people have is a kind of careless permissiveness in the leadership which reduces its supervision to a point where it has very little value. For example, people may be as tardy as they like in attending their church meetings. Most of what is said in the public meetings is either not spoken loudly enough to be heard by the people, or not expressed clearly enough to be understood, or drowned out by noise and confusion. This particular religious association is on a kind of basis where everyone endlessly "does his own thing" with no apparent interest or visible help from anybody else—including the leadership.

This religious organization is a teaching organization, yet no one ever discusses clarity of speech, or proper enunciation, nor are the speakers and teachers taught to speak loudly enough so that others can hear clearly without straining and missing a large part of what is said. In spite of the unusual amount of disorder and noise among the members, no restraining instruction or encouragement is ever given. The general attitude, as is often the case, seems to be that everyone should have the freedom to do as he pleases in his own way. Assuming a membership of five hundred people in this religious body, and counting all of those that they in turn will influence negatively, just think of the damage that will be done over a generation because one ecclesiastical leader has not properly magnified his office by getting sufficient quality into his supervision, a quality which would automatically increase the strength and value of his leadership.

Paul the apostle indicated that we should have a more tightly knit interest in each other. He said, "Bear ye one another's burdens." (Galatians 6:2.) He intended that we should set each other a good example in love, helpfulness, and righteousness. In a substantial way every man is his brother's keeper, and we should see to it that those who depend upon us do not make too many mistakes. Each of us is also responsible for his brother's encouragement, enthusiasm, and faith. Each of us has some blind spots so far as we ourselves are concerned. Therefore, our "super vision" may be most effective when we are helping someone else.

I know of another body of over twenty-five leaders who meet together regularly in a large meeting room in a kind of board of directors' function. Their avowed purpose is to inform, strengthen and uplift each other. They have no electronic assistance for their voices. Some of these men who are not properly conscious of their responsibility for the meeting's total success speak in such a low tone that much of this important meeting is missed by others. But some have duller ears than others, some, weaker voices, and the fact that we can hear ourselves and understand what we are saying does not mean that the one sitting in the far corner of the room is getting our message loudly enough and clearly enough to be easily understood. A false modesty prompts some to keep secret the fact that they are not hearing well. Thus this group of intelligent men go on year after year missing much of the very benefit for which they meet, because no one is willing to assume the supervisory role of making certain that everyone can hear and be heard.

An important business leader that I know has the habit of holding his hand up in front of his mouth as he is speaking. He is a very intelligent man, but if he had a little supervisory help the good which he does for other people would be greatly increased. Anyone with a little courage and a little diplomacy could sit down with him and help him over this problem, but because of lack of courage, or lack of interest, or for fear of what someone may think, no one does. Again, think of the inexcusable losses that come in learning, in morale, in intelligence, and in several other ways from such a small, easily corrected problem.

When I was a member of the Sunday School general board, I was asked by the Sunday School general superintendent to attend a particular Sunday School stake convention. He pointed out that one of the problems in this particular stake was that, of the sixty officers and teachers in the stake, only five subscribed to the *Instructor*, the teaching magazine of the Church at that time. He asked that I encourage, as effectively as I could, the other fifty-five teachers to subscribe.

Accordingly, I called the stake superintendent on the telephone four weeks in advance of the convention and asked him if he would please take care of the matter before the convention took place. The superintendent's attitude was such that I could easily see why unimaginative teachers did not subscribe. He felt that there was nothing he could do beyond making an apathetic, permissive, halfhearted announcement about subscription.

I suggested that he get his people together and talk to them enthusiastically about this fine teaching magazine which was the best the Church was able to produce. As an alternative, I suggested that he have each of his ward superintendencies make a personal call on their teachers and show them the *Instructor* and read to them from it and give them some personal examples of how teaching effectiveness could be increased by using it. He agreed to make a try.

When I met him at the meeting I asked him how he got along in selling the *Instructor* to his teachers. He said, "Not very well."

"Tell me about it," I said.

"Do you see the man coming in the door?" he asked. "I invited him to subscribe, and he said, 'Do you actually believe I ought to subscribe? I once subscribed to it for three years and never in that time did I break the wrapper or look through a single magazine. Do you think I ought to subscribe again?' "

The stake superintendent said, "No, I suppose there is no point in your subscribing if you are not going to read it." And he seemed to think he had given the right answer.

"All of my life," I said to the superintendent, "I have wanted to hear a teacher teach who did not need any teaching help, and maybe this is my opportunity. Would it be all right with you if I attend his class and listen to him teach?"

He agreed, and both of us went to the class.

This teacher had a class of nine-year-old girls. At that time I had a daughter who was just nine years of age, and the little girl on the end of the row reminded me of her. They all looked so pretty in their new dresses and other Sunday attire. They seemed as though they had been scrubbed and starched and perfumed and decorated. They were coming to this Sunday School class for several reasons. One of them was to learn how to handle the problems that they would meet in the next few years of their lives. Someone has said that the time to get a ship ready for the storm is not when it is in the middle of the ocean being pounded by the waves; the time to get a ship ready for the storm is when the boat is still in the dockyard and the planks are being chosen and the rivets are being driven.

This man stood up before these beautiful young children and for the entire period told them about his war experiences. The stories were poorly told and made no beneficial point. These girls would have been much better off if they had never heard them. This man was *drafted* into the army. He was *forced* to have some war experiences. He could not tell them about his religious experiences because he had not had any. I felt a terrible heartsickness for these fine young people who were someday going to find themselves unfortified for the problems that this Sunday School class was designed to solve in advance.

After the meeting I asked this teacher some loaded questions. I said to him, among other things, "I suppose you have a lot of visitors come into your class to listen to you teach."

He replied, "No, I have taught this class for four years and you are the first visitors I have ever had."

I questioned further. "Of course you don't mean that the bishopric does not come in to hear you, or that you don't have occasional visits from the Sunday School superintendency."

"No," he said, "not one of them has ever been in the room in the four years I have been teaching."

Again I felt a horrible emptiness around my heart that this Sunday School superintendency and the bishopric with their sacred "super vision" responsibilities could so completely ignore their opportunities as to let this man go on without help for all these years, considering the great damage he could do to those wonderful little human souls.

We sometimes accuse our friends in other churches of preaching false doctrine when they say that God made the earth out of nothing. We say that is impossible; no one can make something out of nothing. Yet we teach a more serious kind of false doctrine when we say that you can make a family home evening or an effective home teaching visit out of nothing. Certainly it would be false doctrine to say that you could make a warm, friendly, vitalizing "super vision" out of nothing. We usually don't get more out of a thing than we put into it, and good "super vision" is made up of association, inspection, discussion, and a thorough knowledge of the program to be supervised.

As we make our way through the world, we ought to be conscious of those people from whom we may expect helpful suggestions. That includes just about everybody: our families, our religious officers, etc., etc. We should also be aware of those people for whose success we carry some of the responsibility. Every day we ought to pray to God that, among the great abilities he blesses us with from his personality store, one will be "super vision."

Chapter 14

Personal Coaching

In one of the great statements in the scriptures, Jesus spoke of those who have eyes that don't see and ears that can't hear and hearts that fail to understand. There are many of us to whom this statement has a personal and particular meaning. It is likely that each of us has a few blind spots as well as some deaf and dumb areas so far as some specific problem is concerned.

Shakespeare tries to help us understand this natural human weakness. He has Hamlet counsel the performers "to hold, as 'twere, the mirror up to nature; to show virtue her own feature [and] scorn her own image." And in *Julius Caesar*, Cassius tells Brutus:

> And, since you know you cannot see yourself
> So well as by reflection, I, your glass,
> Will modestly discover to yourself
> That of yourself which you yet know not of.

That is a service we should take as much advantage of as possible.

Anyone who aspires to be a great athlete or a great businessman or a great Latter-day Saint needs to have a coach on the sidelines. A coach can most easily discover what a player's strengths and weaknesses are. His job is to take a personal and expert interest in building up the strengths, eliminating the weaknesses, and increasing the satisfactions of the one being coached. Certainly this is one of the reasons why the Lord sends out missionaries and home teachers two by two, so that they may uplift and motivate each other. The Lord said: "And if any man among you be strong in the Spirit, let him take with him him that is weak, that he may be edified in all meekness, that he may become strong also." (D&C 84:106.)

John Greenleaf Whittier was speaking on this subject when in his quaint Quaker style he said: "Me lift thee and thee lift me and we'll both ascend together." While that may not be possible in a physical way, it is the essence of moral and spiritual development. We lift each other simultaneously.

Among the greatest benefactors in my life were my counselors in the bishopric. In a very frank and constructive way they used to have their mirrors out a great deal of the time, helping me to see my problems. A person's judgment is no better than his information, and if we are not getting all of the necessary information about ourselves honestly and frankly, our judgment is bound to be faulty. Receiving a lot of misleading pats on the back is not a very good way to correct faults.

A high school student was once asked by the teacher of his physics laboratory class to come to his office at the close of the period. This was a very good student who was president of the senior class. He might have imagined that the teacher was going to commend him for his work. Instead, the teacher said, "You are the most disturbing influence in this class." The student was dumbfounded. He loved the teacher, he loved the subject. He received "A" grades, but he had some blind spots that were causing others to be distracted. He usually finished his experiments before the others, and in returning his equipment he stopped and visited along the way. His whispers were much louder to the ears of others than they were to his own. And his deaf spots were causing problems for others.

In a kindly way, the teacher talked to the student about his problem. This student wanted to do right, and this personal coaching was of great and lasting benefit to him. It also helped the other members of the class. A personal, individual interview is much more effective than aiming a shotgun blast at the whole class. A good bishop or a good Sunday School superintendent or anyone else who wants to be effective should develop ability and courage in his personal coaching procedures for the benefit of those under his direction.

I saw a young man in a Church leadership position with an unkempt and unbecoming hairdo. The other people in the meeting were properly groomed. I don't know what this young man was trying to prove or who he was rebelling against, but something unpleasant inside was manifesting itself on the outside. It may have been that he was merely trying to attract attention or advise other people that he was different, but consciously or subconsciously he was disrupting other people and was signaling for help. He was so far out that many people felt sorry for him. Of course, everyone tried to be nice to him and treat him as though they didn't think there was anything wrong, but he was flashing to their minds an image of rebellion and evil. He was lowering the general prestige and was causing disharmony in the group and great damage to his own public relations with this particular group of people.

What a great help it could be to him if the bishop would sit down with him and try to find out what his problem is! This young man may be having trouble at home, or may have some anti-social problems that the bishop could help straighten out. There are many troubled people who would welcome the chance to talk about their difficulties with someone whom they trusted and loved. Some people have moral problems or Word of Wisdom problems or other problems of behavior that can be eliminated by talking with someone who stands high in their regard.

For several months, one good mother had been offending many fellow ward members because she had been allowing her children to be disorderly in church. Her children were also disrupting the other children in their classes. The bishop sat down with this woman and her husband and helped them to see the problem. This couple were creating many antagonisms for themselves and their family by offending other ward members. Like the high school student, when they understood the situation they were able to solve the problem. In so doing, they helped themselves, their children, and everyone else in the ward.

The chief function of a bishop or a teacher or a sales manager or anyone else who is responsible for the success of others is not merely to conduct a meeting or teach a class. He is expected to be skilled in several other kinds of communication. One of these is example. But the chief business of leadership is usually in the area of individual coaching, training, and management. This individual attention to his ward members gives the bishop a chance to inspire and motivate them. People spend a lot of money for doctors, psychiatrists and counselors. For this money they want individual, personal attention to their specific problems. In the Church we have personal interviews for those who are to receive recommends, be advanced in the priesthood, or appointed to or released from office. In large part, these interviews may involve counseling. Certainly we ought to have some "personal coaching" for those who have individual problems.

To make general announcements about problems doesn't usually help solve the problems, because the people involved don't recognize themselves as part of the problem. Even if they do, it may not have personal significance to them. They may say, "I am not the only one." It is probably in the field of personal coaching that good leaders can do the greatest amount of good. The greatest leader is the one who can guarantee the greatest amount of benefit to his followers, and that can best be done with an adequate amount of individual, personal attention to specific problems.

Chapter 15

The
Penicillin Cures

Some years ago, I contracted a common cold. The cold hung on a little longer than my wife thought it should have, and she suggested that I ought to see the doctor and have him help me to get rid of the slight cough that still remained. Taking her suggestion, I visited the doctor's office and, without testing my medical allergies, the doctor gave me a good strong shot of penicillin, which he expected would administer the knockout blow to what remained of my cold. The treatment got rid of the cold in short order, and it almost got rid of me.

What neither I nor the doctor knew was that I had a powerful allergy to penicillin, and during the next several weeks I didn't know whether I would make it or not. I had a terrible rash break out on every part of my body, and I was very sick. My wife called the doctor who had given me the treatment, but he had gone out of town. So she got another doctor to try to cure me of the treatment given by the first doctor. Later, I received the bill for both of these doctors' services in the same mail. The one who cured me of the cold charged me ten dollars. The one who cured me of the treatment charged me fifty dollars. Not only was the cure more expensive than the disease, but it was also a lot more painful and a lot more damaging to my system. I have been advised by several doctors to carry some identification so that, in case I should be treated while I am unconscious, the doctor will know about my allergy and will not destroy my life while he is trying to save it.

This phenomenon of the cure being worse than the disease is not limited to penicillin and the common cold. This damaging circumstance works about the same way in many other situations. We had a national example when some Republicans tried to learn some of the political secrets of the Democrats by wiretapping. Without helping the Republicans or harming the Democrats, the entire country was given a dose of penicillin with all the resulting horrors which we now know as Watergate. We strained at a gnat and swallowed a whole caravan of camels, and in the process we almost wrecked our national integrity and harmony in the minds of a great many people. On this one incident and its aftermath which apparently did not do anyone any good, we spent hundreds of millions of dollars of taxpayers' money. People were put out of office, others were put in prison, and many experienced the destruction of their political careers and social prestige. This ought to remind us that each of us similarly is eligible to make some serious mistakes in his own affairs, and we ought therefore to find the proper way of doing a thing before we dive into it with all our strength.

A similar penicillin error was responsible for the inscription on one man's tombstone which said, "Hanged by mistake." I read an article about yet another penicillin cure, effected by the prison system operating in parts of our great country. It told of the conditions inside a certain United States prison. The officials inside this particular prison were very zealous in their desire to reform criminals. Their problem was that they did not know how to go about it. They reasoned that, if confinement was a good thing for the prisoner, it must be true that beating and starving him would be better. This brutality built up great bitterness and hate in the minds and hearts of the prisoners, and when a term of imprisonment had been fulfilled, instead of an inmate being cleansed of the wrong he had committed, the only thing to show for all the taxpayers' money was a bitter, hardened, resentful criminal. This is not exceptional. There are thousands who have gone into the penitentiary for the disease of a minor infraction and have come out many years later far worse than they were before receiving the treatment which was supposed to cure them. One of the important facts of our personal life too is that our treatments should not be such as to produce an effect many times worse than the diseases they are intended to eliminate.

A far different situation was reported from ancient Greece when a young, ruthless hoodlum put out one of the eyes of the great statesman, Pericles. The law of ancient Greece gave the wronged man absolute power over the criminal who had done him harm. Pericles could have enslaved or killed or imprisoned or beaten the one who had done him the damage. Instead, Pericles took the hoodlum into his home and taught him the principles of righteousness and love. By his kindness and helpfulness, Pericles gained the everlasting devotion of this young man and in the process drained all the violence out of his soul.

A few years later, Pericles took this young man back to the city fathers and said to them, in substance, "I received this young man from your hands filled with bitterness, hate, and violence. I now restore him to your custody, a man of honor and righteousness who will serve Athens as a model citizen for the rest of his days."

In the Doctrine and Covenants (121:39) it is stated: "We have learned by sad experience that it is the nature and disposition of almost all men, as soon as they get a little authority, as they suppose, they will immediately begin to exercise unrighteous dominion." This sin of unrighteous dominion, like the penicillin cure, is one of the things we should guard against in the government, in marriage, in our social affairs, and in our religious activities.

The doctor who gave me the penicillin was a highly qualified man, but he made a mistake and I almost lost my life as a consequence. And for this service he charged me ten dollars. With equal ignorance, however, and frequently with some maliciousness, we may try to discipline people, or mete out punishments to them, or we withdraw our approval and exert other sanctions against them and thus make the cure many times worse than the disease. A wife or husband sometimes retaliates bitterly against the real or imagined faults of the other, and this usually makes their situation worse rather than better.

President Hugh B. Brown gave an account of a time when he was a counselor to Bishop Dennison Harris in Canada. Brother Brown and the other counselor were both young men, whereas Bishop Harris was a little older and more mature in his spirituality. One evening, a young woman was brought before the bishopric accused of a very serious sin. She confessed to it, and was repentant and contrite. After hearing the case, the bishopric asked the woman to wait in the outer office. Bishop Harris then consulted with his counselors as to what course they should take, and both recommended excommunication. But Bishop Harris asked the woman to come back in, and after some discussion with her, he told her they would like to settle the matter by the bishopric uniting to give her a blessing.

With great wisdom, love, and kindness, the bishop discussed a plan with her for her to be more active in her Church work and in the social relationships of the ward. Because kindness is a powerful instrument of leadership, this woman accepted the constructive program outlined by the bishop with great enthusiasm. She also left the meeting more humble, more happy, more grateful and more determined to be worthy of the bishop's blessing than she had ever been before. That is, instead of a possibly demoralizing penicillin shot, they had given her a vitalizing, life-giving treatment of love, righteousness, and faith.

Many years later, when Elder Brown was a General Authority of the Church, he was assigned to a conference in Canada. While there, he discovered that this woman was one of the stalwarts of the stake. She was the stake Relief Society president, had raised an outstanding family, had sent four sons on missions after her husband's death, and had been faithful and true all along. The kindness of Bishop Harris had paid off in actual practice a thousandfold, just as the kindness of Pericles had enriched Athens many centuries before. In commenting upon this instance, Elder Brown said that he was "glad that God is an older man" (words Bishop

Harris had used those many years before), and that he would be fortunate enough to have God as his judge rather than a young whippersnapper similar to the one that he may have previously been.

Of course, kindness, reason, good judgment and generosity are not virtues that are brought on by age alone. Sometimes our attitudes of unrighteous dominion increase with our years. Someone once said that if he could add one more commandment to the ten that came down from Sinai, it would be "Thou shalt not be unkind." Neither high position nor old age nor Church membership by themselves take away this tendency to shoot someone full of spiritual penicillin even though it is going to cause his death. Not all the people who are trigger-happy are gunmen. There are too many people who vote for hanging, excommunication, and slander, and too few are giving people encouragement and blessings and confidence in each other. It is not just generous to be kind. Kindness is also the course of wisdom and self-preservation. The Lord has said, "For with what judgment ye judge, ye shall be judged; and with what measure ye mete, it shall be measured to you again." (Matthew 7:2.)

It may be that by his kindness Pericles saved a hundred generations of the posterity of the young man that he transformed from a hoodlum to a good citizen. And some different kind of treatment by Bishop Harris could have destroyed the woman as well as that great multitude of her posterity and those whom she influenced for good. The great apostle Paul gave us a life-saving line when he said to the Romans, "Recompense to no man evil for evil." (Romans 12:17.) Sometimes we deal out evil where, if punishment is called for, we ourselves should be the ones to receive it.

A very wise man once said that we are guilty of all the good we could but do not do. We are also judged for our negative influence. And if the facts could be known, there would probably be a list of names of people responsible for the downfall of each person who falls below what he should be. It just may be that our name is on the list as having made evil contributions to the lives of many others without meaning to do so.

God wants to bless us, and it is our responsibility to bless other people, not to hurt them. I have never seen anyone yet for whom I thought some kindness or helpfulness was not better than a kick or a slander or a hurt. To be bearers of evil and dispensers of punishment have never been very profitable undertakings. One of the most important purposes of the Church is to bless, not to destroy or to deal in evil publicity and the magnification of shame. Yet as long as we deal with human beings we are in danger of using our penicillin shots at the wrong time.

Satan himself was once the light bearer, a brilliant son of the morning, one high in authority, before he rebelled against God. In attempting to exalt himself, he said, ". . . I will ascend into heaven, I will exalt my throne above the stars of God: . . . I will be like the most High." (Isaiah 14:13-14.) Because of his unrighteous ambition, he emptied heaven of one-third of its inhabitants. That is, his influence upon his friends, who had confidence in him, was like a giant shot of penicillin, and because they took his evil into themselves they all ended up with him in hell. This satanic action was taken in the interest of religion, as Satan claimed that he was going to save everyone by compulsion.

Jesus was kind to the adulteress who was brought to him by the scribes and Pharisees who were ready to beat out her life by the awful death of stoning. Jesus had a sympathetic interest in the thief on the cross who wanted to do better and he said to him, "Today shalt thou be with me in paradise"— that is, in the world of spirits.

The Savior's own crucifixion is the most flagrant example of how penicillin should not be administered. Here are the words of Elder James E. Talmage:

"A body of Roman soldiers had the condemned Christ in charge; and as the procession moved out from the governor's palace, a motley crowd comprising priestly officials, rulers of the Jews, and people of many nationalities, followed. Two convicted criminals, who had been sentenced to the cross for robbery, were led forth to death at the same time; there was to be a triple execution; and the prospective scene of horror attracted the morbidly minded, such as delight to gloat over the sufferings of their fellows. . . . It was the Roman custom to make the execution of convicts as public as possible, under the mistaken and anti-psychological assumption that the spectacle of dreadful punishment would be of deterrent effect. This misconception of human nature has not yet become entirely obsolete.

"The sentence of death by crucifixion required that the condemned person carry the cross upon which he was to suffer." (James E. Talmage, *Jesus the Christ* [Salt Lake City: Deseret Book Co., 1962], page 652.)

Many other troubles have come upon our world in the name of religion. Religious wars have been some of the most bitter in history. Family feuds can grow into civil wars in their bitterness. When we have reason to correct someone in our Church jurisdiction, or when we feel that we ought to punish them or cause them suffering, we ought to remember kindness and remember the fact that God is the final judge, and that all of his children need a lift much more than they need a kick.

It is necessary that we have firm opinions. The Lord said: "Reproving betimes with sharpness, when moved upon by the Holy Ghost; and then showing forth afterwards an increase of love toward him whom thou has reproved, lest he esteem thee to be his enemy." (D&C 121:43.) There are far too many people who, because of bungling or some real or imagined slight or some rebuke that backfired, think of those who should be their Church leaders as their enemies, and thus the leadership is shorn of its power. Too many apostate enemies of the Church and too many inactive members are penicillin victims. Jesus said, "It is impossible but that offenses will come: but woe unto him, through whom they come!" (Luke 17:1.) Prison officials are on unstable ground when they think of beating the prisoners and causing them to have the spirit of bitterness and revenge. And when we think of publicity and improperly "handling" Church members and causing an increase in their exposure and feelings of shame and guilt and inferiority, we ought to be pretty sure that *our* penicillin is not going to be worse than *his* disease.

A great businessman once stated his personal philosophy of dealing with all people: at every contact we ought to have something worthwhile to give the person being contacted. On every contact, the contactee should be made better and more enthusiastic than he otherwise would have been.

May God help us to be kind. President David O. McKay used to say that the purpose of the gospel is to make bad men good and good men better. It seems to follow naturally that anything that reverses this procedure and makes good men bad and bad men worse should be discouraged.

Chapter 16

Recruiting to a Standard

A prominent sales managers' organization once asked their most famous member to explain to them how he had built such a high-grade organization of salesmen. He explained that in his recruiting he had very high standards of selection; he only hired men of outstanding character with the highest success possibilities. He said he got this idea from his hunting experience. When he went hunting ducks, he took some painted wooden duck decoys and set them out on the water in front of the blind to attract the kind of ducks that he wanted to hunt. He said that if he had used scarecrows or barking dogs as decoys, the ducks would have been frightened away.

There are some interesting selection processes going on all around us in every part of our activity. We like our children to select their friends from among those people who have solid characters, good judgment, high ethical standards, and great intelligence, because it is a natural law that we become like those with whom we associate.

This sales manager insisted on high-grade salesmen, people who were highly successful, who looked and acted the part. He did not want any grubs or anyone who would be dishonest and reflect discredit on his organization. Because like attracts like, everyone was proud to be a part of his organization.

My father used to have an apple orchard, and he could get a better price for his fruit if he had all perfect apples of uniform size and color. It would be a marketing disaster to put a lot of little, scrubby, colorless, wormy apples in the same box with prize fruit.

In the seventy-sixth section of the Doctrine and Covenants, the Lord tells us the kind of people that will be in each of the three degrees of glory. The telestial will be as far below the celestial as the twinkle of a tiny star is below the blaze of the noon-day sun. We have those same differences in this life. There are certain people who, by their lack of standards, make it impossible for them to be members of Christ's church. The Church also does better when they carefully select leaders and missionaries who are intelligent and capable, with good character and a fine appearance.

About the most disastrous thing that can happen to a social group, a business organization, or a church congregation is to fill it up with people who have too many defects. We know the story of what the rotten apple does in the barrel. A dishonest or immoral or unsuccessful missionary in the mission field can do great damage to everyone else by reducing the morale of the total. As the speed of the convoy is set by the slowest ship, so sometimes the reputation of a group is determined by its least prestigious members. While no one ever thinks of himself as being the rotten apple in the barrel or the scarecrow to scare the good ducks away, we ought to make sure that we make positive contributions as a member of the group so that others will see our good works and regard the whole group with favor as a consequence.

Chapter 17

Leadership and Youth

Sometimes we put off our leadership preparation until the job that we should be preparing for actually presents itself. By that time, it is frequently too late for a maximum amount of preparation for the accomplishment desired. When the time for performance has arrived, the time for preparation has passed.

A woman once asked her doctor when was the proper time to start teaching her child to be honest.

The doctor asked, "How old is he now?"

The mother replied, "One year."

"You are already twelve months late in starting," said the doctor.

When should one start teaching character, spiritual participation, and Church leadership? A large part of success begins at a very early age.

Many have entered upon their life's work when still very young. Horatio Nelson was one of nine children and was left motherless at the age of nine. Horatio, the most sickly of the brood, went to sea as a stowaway at the age of twelve. He went to the Arctic and came back a second mate at age nineteen. He was a lieutenant at twenty, a lieutenant commander at twenty-one, a captain at twenty-three, in charge of his own ship. On one occasion, the Prince of Denmark came aboard his ship and asked for the captain. The prince said: "I was shown a boy in a captain's uniform, the youngest man to look upon I ever saw holding a like position."

Before he was twenty-six years old, Nelson had fought pirates, savages, Spaniards, and Frenchmen. Physically he was too weak to meet his competitors on an equal level, so he pitted his brain against their brawn. He studied while his companions gambled and caroused and "saw the town." Sir William Hamilton, British envoy at the Court of Naples, said after meeting Nelson for the first time, "The world will yet ring with the name of Horatio Nelson." Admiral Hood said of him, "Nelson is the only absolutely invincible fighter in the British navy."

When a crew mutinied, they placed Nelson in charge of the ship if he was within call. Nelson was advanced step by step until he became Admiral of the Fleet. If he had not had any motivation or training in leadership until he was old enough to be admiral, that leadership spark may have died.

Alexander the Great conquered the world by the time he was twenty-six. Joan of Arc was in charge of a great national French army by age seventeen.

Mozart was a musical child prodigy. Someone once asked him, "Would you teach me how to write symphonies?" Mozart replied, "You are too young to write symphonies." The inquirer said, "But you were writing symphonies when you were fifteen years younger than I now am." Mozart responded, "But I didn't have to ask anyone to teach me." Mozart, Schubert, and Mendelssohn all began to compose before the age of twelve. Some others have given concerts and astounded audiences before the age of ten. Many have also received divine appointment at a very early age.

Mormon was called by the prophet Ammaron and told what his life's work was to be when he was only ten. His job was to accumulate the records that should later be translated into the Book of Mormon and preserved for us. Mormon had a personal visitation from the Lord at age fifteen, and at age sixteen he was appointed leader of the great Nephite army. His career lasted from the time he was sixteen to the time he was seventy-four, a period of fifty-eight years, which is probably one of the longest military careers in history.

Noah was ordained under the hand of Methuselah at age ten. (D&C 107:52.) Samuel was called at approximately age twelve. David was anointed king when he was just a shepherd boy, and then went back and worked with the sheep; after that it was some years before his appointment became effective. Solomon was on the throne of ancient Israel when he was just a teenager. Joseph Smith was called when he was a boy of fourteen. About his own call, the prophet Jeremiah said: "Then the word of the Lord came unto me, saying, Before I formed thee in the belly I knew thee; and before thou camest forth out of the womb I sanctified thee, and I ordained thee a prophet unto the nations." (Jeremiah 1:4-5.)

Many and probably all of the great gospel leaders were chosen and ordained even before they were born. The Prophet Joseph Smith said, "Every man who has a calling to minister to the inhabitants of the world was ordained to that very purpose in the Grand Council of heaven before this world was."

We don't always get started on the job when we should, however. By taking some contrary course we make it necessary to do a remodeling job on ourselves before we can assume our proper place later on. The Lord said, "Behold, there are many called, but few are chosen." (D&C 121:34.) The reason may be that we do too many wrong things in the beginning for which there is no adequate remodeling job available. Jeremiah himself resisted the Lord's call: "Then said I, Ah, Lord God! behold, I cannot speak: for I am a child. But the Lord said unto me, Say not, I am a child: for thou shall go to all that I shall send thee, and whatsoever I command thee thou shalt speak. Be not afraid of their faces: for I am with thee to deliver thee, saith the Lord." (Jeremiah 1:6-8.)

Joseph was sent by the Lord into Egypt when he was seventeen to build up the granaries and avert the effects of the famine which was coming. Later, in discussing his life's mission with his brothers who had sold him to the Midianites who took him into Egypt, he said, "Be not grieved, nor angry with yourselves that ye sold me hither: for God did send me before you to preserve life." (Genesis 45:5.)

Jesus got started on his life's mission at a very early age. He was teaching the wise men in the temple at age twelve, and in answer to his mother's rebuke he said, "Wist ye not that I must be about my Father's business."

One of the advantages of getting started on the straight and narrow path of success as early in life as possible is that you don't have too many bad habits to overcome at a later date. One of the advantages of building our leadership house to the proper specifications to begin with is that extensive remodeling jobs take a lot of time and are very expensive.

One of the greatest pieces of good fortune in the lives of Latter-day Saints is that we are supposed to get started young. Our parents are instructed to give us the right start by teaching us the reverence and righteousness that will make us responsible by the time we are eight years old. If male members are faithful, they may hold the priesthood at age twelve and go on a mission as an authorized preaching and baptizing minister of the gospel at age nineteen.

If we have too much drug addiction, immorality or ignorance to overcome, the total result may be thrown off course. It doesn't make very much sense to wait until we are old enough to go on a mission before we start thinking about reformation and progression. Nor does it help us to be successful if we first get our lives all messed up with things that are contrary to the ultimate objectives of life which we propose to sponsor.

When someone is called to be a bishop, it might be more helpful if he had gained a mastery of the bishop's training course before the call rather than afterward. It is particularly not an advantage to allow oneself to be over-age before he is baptized or ordained. Every young man ought to study some good books on leadership before any call presents itself.

Young Abraham Lincoln had the right idea about leadership training when he lay before the fireplace on the dirt floor of his parents' backwoods cabin reading the Bible and the *Life of Washington*. He said: "What I want to know is in books, and my best friend is the one who will get me a book I haven't read. I will prepare now and take my chances when the opportunity arrives."

That would be a very profitable attitude for every prospective church leader. The Lord himself has said that the Church has need of every member. It is much more profitable for every member to get himself well prepared for every possibility in advance. That is, every deacons quorum president ought to be in preparation to run the elders quorum, and every elders quorum president should be prepared to be the bishop, and every bishop should be prepared to be the stake president.

The Lord said, "If you are prepared, you shall not fear," and if you are prepared you shall not make a lot of the other mistakes that are common when preparation begins after the assignments are handed out. When we hold leadership meetings in the wards and stakes, we usually invite only those who are already in office. Some of them may be 65 years old with 50 years of service and do not have the same need for training as some young man who has never had any leadership responsibility. We sometimes train the ones whose need is the least and leave untrained those whose need is the greatest. We invite the ones with the greatest experience to the leadership meeting. But what about the one who is going to be appointed to one of these offices next month or next year? Before delivering the Book of Mormon records to Joseph Smith, the angel Moroni had him go through a kind of four-year training course. While he only met with Moroni once a year, the young prophet knew what his future responsibilities were going to be and he was doing a lot of things to get himself qualified and ready. This principle of preparation also applies in every other field of our success in life.

Many years ago we had a doctor for a neighbor. This doctor had five sons. All of them wanted to be doctors. They read their father's magazines and heard him tell about his experiences with patients. What a tremendous advantage it was for them to have the spirit of medicine—the spirit of service. While they were yet too young to understand, they were not too young to form those attitudes that would make them great in their later years. All of them are now doctors, and each one is eminent in his field. They had a great advantage over those students who were partway through medical school before fully making up their minds about medicine.

In our church and in our lives we ought to make some good leadership books available for our children. We ought to give them the kind of advantage that Abraham Lincoln and Mormon and my doctor's sons and Joseph Smith had. It would be very helpful in many cases if, instead of giving our leadership attention only to those whose lives are set and established and who are presently in office, we could also give some kind of leadership preparation to those who are going to be in office in two or three years from now. It may be possible to do that by having some good books available on character development, the importance of salesmanship and the desirability of developing our initiative and leadership skills. One of Lincoln's favorite books was the Bible, and the other books that inspired Abraham Lincoln's success are still available.

My patriarchal blessing, received in my early youth, said, "Prepare yourself for the positions in the Church which await you." That is what the Lord was saying when he called attention to the fact that the church has need of every member. Every president of the Church in his time has indicated that everyone in the Church, of every age, should be engaged in missionary work. We all have a genealogical responsibility. Everyone is responsible for the welfare of his family members, his friends and his associates.

Five years before the Savior was born in Jerusalem, he sent Samuel the Lamanite among the people who lived upon the western continent telling them to get ready. Immediately prior to his birth, he gave them a sign lasting two days, a day and a night and a day, in which there was no darkness. At his crucifixion a great tempest and other disturbances warned them that they were not prepared. And after his resurrection, he appeared among those who were spared from the destruction and organized his Church upon this continent, but unlike Abraham Lincoln they were not ready. After having met with them for a short time, the Lord said to them: "I perceive that ye are weak, that ye cannot understand all my words which I am commanded of the Father to speak unto you at this time. Therefore, go ye unto your homes, and ponder upon the things which I have said, and ask of the Father, in my name, that ye may understand, and prepare your minds for the morrow, and I come unto you again." (3 Nephi 17:2-3.)

Some of these unprepared people sat up all that night in order to get ready for their meeting with the Savior the next day. They had had the period of his earthly lifetime plus five years to get ready, yet when he came they were unprepared.

Largely, that is the sad story of our lives. Sometimes, with too many remodeling jobs to be done before the building can be started, we never do actually get ready.

Part Four

Motivation

Factors of Leadership Power
Leadership Inventory
The Sales Function of Leadership
Pride in Your Outfit
Being Competitive
Sales Points for the Law of the Fast

Chapter 18

Factors of
Leadership Power

We live in the greatest age that has ever been known in the world. We are the beneficiaries of the greatest knowledge explosion that has ever occurred upon our earth since God said, "Let there be light." (Genesis 1:3.) We live in the very center of power, culture, and accomplishment. Our fore-fathers lived on a flat, stationary earth and plowed their ground with a wooden stick, but we live on an earth of power steering and jet propulsion, and we need personality and character qualities to match the times and conditions.

As the Son of God was trying to establish his church upon the earth, in recruiting those who would carry out his enterprises he called doers. Thinkers are important and talkers are necessary, but the great accomplishments of the world will always be made by those who can effectively get the ship into port. The great men of the world are the men with initiative who have the power and industry to get the job done. We need high objectives and determined ambitions. Someone once said, "There are no lazy salesmen, there are just salesmen who lack motive power." More than anything else we need the power of motion.

Someone has explained that the science of crime detection is the science of achievement in reverse. The detective takes an act and works backward to find a motive. If the motive can be discovered, the criminal can usually be identified. On the other hand, the effective leader takes a motive and works forward to an accomplishment.

The wise man, Solomon, once said: "Wisdom is the principal thing; therefore get wisdom: and with all thy getting get understanding." (Proverbs 4:7.) Someone, who must have been even wiser than Solomon, said: "Industry is the principle thing, therefore get industry; and with all thy getting, get going." Motivation has been described as morale in gear. It is the good seedbed and the good seed.

When appraising the prospects of any projected accomplishment, it is a good idea to give some detailed consideration to the many success factors that need to be provided for. There are financial factors, health factors, market conditions, the influences of government and competition. Probably the most important factors of any successful undertaking are the "M" factors or the motive factors. These are those internal factors that guarantee the generation of sufficient power. They provide the impulses that give the booster shots when the fuel might be low. The greatest motivation is self-motivation. Socrates once said, "He who would move the world must first move himself."

In 1929, a young unknown ex-German army corporal by the name of Adolf Hitler was sitting in his prison cell in Germany writing his book *Mein Kampf*. His plan was to make Germany the greatest nation in the world. The fact that, starting out single-handed, he almost upset the world indicated that he did have something. How did he do it? The answer is in his book. He said, "The question of Germany regaining her power is not how to manufacture or distribute arms, but how to produce in people that will to win, that spirit of determination which produces a thousand different methods, each of which ends with arms." It is a well-known fact that you don't win wars merely with tanks or guns or airplanes or oil. You win wars with that spirit of determination inside of people. And that is how you save souls, raise the level of education, culture, spirituality and material welfare, and do almost every other worthwhile thing in the world.

Some people think of Ralph Waldo Emerson as the greatest thinker that America has produced. Ralph Waldo

Emerson indicated that his greatest need was to be motivated into activity.

With this same need, a salesman once went to his sales manager and asked him how to succeed. The sales manager said, "I can immediately quadruple your income if you will just follow two little, simple rules." The salesman was delighted, and agreed to do anything if he could just make himself successful.

"Here is rule number one," the sales manager said. "Immediately stop doing all of those things which you yourself know for sure you should not be doing. Rule number two: Immediately start doing all of those things that you are positively sure you ought to be doing." Following these rules would make anyone successful in short order in any field.

Suppose that in America we all stopped doing the things we know for sure we should not do. Immediately there would be no alcoholics, no dope addicts, no crime waves, no dishonesties, no slackers, nobody trying to cheat the government or do any other harmful thing. This world would soon be God's paradise. Then, suppose that every person immediately began doing all of those things that he knew for sure he ought to do. We would soon have a society that had reached complete success.

The way to this utopia is to develop the "M" factors or motive factors of success and keep them going with full power, not for a minute or a week or a year but all of the time. God has given us the key of one of his most important success factors in pointing out that he himself builds habits around his successes, so that he is the same yesterday, today, and forever. That is what our success ought to be, not something that flashes hot or cold depending upon which breeze is blowing at the moment. We need to install a good set of powerful "M" factors and then develop them to the limit so that they can easily carry the full load of our success. One of the strongest of these factors is to make up our minds on issues and develop the right kind of ideas.

It is difficult to make a success out of someone who cannot think logically, who has no convictions, who does not have mastery over a good set of ideas. The idea might be compared to the water that turns the waterwheel or the air that makes the windmill do its work, and as one of the ingredients of success we might ask ourselves, What are the things that motivate us? Once we have that information, and get a full development of our own "M" factors, we are well on our way toward success.

The following are six suggestions that may be helpful in providing ourselves with motivation.

First, we are motivated by ideas. Man is primarily a thinking being. Solomon said, "For as he thinketh in his heart, so is he." (Proverbs 23:7.) The most valuable material possessions I have in the world are my twenty-five idea notebooks containing the ideas that I live by. They are regular 8½-by-11-inch, three-ring binders with about three hundred pages in each book. For fifty years I have been storing away in these idea banks the most usable ideas I have ever read or heard or thought. Fifty years ago, as I was starting in the life insurance business, I heard someone say that the first investment of every salesman should be made in a pair of scissors and a pot of glue. There are some who think that a person's brain is a baggage room or storehouse, but that is not true. Your brain is a machine, a workshop, and it can be kept going from the fuel stored in this idea bank. I have a vast paper memory of seventy-five hundred pages of ideas, all tailored and chiseled and polished to meet my needs. These include the great motivating ideas, the answers to objections, the tested sentences.

One of the great experiences of my life occurred many years ago as the Japanese War was coming to an end. I heard Dr. Adam S. Bennion give a lecture on the value of great literature. You can persuade anyone of the value of great ideas, of great human thought; but most people miss their benefits by saying, "I don't have time to read, to study, to memorize, to perfect and preserve ideas." To overcome this objection, Dr. Bennion said, "Suppose that you were going to be a prisoner in a Japanese concentration camp for the next four years, and you could take with you the works of any ten authors. Which would you take, and what would you expect to get out of it?"

In a concentration camp, where they are not readily available, prisoners get very hungry for ideas. Dr. Bennion's program was to take the complete works of the men that you would like most to resemble, and exhaust each one in turn. That is, you rethink the greatest ideas that he ever thought. You run the strongest motivations through your mind that ever went through his mind.

I recognized this as a valuable idea; and, even though I was pretty busy, fortunately the idea didn't go away. At that time I was teaching a class in salesmanship, and I decided to reread the Bible with the idea of getting out of it its salesmanship. The Bible has served as the world's first book of religion. It is the world's first book of knowledge, the world's first book of wisdom, the world's first book of poetry, the world's first book of literature. But it is also the world's finest sales manual. That is, the best way there is to be a good salesman is to be a good man. (Incidentally, that's also the best way to be a good lawyer or a good teacher or a good bank president or a good husband.) So I decided to reread the Bible, and when you read the Bible to get its salesmanship it becomes a different book from what it is when you read it to get its theology or its history or even its wisdom. I had a thrilling experience with the Bible.

I got a thrill out of mentally following the young Carpenter as he went around saying to people, "Be not afraid." "Why are ye troubled?" "Why do thoughts arise in your hearts?" "Be of good cheer." The Bible is filled with the greatest success principles and it has a great many productive sales methods. Let me just give you one.

As Moses was preparing to cross the desert with his large group of former slaves, he needed someone who knew the desert and who would be their guide. Moses tried to recruit Hobab, a man living on the edge of the desert, to be that guide, to show them the way in the desert. In his first approach he said, "Hobab, come with us and we will do thee good." But Hobab said, "I will not go."

Moses needed Hobab, so he tried again. This time he used a more effective approach. He said, "Hobab, come with us that thou mayest be as eyes to us in the wilderness." Now, that's a completely different idea. (See Numbers 10:29-31.)

We make these same kinds of approaches in Church work. We say to someone, "Come to church with us, and we will do you good." That is, it will be a good thing for you to associate with nice people like us. That may be a great idea, but it isn't very interesting to most people. Sometimes we try again, and say: "Come and teach this class. We don't have anyone that can do it as well as you." That is, we use the service appeal instead of the "we will do you good" approach. Moses said, in effect, "Hobab, you come and lead us in the wilderness, you show us the way. Without you we will probably get lost and starve out there in the desert." Before Moses had finished his presentation, Hobab had on his hat and was on his way.

Anyway, I had a thrilling experience with the Bible, and I have since done a little writing under the title of "The Salesmanship of the Bible." Having had the practice with the Bible, I got the courage to take up Shakespeare. Shakespeare comes near the top of most people's list of nonscriptural authors. But he wrote a long time ago, and I didn't have much of a background in literature. I almost decided to discard the idea on several occasions, but because I had made a pledge to myself I kept working at it. I reread some of the material many times and researched it and talked about it. Finally, the clouds began to part and a little bit of the light began to come through. I had a thrilling experience with Shakespeare. Shakespeare is a great idea-man.

I always read with my pen and mark everything I think is worth memorizing. I rethought every idea that Shakespeare ever thought, or at least the ones he put down on paper. Out of my 7,500 pages of notes, 214 of them are my Shakespeare notes, and I have gone back and memorized many of them. I could probably recite you one hundred pages of what to me are Shakespeare's greatest speeches and his most powerful ideas. Let me give you one great one.

When Henry V was King of England he laid claim to the throne of France. He took a little army and sailed across the Channel to enforce that claim. The problems proved to be a little bigger than he had expected. Landing in France with about twenty thousand men, he lost thousands of them to dysentery. One October night, after a march across France in the mud of a rainy autumn, he found himself at Agincourt—

perhaps twelve thousand weary Englishmen, many of them sick, facing an army of sixty thousand well-fed, well-armed, well-horsed, and well-armored Frenchmen intent on wiping them out.

In this kind of a leadership situation what would you have done? One alternative would be to surrender. That is not what Henry did, however. In Shakespeare's reproduction of the events, collectively and individually Henry gave his soldiers pep talks. In the quotations below, taken from the play *Henry V*, I have woven together some of Henry's comments as well as some of those of his generals.

> Once more into the breach, dear friends,
> Once more the blast of war blows in our ears.
> The French are bravely in their battle set and
> Will, with all expedience, charge upon us.
> 'Tis fearful odds, there's five to one,
> Besides they are all fresh. 'Tis true
> There is great danger. The greater, therefore,
> Must our courage be.

Then he said,

> O, God, of battles! Steel my soldiers' hearts
> Possess them not with fear. . . .
> Princes all, God be with you. We may never
> Meet again till we shall meet in heaven.
> God's arm strikes with us. All things are
> Ready if our minds be so. Perish the man
> Whose mind is backward now.

Then he said,

> On, on ye noble English. I see you
> Stand like greyhounds in the slips,
> Straining upon the start. The prey's afoot:
> Follow your spirit, I'll to my task.
> There's work to be done. . . .

Henry didn't say it would be an easy battle. He said, in substance: "Maybe none of us will live until sundown. In that case we shall never meet again until we shall meet in heaven.

But we're Englishmen. We came over here to do a job and we are not going home unless the job is done." He had made up his mind. Someone once said, "All things are ready if our minds be so." The most important part of any success is to make up our minds about it.

One of Henry's captains reminded him that a lot of Englishmen across the Channel were asleep in bed at that very minute, and he suggested that the presence of ten thousand of them now would be just right for winning the war. Henry wouldn't have this. He said that would dilute the honor of his little army. To him, if twelve thousand Englishmen, many of them weak and sick, could beat sixty thousand Frenchmen, that was honor; but there would have been no honor in a million Englishmen whipping sixty thousand Frenchmen. After Henry's pep talk to this backward looking soldier, the man responded:

> God's will! my leige, would you and I alone,
> Without more help, might fight this battle out!

That is, he is saying that he now wished that he and the king alone could fight those sixty thousand Frenchmen. Now, that may not be good judgment, but it is courage. And courage is the thing that most of us need more than almost any other thing.

It happened that the Battle of Agincourt was fought on St. Crispin's Day. (Crispin had been a Christian martyr a few hundred years earlier, and his martyrdom was commemorated by the Feast of St. Crispin.) Just before the battle, Henry said, in substance: "This day is called the Feast of Crispin, and he who survives this day and comes safe home will in time to come stand on tiptoe when this day is named. And those men in England now asleep in bed will count themselves accursed they were not here to fight with us on this, St. Crispin's Day."

The English won the Battle of Agincourt. Great courage and great ideas on great subjects can also help us win our battles.

What a thrilling realization—that we can run through our minds the greatest courage, integrity, and heroism that can be developed in the minds of the greatest men taken in all ages!

When I had finished reading Shakespeare, I read twenty-eight volumes of Elbert Hubbard; and I love Elbert Hubbard. I read the fifty volumes of the Harvard Classics and made notes on every idea that strongly impressed me. I read the complete works of Ralph Waldo Emerson, whom President McKay called the greatest thinker that America ever produced. If you want something to give you a thrill, just reflect on the concept that I can run through my little weak brain the greatest ideas that went through the brain of the greatest thinker America ever produced.

In my notebooks are the quotations that I want to memorize, that I have selected from 987 books. These are the great books of the world, the classics, books that have survived the ages. The psychologists tell us that when a person runs an idea through his mind it makes an impression or engram; thus, if you run the right kind of ideas through your brain, you yourself can raise the quality and enthusiasm and power of your own mind. If you think negative thoughts, your mind becomes negative. If you think depraved thoughts, your mind becomes depraved.

On the other hand, we can think the most motivating and godly success thoughts that have ever occupied the minds of the greatest men in any age. When we think the most motivating and inspiring ideas known in our world, our minds will respond accordingly. If we think the same kind of thoughts that were thought by the great prophets, the greatest poets, the greatest captains of industry, our minds will begin to respond as their minds responded.

Grantland Rice has always been a hero of mine. For fifty years he traveled around the country with the sports champions, trying to isolate those qualities which made some athletes great. Then he wrote seven hundred poems trying to make these qualities negotiable in the lives of other people. One of his poems is entitled "Courage." In it he said:

I'd like to think that I can look at death and smile and say,
"All I have left now is my final breath, take that away
And you must either leave me dust or dreams or in far flight,
The soul that wanders where the stardust streams through
    endless night."

But, he added:

I'd rather think that I can look at life with this to say,
Send what you will of struggle or of strife, blue skies or gray,
I'll stand against the final charge of hate by peak and pit,
And nothing in the steel-clad fist of fate can make me quit.

The mind acquires the courage and abilities of what it thinks, hence leaders should regularly run through their minds the attitudes and ambitions that will make their work more productive.

William Ernest Henley was a cripple when he wrote "Invictus." His poem can perhaps transfer to us some of his determination to be at his best even in the face of serious obstacles.

Out of the night that covers me,
Black as the pit from pole to pole,
I thank whatever gods may be
For my unconquerable soul.

In the fell clutch of circumstance
I have not winced nor cried aloud.
Under the bludgeonings of chance
My head is bloody, but unbowed.

Beyond this place of wrath and tears
Looms but the horror of the shade,
And yet the menace of the years
Finds, and shall find, me unafraid.

It matters not how strait the gate,
How charged with punishments the scroll,
I am the master of my fate;
I am the captain of my soul.

When strong, vigorous ideas occupy one's mind with the right kind of spirit, the result may help to banish such enemies of success as discouragement, fear, lethargy and sloth. Think of the stimulation that may be transferred to us from the following lines entitled, "The Champion."

The average runner sprints until the breath in him is gone
But the champion has the iron will that makes him carry on.
For rest the average runner begs when limp his muscles grow.
But the champion runs on leaden legs, his spirit makes them
  go.
The average man's complacent when he's done his best to
  score.
But the champion does his best, and then he does a little
  more.

Motive factor number one is to have your mind and
personality loaded and charged with great ideas.

Motive factor number two might be people. We work
harder for people than we do for money. People are the
beginning and the end of the work of the Church as well as
the purpose behind most other activities. Under the title of
"The Purpose," Edgar A. Guest put down in writing this idea
about our people motivations.

> "Why do you peddle the fruits?" said I
> To a huckster of melons passing by.
> "Why do you shout from dawn till gloam?"
> Said he, "For the wife and the kids at home."
> "Why do you dig in the ditch?" I asked
> Of a grimy laborer sorely tasked.
> And this was the reason such work he did.
> "I gotta da wife, I gotta da kid."
> On they go, down that busy street,
> Eager toilers with hurrying feet.
> Butcher, baker, and banker grave.
> Why do they work, why do they slave?
> What is it that moves them to work and plan?
> What is the motive of every man?
> Stop him and ask him what holds him fast.
> Dreaming and striving to serve at last.
> And with polished speech and accent queer
> This is the purpose that you will hear,
> Each will say as the digger did,
> "I gotta da wife, I gotta da kid."
> And that's the purpose that moves us all,
> A home, a wife, and children small.

I heard a story of a young football quarterback whose father died just before the crucial game of the year. The coach said to him, "Bill, you take some time off and be with your family. We'll get along all right without you at the game Friday, and you won't need to come to any practices." But the boy didn't like that idea at all. He said: "No, I want to play, and I'm able to play. And I'll be here Friday."

The coach didn't understand it, but the boy seemed to know what he was doing, so the coach said, "Okay, if you feel that way about it we'll let you start and see how you get along." This young man went into the game, he threw passes and ran the ball and kicked punts and blocked tackles and generaled his team like Superman. They won an overwhelming victory.

As they went off the field, the coach put his arm around this young man and said, "Bill, would you like to tell me about it? How is it you could do as you did today under these circumstances?" And the young man replied, "Coach, what you may not know is that my father was blind, and this is the first game that he has ever seen me play."

We can all do better if we know that our Father is watching. We like the praise and applause of our friends and admirers, too, and our wives and children would also like to see us make a touchdown occasionally. One of the powerful motive factors is the confidence of those we serve and those who cheer from the grandstand.

Motive factor number three: One of the strongest of all the motive factors is the consciousness of an outstanding skill. Everyone likes to do that which he does exceedingly well. If you are going to be a football coach and want to have great motivation and high morale among your players, teach each one of them some outstanding skill and make them effective in their play. That is exactly how you develop a good lawyer, or a good salesman, or a good missionary, or a good bishop.

Motive factor number four is the promise of reward. Andrew Carnegie was once asked to speak to a college graduating class. He began his remarks by saying he desired to speak only to those graduates who planned to be millionaires. That is, Andrew Carnegie was stimulated most by those who wanted to go somewhere and be somebody and amount to something. But this promise of rewards for service rendered applies to all departments of life.

In California, I discovered a missionary preaching some false doctrine. He made the statement to one of his contacts that missionaries didn't get paid. He said, "We work for nothing."

After the contact had gone, I said to the missionary: "That is the most ridiculous statement I have ever heard in my lifetime. Who ever told you or how did you ever conclude that missionaries don't get paid? I thought the Lord said that if you labor all of your days and bring but one soul unto him your reward will be great."

I asked him if he remembered the comparison the Lord made between the worth of a soul and the wealth of all of the earth. He did. Then I asked him if he knew what the earth was worth. He didn't. But I had a newspaper clipping that gave the assessed valuation of just one small section of the United States alone as over one trillion dollars. We got a piece of paper and I had the missionary write out the figures representing a trillion dollars. During the previous year, this missionary had been instrumental in bringing twelve converts into the Church. That is, one a month. I had him figure out that if he worked ten hours a day for thirty days it would mean that he worked three hundred hours to save a trillion-dollar soul. I had him divide a trillion by three hundred hours, and he discovered that, on that basis, he might be earning $3 billion, 333 million dollars per hour.

I asked him, "What is the most money per hour that anybody ever paid you before you left home?" "Seventy-five cents," he replied. "Then what did you mean," I said, "when you told that person that missionaries don't get paid?"

There are some people who think that bishops don't get paid, or that good parents don't get paid, or that effective Scoutmasters don't get paid. But there is a fundamental law in the universe we ought to remember and believe, which says that all effort must be paid for. We can no more do a good thing without at some time in some way receiving a reward than we can do an evil thing without suffering a penalty. It just is not possible.

The Lord has never given a commandment to which he

did not attach a blessing. For example, through Malachi the
Lord said that we ought to pay our tithing. He said, "Bring ye
all the tithes into the storehouse. . . ." That is the command.
And then the blessing is attached: ". . . and prove me now
herewith, saith the Lord of hosts, if I will not open you the
windows of heaven, and pour you out a blessing, that there
shall not be room enough to receive it." (Malachi 3:10.) He
says that if we will obey the law, the benefit will be so great
that we will be unable to contain it.

From the top of Mount Sinai, the Lord said, "Honor thy
father and thy mother." That is the command. And the
blessing was attached when he said, "that thy days may be
long upon the land which the Lord thy God giveth thee."
(Exodus 20:12.) That's the reward. Isn't it interesting that you
can't even keep the Sabbath day holy without being paid for
it? That is, everyone who does keep the Sabbath day holy will
be a different kind of person from those who do not. You
can't even think a good thought without receiving a reward.
And you can't think an evil thought without suffering a
penalty. It just is not possible. Every time one builds up his
own ability to do, it is like putting himself out at compound
interest. Everyone was created with instinctive motivation that
comes from the consciousness of a reward.

Motive factor number five is fun. I am a believer in
everyone having fun. The first step toward any accomplishment is to believe in it, and the second is to enjoy doing it.
Shakespeare wrote, "No profit grows where there is no
pleasure taken." (*The Taming of the Shrew.*) If you don't enjoy
doing something, you probably won't do it very well.

Walking up the street one day, I caught up to a friend of
mine. I took him by the arm, and as we walked I said to him,
"Ross, what do you do when you want to have fun?" He
replied, "I go fishing." "Why do you go fishing?" I asked. He
said, "I go fishing to catch fish."

"That is ridiculous," I said, "and I can prove to you that it
is not so." I knew quite a bit about him, and I said, "You make
about so much money per day." "I suppose that is about
right," he agreed. "Now, how many days do you close up your
office and lose this income because you go fishing?" He told

me approximately how many. We multiplied the two figures and added a little for expenses and equipment, and we figured out that it cost him $3,700 a year to go fishing.

Now I said, "How many pounds of fish do you catch?" I knew he couldn't catch very many, because the law wouldn't allow it. He gave me the number and we divided $3,700 by the number of pounds of fish he caught; and we figured out, roughly, that he could have had every fish gold-plated for what it cost to catch them.

"Now, either you are a very bad businessman," I said, "or you are mistaken in your motive, because you couldn't possibly go fishing for the sole purpose of catching fish. If all you wanted was fish, you could buy the whole fishmarket for $3,700. You could provide the whole neighborhood with fish for that amount." He agreed. "I guess that's right."

"But you've got to have a motive," I persisted. "Now, what is the reason?" He responded: "I suppose I go fishing for the fraternity. These three men I go with, they like me and I like them, and we relax and have a good time together. That's it, it's the fraternity."

"That is just as ridiculous as the other answer you gave me," I told him, "and I can prove to you that that isn't so either." I continued: "Now, suppose you went fishing and your friends each caught a big string of fish this long, and you yourself went home with just one little minnow on your hook, two inches long. What kind of a time would you have?"

"That would be the most miserable experience I can imagine."

"Do you mean to tell me that your friends wouldn't be friendly to you just because you didn't catch any fish?"

"No, I suppose they would be really friendly. If I didn't catch any fish they would know there was a crisis, and they would have to be friendly."

"Then if you wanted friendship," I suggested, "what you would do would be to go fishing and not catch any fish." And he said, "I suppose that's right."

After a few minutes, he asked me a question: "Sterling, why is it that I go fishing?" "Fortunately, I can tell you," I replied. "You go fishing out of your desire for accomplishment." This is an inner something with which God seems to have endowed every person upon this earth. There probably isn't anyone alive who doesn't count success as his most pleasant experience.

If you were going to go to school, you would rather get A's than D's. If you were going to be employed, you would rather be promoted and praised than kicked around and fired. If you were going to get married, you would rather live up on a pedestal than sleep out in the doghouse. Because we tend to repeat those experiences that give us pleasure, the Creator has made success pleasant, trying to entice us on from one success to another until he gets us to where he wants us. He is aiming for the great objective mentioned in the Sermon on the Mount, "Be ye therefore perfect, even as your Father which is in heaven is perfect." (Matthew 5:48.) Most of us have a long way to go before we reach that exalted goal.

Motive factor number six: One of the greatest motivations is to work for a cause. That is when we have some deep convictions. That is when we are doing something that we believe in with our whole soul, that we really have our heart in. Let me tell you about a man who had a cause.

On May 10, 1940, eight months after World War II began, Winston Churchill was made the Prime Minister of Great Britain. It was a crucial time for the British. All over the world people were wondering whether the British would be able to hang on for another week or a month. Everybody knew that if there was to be any hope of winning the war, they had to have some new people in the government.

Some people didn't like Winston very well. He had been kicked out of government a time or two. He was a little bossy, but everybody knew that there was no place where the fires of freedom burned with a brighter flame than in this rugged Englishman. So on May 10, 1940, they dumped the burdens of their great, groggy empire on the shoulders of this one man and said, in effect, "Okay, Winston, you go ahead and win the war with your bare hands." That is, he had no more material or equipment or financial resources than the former administration had had, and they had done little if anything to advance the nation's cause in the war.

How would you feel if you had an assignment like that? The only things we are ever asked to do in our Church work are activities like going out and making friends with prospective elders or making some converts to the religion of Christ or doing some other pleasant, easy thing with great rewards attached. Churchill was asked to go out and destroy half the world, if necessary. But this is how he felt about his assignment on that day in May 1940. He said: "As I went to bed at about 3:00 A.M., I was conscious of a profound feeling of relief. At last I had authority to give direction over this whole scene, and I felt as though I were walking with destiny, that my past life had been but a preparation for this hour, for this trial. I could not be reproached either for having made the war or for lack of preparation for it, and yet I felt I knew a good deal about it, and I was sure I would not fail."

Fail to do what? Well, fail to save the world from the greatest mechanized might ever known in the world, "with his bare hands." In the House of Commons and on the radio, Churchill started to make some of those great motivating speeches for which he became famous. At the conclusion of one of them, he said: "We shall not flag or fail. We shall go on to the end, we shall fight in France, on the seas and oceans, we shall fight with growing confidence and growing strength in the air, we shall defend our island, whatever the cost may be, we shall fight on the beaches, we shall fight on the landing grounds, we shall fight in the fields and in the streets, we shall fight in the hills. We shall never surrender. And even if, which I do not for a moment believe, this island or a large part of it were subjugated and starving, then our Empire beyond the seas, armed and guarded by the British fleet, would carry on the struggle, until, in God's good time, the New World, with all its power and might, steps forth to the rescue and the liberation of the old."

It wasn't very long before people on both sides of the conflict discovered that this valiant man didn't have the slightest intention of surrendering, and these motives started to take root in other people. They began to stand a little straighter and work a little harder and think a little more courageously. Production in the factories began to go up. The tide of war began to change, and finally the Allies won the war. No one individually was as responsible for the victory as this staunch Englishman who had convictions about what he was doing. This kind of conviction is the reason for which both patriots and prophets have given their lives.

Some appropriate and beautiful words were written by John Gillespie Magee, who was an American fighter pilot connected with the Royal Canadian Air Force. He was shot down over London in the battle for Britain in the first part of the Second World War. Before going into the service, John Gillespie Magee had done the usual things that seventeen-year-olds do. Then, after his basic training was finished, he felt for the first time in his hands the controls of these powerful engines capable of sending his aircraft through space at stupendous speed. Feeling the exhilaration that came from doing well his part of the work of the world, he wrote a poem entitled, "High Flight," which is now found in the Library of Congress under the title of *Poems of Faith and Freedom.*

I share this with you because you are also engaged in a high flight, not only the high flight of your own success, but the high flight of a cause where the welfare of many other people is in your hands.

Oh, I have slipped the surly bonds of earth
And danced the skies on laughter-silvered wings;
Sunward I've climbed, and joined the tumbling mirth
Of sun-split clouds,—and done a hundred things
You have not dreamed of—wheeled and soared and swung
High in the sunlit silence. Hov'ring there.
I've chased the shouting wind along, and flung
My eager craft through footless halls of air.

Up, up the long, delirious, burning blue
I've topped the wind-swept heights with easy grace
Where never lark, or even eagle flew—
And, while with silent, lifting mind I've trod
The high untrespassed sanctity of space,
Put out my hand, and touched the face of God.

Chapter 19

Leadership Inventory

One of the important parts of any business is its inventory. Anyone is placed at a serious disadvantage who doesn't know how much merchandise he has on his shelves and what its value is. The dictionary says that an inventory is a detailed list of articles which gives for each the code number, description, and value. An inventory is a kind of catalogue. It is a formal list made up each year of the various items of property belonging to a particular person or firm.

The dictionary also indicates that an inventory may be a tally of one's individual personality traits, aptitudes, attitudes, skills, etc. Such a personal inventory may be used for the purpose of planning a person's own life or in analyzing or counseling himself. An inventory may also represent the capital on which one's income is calculated. It may be very helpful to think of our own personal inventory in about that same way.

The scriptures mention many items we should get into our personal inventory on a permanent basis. For example:

"Whatever principle of intelligence we attain unto in this life, it will rise with us in the resurrection.

"And if a person gains more knowledge and intelligence in this life through his diligence and obedience than another, he will have so much the advantage in the world to come." (D&C 130:18-19.)

Intelligence, knowledge, understanding, diligence and obedience are items of great worth which we might want to include in our personal capital. Stock of this kind is not acquired overnight. Over the years I have gone through an interesting process of making up a kind of literary inventory. Some of the headings are as follows:

1. *My idea books.* Abraham Lincoln once said, "What I want to know is in books, and my best friend is the one who will get me a book that I haven't read." What wonderful treasures we have in the holy scriptures, the great biographies, the great histories, the great books of science, the great books of inspiration, and even the great fiction! We ought to keep at our fingertips, in especially prepared idea books, the great thoughts which we love and which we can use to motivate and exalt other people.

2. *My heroes.* In 1899, a large sum of money was given to the New York University which was used to build the Hall of Fame for Great Americans. Since its establishment, the electors have voted 102 great Americans into membership. In this famous building, each of those elected is honored with a pedestal, a bronze bust, and an explanatory tablet memorializing his great qualities. The Hall of Fame for Great Americans contains one of the greatest collection of statuary to be found upon this earth. It also houses the most imposing company of great men and women that there is in the world.

The ancient Greeks performed this function of memorializing greatness by setting aside the top of Mount Olympus, which reaches some ten thousand feet up into the sky of northern Greece, as a home for their national heroes and supermortals. They used these heroes as a pattern after which to model their own lives. The people of Sparta could tolerate no weakness in themselves because they believed themselves to be the children of Hercules.

I am grateful for those fine men and women memorialized in the American Hall of Fame. Included are many of America's Founding Fathers and the other men who have helped to make America and Americans great. It is also a joy for me to be able to lose myself in the interesting mythology of the Golden Age of Greece. I have an even finer group of heroes in my own hall of fame, however, which I carry around with me in my own mind and heart.

My hall of fame is peopled with heroes of my own choosing. But I have carried this a little further and have written down the life stories of some 101 men and women who personify skills, abilities and virtues that I would like to remember. These I not only carry in my mind, but I have recorded them in three manuscript volumes under the title *My Hall of Fame*. I have personally carved their mental and spiritual portraits and written their explanatory tablets. Each of my tablets takes about sixteen minutes to read. I can spend a few hours in my hall of fame and run the greatness of my heroes through my own mind again and again.

I am sure that Carl Sandburg loved Abraham Lincoln far more because he was Lincoln's biographer. And as I can be most thoroughly thrilled by the great music and the beautiful art with which I am most intimately familiar, so I can be most readily inspired by the biographies that I myself have written. To enjoy an interview with them, I am never kept waiting in anterooms or outer offices. My heroes always have the time to give me all the attention I need, and our interviews are on the most intimate and friendly basis.

I have included in my hall of fame many of the great prophets, some of the captains of industry, some of the great athletes, writers, scholars, and leaders of nations. I have included Joan of Arc, Madame Curie, Winston Churchill, Mohandas K. Gandhi, and in an especially favored place I have carved the portrait and written the tablet of my mother.

3. *My success stories*. One of the most important ingredients of success is success itself. Nothing succeeds like success. Nothing is as valuable as success. Nothing is as motivating as success. Nothing is as pleasant as success. And every human being is supposed to do something better than anyone else can do it. We should make a written collection of these little segments of success as they appear like shining jewels in the life and personality of someone else. Because

possession is nine-tenths of the law, it follows that we can develop a kind of natural patent on the greatest success segments that may be developed by others. Because these spare parts are interchangeable, our collection may be amended and expanded to fit circumstances. If we collect and utilize them properly, these important success elements may become a part of our own success bloodstream. Because of the greater success caused by them, more people will qualify for the celestial kingdom and glory will also be added upon our heads forever and ever.

4. *My gallery of art.* Pictures have always been very helpful. It is said that one picture is worth a thousand words. The Mona Lisa was lent by the French government for exhibition in New York and Washington, D.C., in early 1963. At that time it was appraised for insurance purposes as having a value of $100 million. That is a great amount of money, but other pictures carried in the minds and hearts of people have had an even greater value.

On March 17, 1941, President Franklin D. Roosevelt dedicated our first national gallery of art. It is located in Washington, D.C. The building cost $16 million to build and houses a collection of 126 paintings by the old masters and 26 pieces of sculpture that were valued at that time at approximately $80 million, or an average of $500,000 each. The gallery and an endowment fund to maintain it were presented to the American people as a gift by the late Andrew W. Mellon.

We may compile some inspiring picture books containing pictures of our own. In addition, we may have a few five-hundred-thousand-dollar pictures painted in our minds and hearts.

5. *My word pictures.* Probably the most inspiring pictures are not those painted with paint on canvasses. They are painted with words and emotions on human minds and souls. For my own inspiration I have collected some word pictures of such subjects as loyalty, integrity, dependability, faith, beauty, and devotion to God, which have the ability to stir my

soul and charge with power my ambition. Among the great pictures from the scriptures, I see Jesus dressed in shining garments on the Mount of Transfiguration. I have many other pictures that tend to enrich the courage, righteousness and industry of my own activity and faith.

May God help us all to enrich the inventories of our leadership as well as our own personal lives.

Chapter 20

The Sales Function of Leadership

We use a very important term in our business affairs called salesmanship. It is an educational process whereby we build desires for certain things in the minds and hearts of people, backed by enough conviction to motivate their positive action.

Our great commercial world is made up of those who sell food and clothing, automobiles and homes, life insurance and real estate, stocks and bonds. In fact, the success of our economy depends largely upon the salesman. That is, if the General Motors salesmen stopped selling automobiles, their factories would close down and many people would be out of work. The thing that every business wants more than anything else is customers, and that is also what the Church wants. But nothing ever happens until someone sells something, either a commodity, a service, an ideal, or an idea. The freight train is sent on its way down the track because salesmen have been at work. In fact, it has been said that one of the chief differences between America and some other less progressive nations is that America is a nation of salesmen.

Each day we have millions of salesmen sitting down in the homes, offices, and factories of America teaching people an improved use of those things which best serve their needs. It is a very interesting fact that many of the most worthwhile things need to be sold. Even the most fundamentally useful things were not automatically accepted when they were first made available. Some of our current necessities more or less force themselves upon us. We buy groceries when we get hungry. We buy overcoats when we get cold. We go to the doctor when we get sick. But there are many of our needs covered by what we call intangibles. For example, the great life insurance industry is one of the biggest businesses in the world, yet the benefits of life insurance must be sold by salesmen. If the life insurance business were operated as are our grocery stores, where someone waits for people to come in and buy what they need, there would not be very much life insurance sold. People also need to be persuaded and worked with in order to make them want to get an education. Yet in spite of all the education promotion that we are able to do, our country is plagued by ignorance, educational dropouts, and incompetence.

As a counterpart for our material affairs, we have a great spiritual realm where there is an even more urgent need for some effective sales procedures. In our mental and spiritual affairs, however, the words *salesman* and *salesmanship* may not have a very creditable standing. In the Church, those who do these persuasion and conversion jobs are called missionaries or home teachers or leaders or exemplars. But with these titles we sometimes do not put the same emphasis on success as we do in our material affairs, and usually, we are not as effective. There are many who feel that if we conducted our business affairs the way many people conduct their Church activity, we would bring on world turmoil and bankruptcy in a short time.

For example, the Lord sent Noah to deliver a message, and in 120 years he was unsuccessful in converting anybody except his own family. All the rest were wiped out by the Flood. Jonah did a little better when the Lord sent him to Nineveh with an idea to deliver about repentance. Jonah went grudgingly and unenthusiastically, yet he got his idea over pretty well, and the city was temporarily saved. As a salesman, Moses had a pretty bad inferiority complex. He said to the Lord, "I am not eloquent. . . . but I am slow of speech, and of a slow tongue." (Exodus 4:10.) The anger of the Lord was kindled against Moses, and he said, "Who hath made man's mouth? . . . have not I the Lord?" (Exodus 4:11.) Most of our mouths would do a lot better if we would work at our jobs of communication more vigorously.

Those who were responsible for carrying the message to Babylon, Tyre and Sidon, Sodom and Gomorrah, Greece and Rome, were not successful enough to get the condemned population spared. And even in our day, after a full restoration of the gospel, our leadership effort in the sales department leaves much to be desired.

For example, in 1960 the Church had 228,516 Melchizedek Priesthood bearers. At the end of 1975 this number had risen to 447,786, which is an increase of 96 percent. But in 1960 we had 125,000 prospective elders, whereas we had 417,982 in 1975, an increase of 234 percent. That is, the increase has been greatest where there should have been a decrease. The purpose of the Church is to build success and to make people happier and more useful. But we need spiritual converters and motivators with a higher degree of success orientation than we frequently have. A good example was set for us in Enoch's day when sin was eliminated in his city and his people qualified themselves for translation.

In the Church, we have many advantages over a commercial enterprise in that we have an almost unlimited selection of salesmen. That is, the bishop or the stake president or the missionary or the home teacher can be called to their positions from among the membership, whereas a sales organization does not have such an unlimited selection opportunity. Sometimes a home teacher carries out what would correspond to the sales function in business, but frequently he goes back again and again, month after month after month, making visits but getting no sales. That is, our conversion percentage as teachers and missionaries would not be very satisfactory if we were part of an aggressive, high-quality commercial sales organization. It might greatly improve the success of our Church functions if we thought of ourselves a little more as productive salesmen. For example, it is a home teacher's job not merely to make visits, but to change lives and produce activity.

The leader of young people needs to know how to actually build character, produce righteousness, train young men to go on missions, and get young people to marry in the temple. The large and growing segment of inactive Church members known as prospective elders needs much more effective leadership. In the Church we have by far the most valuable products to sell, including eternal families, eternal success, eternal happiness and eternal life. But there are far too many people inside the Church who are still walking along that broad, meandering road which leads us to the place where no one wants to go. We could have a much better score if we were more expert in our persuasion techniques. With good, highly trained, industrious men and women in our leadership positions, we would be capable of miraculous actions. We have the greatest possible benefits for people at a cost which is less than nothing. And we are capable of much more than we are presently doing. When Jesus prayed that the Lord's will should be done in the earth as it was done in heaven, he could have been thinking about better teaching and better leadership.

Suppose we take some of our Church assignments and think of the sales possibilities they contain. If a person decides to be a doctor or a lawyer, he must determine what kind of medicine or law he desires to practice and then train himself in the skills required for that particular calling. With this need for preparation in mind, suppose we think of some of the sales opportunities in the Church.

1. *Selling reading.* One Sunday when I was eight years old I was attending a sacrament meeting when I heard a speaker discuss an article in the *Improvement Era* which had been written by President Heber J. Grant. I didn't understand all of the points the speaker made about it, but I was impressed that I wanted to know more. We didn't have an *Improvement Era* in our home; but there was a man who owed me a couple of dollars for thinning some sugar beets, and I went and asked him to pay me my money so that I could subscribe to the *Improvement Era*.

I don't read as much as I ought to now, but back in those cowherding days I had a little more time, and a little better eyesight, and for many years I read everything that was published in the *Era*. The magazine included articles by Heber J. Grant, David O. McKay, Joseph Fielding Smith, Brigham Young, Joseph Smith the Prophet, and many others; so as a young boy I had the opportunity of sitting down with the ideas, ambitions, and ideals of the greatest people in and out of the Church and could absorb their ideas and attitudes for my own good and benefit.

Certainly we have enough literary ability in the Church to make the best ideas available in printed form, and we ought to have the salesmanship to see that they are studied, believed in, and practiced by every member of the Church as well as being made available to every nonmember. Not only should we make our ideas available, but we need to see to it that they are read, understood, believed, accepted, and practiced. What a great idea it is that if I were appointed as the ward's *Ensign* director or the salesman of the *New Era* or *Friend*, and if I were effective in my job, I could not only persuade people to subscribe but could persuade them to read, understand and obey.

2. *Selling missionary work.* If a person is going to be a successful life insurance salesman, he ought to believe in his product. Someone has said the best way to *sell* a large insurance policy is to first *buy* a large insurance policy. That is about what the Lord said to Peter when he said, "When thou art converted, strengthen thy brethren." (Luke 22:32.) The time to prepare a ship for the storm is while the boat is still in the dockyard, and the time to prepare a missionary for missionary work is not after he turns nineteen years of age. His training ought to start the day he is born. The advisors of young men ought to be good salesmen, and the building job should be continuous in the nineteen years preceding the time when he actually takes up the work. Someone has said, "It is a lot easier to make a salesman out of a man than it is to make a man out of a salesman." And it is much easier to make a missionary out of a full-time Latter-day Saint than it is to try to make a change at age nineteen after he has been trained in disobedience, Word of Wisdom violation, fornication, and other sins, delinquencies and weaknesses.

3. *Selling ward maintenance:* The young boy who has made regular deductions from his newspaper-carrying income to save for his mission is much more likely to honor the principles he will later teach to other people. It is an interesting fact that those people who regularly pay their fair share of the ward maintenance will be far better Church attenders than those who pay nothing. One very successful bishopric started out their new ward on the premise that they would get every single member of the ward, including every prospective elder and every part-member family, to pay their ward maintenance. Very few people would pay regular ward maintenance and then stay away from church. There is a very high correlation between non-payers and non-attenders. And if you can change the non-payers to payers, the non-attenders will change more or less automatically.

4. *Selling missionary contributions.* One bishop had a member who would not keep the Word of Wisdom and who had a number of other weaknesses and problems. The bishop called at his home by appointment, and the curious member said, "What are you going to do to me?"

The bishop replied, "I am going to call you on a mission."

"I am not afraid of that," said the member. "You know even better than I do that I could not get a recommend. You know that I smoke and I drink a little and I have done some other things of which I am not very proud." "Bill," the bishop responded, "I know that, and your neighbors all know it, and the Lord knows it. But I am still going to call you on a mission. At least, I am going to call part of you on a mission. We have some men in this ward who are just fractional men. For example, one of these men is a natural-born missionary. If he went on a mission he would probably bring forty new families into the Church. But he can't go on a mission on his own power because he is only a fractional man. He hasn't any money and could not support himself. You are another of these fractional men. You have the money to go on a mission, but you are unable to get a recommend. And so I am going to put the best parts of each of you together to make one full missionary. I am going to call his recommend and your money."

If the bishop had stopped there, the sale would not have been complete. He continued: "Bill, you have mentioned that you smoke and drink and do some other things that you are not very proud of. Someday each of us is going to have to face up to this situation. You have said that you are not very pleased about it and certainly the Lord may not be very pleased about it. Someday he may want to discuss it with you a little more, and if you still have these liabilities and have no compensating assets you may feel very embarrassed about it. It seems to me that this missionary opportunity is going to supply you with some very satisfying assets. After you have said to the Lord how sorry you are about your liabilities, it may be he will turn over to the page where assets built up by the missionary service are listed. Suppose that, because you make this mission call possible for this fine young missionary, the Lord gives you half credit for these forty families that together you will be responsible for bringing into the Church. That is, you will have been responsible for getting the members of twenty families not to do those wrong things that you yourself have done."

Through Moses, the Lord gave ancient Israel a very interesting arrangement that might be called the law of compensation. He said that if a man wants to make amends for stealing another man's sheep, he may do so by returning the stolen sheep and giving the injured man four additional sheep for damages. That is, if someone stole a sheep and by doing so forced the one who had been wronged to hire a detective, track down the one doing the stealing and take him to court, even if the wronged person won the case and got his sheep back he would still be the loser. But if the one doing the stealing repented and returned the sheep with four other sheep as payment for damages, the injured man might be very pleased with the entire transaction. When the Lord made this suggestion of compensation for damages, he was not thinking about stolen sheep but lost souls.

The bishop suggested to his ward member that, short of the man changing his own conduct, the best thing he could do would be to help somebody else avoid those same mistakes. The tears began running down this man's face. For several years he had been very unhappy about his situation but had lacked the strength to do very much about it on his own power. He was delighted that the bishop had given him some opportunity not only to do good but to make some compensation for the damage he had done to himself. Later the missionary he financed shared with him the details of some of his conversions and other faith-promoting experiences. It wasn't very long before the man doing the financing was able to stop his own bad habits and become active in the Church. This demonstrates that the best way to help oneself is to help somebody else. The best way to become a believer is to persuade somebody else to believe. And that is the primary function of a salesman.

There are a lot of people who will buy life insurance or automobiles or education if a good salesman is there to give them suggestions and encouragement. A good salesman is one who is friendly and who is interested in other people. He is one who has strong convictions and good judgments and can effectively merchandise great ideas. Primarily he is one who is regularly on the job with profitable ideas that will help the one being encouraged to buy. A good salesman is one who can identify human needs and can effectively bring about the necessary improvements. It might be a very good idea for each one of us to sit down and make an inventory of those ideas that the Lord would like to be established in the hearts of his children. The Lord has said that it is given to us as Church members to be the salt of the earth. We are the light of the world; we represent the city that is built upon the hill. The spirit of man is the candle of the Lord. We are also his messengers and his managers and his salesmen.

The great field of athletics hires coaches to develop the bodies and minds and attitudes of the players under their direction. But it is also nice to win games. So it is to be successful in business. We ought to have more religion in business, but we ought to be more businesslike in the Church. Certainly we must not fall down in any part of that supreme, divine enterprise of human betterment.

Chapter 21

Pride in Your Outfit

Ernie Pyle was a war correspondent during World War II. He traveled extensively and lived for long periods with the troops. He knew a lot about war and a lot about the character traits that make men good soldiers. On one occasion, he said that nine-tenths of morale is made up of pride in your outfit and confidence in your leaders. We know that a high morale is one of the fundamental elements in military success, but it is also one of the most vital of all success factors in any undertaking. It would be pretty difficult to have a successful business or good public relations or a high degree of accomplishment without high morale. The ability to produce this morale in our wards, our quorums, our businesses, and in our own lives is a goal for which we should strive most ardently. Ernie Pyle tried to indicate to us the overwhelming importance of pride in our outfit and confidence in our leaders.

Like so many other terms, *pride* is a combination word and in its genuine form is made up of love, desire, a feeling of elation, and a sense of intense satisfaction. This principle touches every interest in our lives. Everyone likes to be a part of a going concern. We want to conduct our lives so that they will be above any possible reproach. We need pride in our country, pride in our work, pride in our associates, pride in our family, pride in our faith, and pride in ourselves.

The scriptures point out that there is great joy in heaven when we are righteous and do our work effectively. On four separate occasions God said of his Firstborn Son in the spirit, "This is my beloved Son, in whom I am well pleased." (Matthew 3:17.) In this statement we can feel the pride that the Father felt in his Son. It would probably make the Father feel similarly proud to be able to say that about any of his children. As he has indicated, there is more joy in heaven over one soul that repents than over many righteous people who need no repentance. (Luke 15:7, 10.)

The opposite of pride is shame. By way of contrast, we might imagine how the Lord felt about the Laodiceans mentioned in the scripture who had aroused his disgust and caused him to say: "I know thy works, that thou art neither cold nor hot: I would thou wert cold or hot. So then because thou art lukewarm . . . I will spue thee out of my mouth. Because thou sayest, I am rich, and increased with goods, and have need of nothing; and knowest not that thou art wretched, and miserable, and poor, and blind, and naked." (Revelation 3:15-17.)

The Lord has also said that in the Judgment he will say to those found on his left hand, "Depart from me, ye cursed, into everlasting fire, prepared for the devil and his angels." (D&C 28:28.)

Jesus asked us a very important question when he said, "Therefore what manner of men ought ye to be?" And then he answered his own question by saying, "Even as I am." (3 Nephi 27:27.) That condition in us would immediately produce high morale. We ought to have confidence in God, but we ought to so live that he will have confidence in us.

How awful it would be to have God ashamed of us, and how depressing it is to be ashamed of people with whom one worships! What a dreadful thing to feel incompetence and mediocrity in those who lead! But it would be even worse to cause others to be ashamed of us and to know they have no confidence in what we do or say.

A man once told me that the president and vice president of his company were coming to his city to attend a business meeting. They were very interested in the Church, and they

had told him that they would like to attend some of his
church meetings and see his church in actual operation. He
asked me, "Do you know of some very successful ward where
I could take them?" I said, "I know exactly the place. You
take them to your own ward." He responded, "Oh, I couldn't
do that."

I asked him why, and he told me about the lackadaisical
leadership, the poor organization, the indifferent membership, the lack of attendance, the disorder, and the irreverence. The building that had been dedicated as a house of
worship was shabby and uncared for, which was a reflection
of the uncared-for look of the people themselves. He felt that
many of the people in the ward neither looked nor acted like
Latter-day Saints.

If this man was ashamed to take the president of his
company to his ward, in which he was an officer, how would
he feel if the Lord himself should visit his ward? How would
you feel to know that the Lord felt as ashamed of your ward
as he did of the one at Laodicea? Or suppose he said to us
what he said in the scriptures of those who highly displeased
him. (See D&C 28:28.) How terrible it would be to have the
Lord ashamed of our ward! What if he could have no
confidence in the bishopric or the home teachers or the
parents because of our sins and halfheartedness, and because
we had infected others with a kind of Laodicean lukewarm-
ness? He might then consider us also to be wretched, and
miserable, and poor, and blind, and naked. Certainly the
Lord would not be very pleased to inspect our tithing record
or know of our lethargy, our indifference, and our lack of
faith. One of our most inspiring opportunities is to live so that
our families and our friends and our God will have sincere
pride in us.

The people of ancient Athens were very proud of their
city. Their young men used to stand up and take a sacred
Athenian oath in which they promised never to cause any
Athenian any injury nor bring any disgrace upon their city.
They also took a sacred oath never to bring dishonor upon
themselves. These ancient Greeks could tolerate no weakness
in themselves because of the great satisfaction they had in

their progenitors and the fathers of their city. This kind of pride and ambition in the hearts of people brought on the Golden Age of Greece. The same qualities can bring on a golden age in our day.

When we pray to the Lord we always ask him to bless us. This might be pretty difficult for him to do if he is ashamed of us. We ought to find out as much as possible about this great Ernie Pyle formula in all of its aspects. Someone has tried to describe morale as that mood most conducive to a dependable performance. It indicates a steady, continuous, personal self-control. It identifies a courageous, enthusiastic determination which prevails in spite of all privations or dangers. It rules out those great sins of fractional devotion with marginal morals, a maximum of permissiveness and a minimum of performance.

High morale is based upon a person's faith in a cause and a conviction that he is doing his best. It is manifest in a confident, aggressive, resolute, buoyant spirit of whole-hearted cooperation. And it is particularly attended by zeal, the willingness for self-sacrifice, and the power of indomitability. In effective combination, all of these seem to add up to pride in your outfit and confidence in your leaders.

To be able to control the whole, we need to thoroughly understand the ingredients, and we always come back to this quality of genuine pride. The dictionary motivates us with the thought that true pride is one of our finest, most beautiful, and most lovely characteristics. It is one of our most exalting mental and personality traits. It describes the holy passion of joy that a mother might feel in a noble son, one that she has nursed and trained through his early years so that in the full glory of a righteous, grateful, honest manhood he may effectively serve his family, his country, and his God.

God has given us an ability that will earn for us the right to believe in ourselves. For when we do what is right, we always feel an exalting sense of our own worth. And just as intense misery comes from guilt, so we get extreme happiness from those things that build up our self-respect. A most pleasant sense of delight and elation always comes when we feel worthy of our better selves.

On the other hand, the one burden that is too heavy for anyone to bear is to feel that his own life is not worthwhile. A serious burden can be put on a person's soul when he distrusts and dislikes other people, whereas real confidence and trust in others are among the most ennobling of all emotions. These traits identify us as a person who is sure of his ground. We can get great joy when we feel dependable and responsible and are actually able to get the job done on time. Confidence is the proven assurance of good in those with whom we identify. And as much as possible we ought to have a lot of firsthand personal experience with these great feelings of love, pride, and confidence in others.

The story is told of two brothers who fought in World War I. They had grown up together. They went to school together. They loved each other. They enlisted in the army together and then they went "over the top" many times together. After one of their excursions into no-man's-land, one of the brothers did not return.

Immediately, Jim went to the officer in charge and said: "Sir, I would like to go out into no-man's-land and find my brother." But the officer said: "No, it would be a useless risk. Your brother is probably dead, and another loss would be the only result." After the passage of a few hours, Jim returned to the officer and said, "Sir, I would like to go out into no-man's-land and find my brother." Again, he was refused. Then again, as it was getting dark, Jim returned to the officer and said, "Sir, I would like to go out into no-man's-land and find my brother." Annoyed and irritated, the officer said, "O.K., it's your life. If you want to throw it away, go ahead."

So Jim climbed out of the trench. On his hands and knees he crawled under the barbed wire and disappeared into the darkness of no-man's-land. Hours passed and he didn't return. Midnight came and went and no sign of Jim. Then, just before it began to get light, a movement was discerned in the darkness of no-man's land, and when Jim had satisfied the sentry's challenge he was helped back down into the trench. Immediately he went to make his report.

When the officer saw him coming, he said: "Well, I hope you are satisfied. He's dead, isn't he?" Jim replied, "Yes, he's dead, but he wasn't dead when I found him." And then he told how all night long he had searched among the dead of yesterday's battle and finally had found his brother unconscious in a shell hole. With the water from his canteen he washed the mud from his brother's face and gave him a drink. His brother regained consciousness just long enough to say five words. He looked up into his brother's face and said, "Jim, I knew you'd come." After relating the experience, Jim said to the officer, "Sir, I would rather have died a thousand times than to have had my brother waiting out there in no-man's-land expecting me and know that he died in disappointment."

There are a lot of our antemortal brothers still waiting for us out in the no-man's-land of this world.

Those who qualify for the celestial kingdom will be those who are faithful and diligent in keeping all of God's commandments. What a great compliment it would be when we enter those mansions in heaven to have the Lord take us by the hand and say, "Jim, I knew you'd come!" On the other hand, it might be one of our greatest sins to let other people down and allow their confidence in us to be destroyed. It is particularly unfortunate when confidence is uprooted in the soft soil of our relationships with our children, our spouses, and our parents.

The story is told of a great king who, when his only son was born, took him to the far corner of the kingdom and handed him over to a poor peasant couple with the instruction that they were to rear him as though he were their own son. They were not to tell him who he was until he was old enough to reign, and then his father would come back and make his identity known. Now, suppose that you are that boy and the time has come when, for the first time, you stand before your father and mother and all of your people, knowing who you are. And then suppose that you show yourself before them as unclean, undependable, and unworthy.

One of the advantages we have when we act out a situation in advance is that if we don't like what we see we can reset the stage and come in again. You know that you would not like to show yourself before God as undeserving, so in imagination you might relive your life and come in again. This time you see the great joy in your parents' faces that even though you didn't know you were a king, you behaved like a king; and even though you didn't know you were destined to handle great power and wealth, you showed yourself fully capable and worthy of handling great power and wealth. Then you may feel that great pride and love that everyone had in your accomplishment.

Someone has said that this parable is exactly what life is, except that we are not just the children of a great king; we are the children of the great God who created the earth. We are traveling through life incognito, and someday we are going to find out who we are. Then the earth itself will probably not contain our joy if we have been faithful. Such a thought once prompted this simple prayer:

> Great God, I ask thee for no meaner pelf
> Than that I may not disappoint myself.

It is probable that the greatest opportunity of our lives is to win the unquestioned confidence of our families, our associates and God. What a thrill it would someday be to feel God's hand on our shoulder and hear him approve the activities of our second estate!

Chapter 22

Being Competitive

Every human life is made up of many different factors. Our individual work is made profitable to ourselves or to others by how we rate in those various areas of character, ambition, righteousness, productivity, and the ability to get along with other people.

Before we buy an automobile or a home or some equities listed on the stock market, we make comparisons between the various choices available and then take the one that seems to us to represent the greatest values. There is a continuing adaptation made among us reminiscent of that ancient law known as the survival of the fittest. Those who are unprepared to survive are either eliminated or relegated to some lower level where they can compete with those of their own standards and industry. For example, in the United States there have been over twenty-four hundred makes of automobiles manufactured during this century. All of these companies except a very few have gone out of business. For one reason or another, the discontinued company was unable to compete with those who were better qualified for success.

Clearly, one of the greatest powers in the world is the gigantic force of competition in the different areas of our lives. As various stocks vie with each other for favor in the marketplace, they go up or down in price according to which shows the greatest promise. The old law of supply and demand says that as the demand increases and the supply diminishes, the price goes up. The various articles and services which we have for sale are constantly competing for the confidence and favor of the people.

This law of competition also has great significance in the personal lives of human beings. From the beginning people have been divided up to work and live together in such smaller groups as races, nations, communities, occupations, teams, and families, that they might better stimulate, motivate, teach, and help each other.

The Lord himself has said that man does not live unto himself alone. That is, it is not good for people to live alone or work alone or worship alone, because then they lose the example, friendship and motivation of others.

For a very good purpose, God has planted in our natures this powerful competitive instinct. This does not apply to man alone; it is also a part of animal life. For example, if one horse tries to pass another horse on the track, the horse being passed will more or less automatically try to increase his speed in order to maintain his position. This instinct has a much stronger application to human beings, however. From the earliest times, men have been familiar with an interesting phenomenon which we refer to as keeping up with the Joneses. When the Joneses get a new automobile, we feel the urge within ourselves to get a new automobile. When their children go to college, we want our children to go to college. When they develop higher standards of living, that is a great incentive for us to increase our own efforts in that area. We don't want to fall too far behind the parade.

Not only is example one of the greatest influences in our lives, but its power is increased by this competitive instinct which makes it pleasant not only for us to follow but to lead. We want to keep up with the Joneses, but it's even more fun to go ahead of them. This is a particularly helpful instinct in the important categories of our faith and good works. When one of our associates learns to do something well, he contributes to our success because our competitive instinct makes us want to do it a little better. When someone runs the mile in four minutes or less, someone else is sure to try to break the record. When one of the people we admire believes the gospel and goes on a mission, then we also tend to want to live the gospel and go on a mission. When the tide of faith comes in, all of the ships in the harbor are lifted up. This is a fundamental law of life.

The great purpose of life is to succeed, and creation has tried to help us toward this objective by endowing us with this divine competitive instinct. If properly cultivated and directed, this gift offers each one of us the possibility of greatly increased power and happiness. If we want to be a great soul in heaven, we ought to practice being a great soul here.

The quality that most coaches would look for in someone to play on one of their athletic teams would be a strong desire to win. One of the best examples of motivation that we know of is found in an amateur athlete. More than anyone else, the amateur football quarterback works at the very limit of his ability, and does it without monetary compensation. He exposes himself to great physical risks in order to win for the school. But if you were to take away the competition and the possibility of victory, disregard the statistics and not keep score, you would kill most of the interest and desire to play; whereas, you produce undreamed-of power when you develop a competitive spirit, a high morale, with a powerful urge for excellence and the consciousness of a high skill.

Schools compete with each other, but individual players also compete with each other, and the position of each one will depend on how successfully he compares with other players. To a champion runner, it is very important whether he can run the mile in three minutes and fifty-five seconds or whether it takes him four minutes and one second. That is, to gain six seconds in a mile can be all-important. This competition factor is also very important in our business, social, and religious activities, and in life generally.

There is no question that competition helps trade. The construction companies bid against each other for jobs they do. Automobile companies, merchandise manufacturers and retailers, life insurance companies, and many other organizations carry on a very intense and helpful competition, and our total accomplishment is improved as a consequence. Some good competition also makes the game a lot more fun. If a person expects to make the greatest progress, he must see to it that his goods and services are competitive with the best. It is natural that some people do not like competition, because it forces them to be on their toes and to improve the quality of their own efforts. When some firm or individual can get a monopoly so that he has no competitors and is not asked to make comparisons, the standards usually drop and the interests of the patrons are hurt. The federal government has enacted some important anti-trust laws against monopolies and collusion between companies as being in restraint of trade and detrimental to the public good. The idea of eliminating the great natural competitive urge in human beings is frequently carried over into Church activities. It constitutes a kind of spiritual restraint of trade which may be hurtful to those who, because competition and the will to win has been eliminated, have to live with the lower score.

Competition has many advantages to the competitor himself. In order to compete, he must keep himself alert, take advantage of every possible improvement, maintain the excellence of his product, and give the most satisfying service at the least cost. He must also be the kind of person who will inspire confidence, trust, and affection in those with whom he does business. But this idea of competition is not fully accepted by everyone. We sometimes refer to our competitive world as a "rat race," or "dog-eat-dog" situation. We sometimes try to cover up our own weaknesses and failures by belittling those who excel us. But try to imagine what our world would be like if we did not feel the need to compete in anything and no comparisons were permitted.

I once visited the home of a couple who have excluded themselves from the outside world and live more or less as hermits. They are both far past middle age. They have many acres of valuable land on which they can hardly pay the taxes because of their antiquated methods of farming. They live in an unimproved house that has no inside plumbing. They don't like improvement or competition or keeping up with anybody. They don't know the thrill of winning or the excitement that goes with excellence.

We sometimes develop this destructive, unconcerned attitude in our Church leadership. We do away with the score and never check up on ourselves. We adopt the philosophy of the phrase from the song which says: "If we fail, we fail with glory." The result of our Church accomplishment is then approximately what it would be if in an athletic program or a business organization we did away with the statistics and made it against the law to keep the score.

Frequently, because of unbusinesslike attitudes in our political, civic or Church leadership, we lose the stimulation that we get from excellence in our other fields of activity. For example, our home teaching program might be greatly improved if each home teacher had the attitude and motivations of a high-grade salesman.

The same might also be said of other Church workers. If the elders quorum president had the same kind of attitude toward his assignment that an energetic, ambitious sales manager has for his business, there would likely be a great increase in the elders' activities and accomplishments. And if all prospective elders could be encouraged to work as near the limits of their abilities as a high school football quarterback does, there might be a lot more people on schedule for the celestial kingdom.

Some educational institutions use this competitive idea by giving A's to the top group, B's to those of second grade, and so on down to those who are dropped from school. Schools also give special honors to those who turn in an outstanding success, ranging downward from summa cum laude. The Lord himself has established a competitive ranking for our eternal lives. He will segregate us, according to our total success, into three great kingdoms of glory and one kingdom which is not a kingdom of glory. The highest of these is the celestial kingdom.

Below the celestial kingdom is a much larger group that makes up the terrestrial kingdom, which is as far below the celestial as the light of the moon is below the blaze of the noonday sun. Below that kingdom is a kingdom of glory which is called the telestial. Then, below all of these, is a kingdom which is not a kingdom of glory. This is the kingdom which will be inhabited by Satan and his angels, who will be joined by those who become sons of perdition or sons of Satan in this life and are not entitled to a kingdom of glory. Certainly they will not sing, "If we fail, we fail with glory."

We must learn to fight for what we believe, and it may be of great help to us to develop this competitive spirit which creation itself has made a part of every human soul. We must learn to be competitive for righteousness. We must not lose the game to the atheists, to the criminals, to the sinners, or to our own weaknesses. The philosophy of success is to win. The champion always has a competitive spirit and a love of victory. As God will eventually triumph over Satan in every department, so we must win a daily victory in our religious affairs.

The Lord has put into us this great competitive spirit so that we are stimulated by the inspiring examples of others and the good works of those around us. What would be the advantage of a good example or of inspiration itself if we were not motivated by it? We must live the principles of the gospel if we want to qualify for the highest rewards. Every principle and every ordinance of the gospel has to do with the celestial kingdom. If we are only interested in the telestial or the terrestrial kingdom, it is not necessary to be baptized or to be married in the temple or to pay tithing or to keep the Ten Commandments. Many people of lesser ambition can get into these kingdoms after paying the penalties of their disobedience in the spirit prison house.

It is hoped that each one of us will someday discover that we have excelled in enthusiasm and righteousness all of those lower grades occupied by the atheists, the idlers, the inactive, the indifferent, and those who disobey the commandments. Eternal life in the celestial kingdom will incite one of the most worthwhile emotions that we have ever known. May we never have to endure the bitter regrets of failure! In the meantime, we can greatly increase our leadership success by being more businesslike in this greatest of all enterprises—the salvation of our own souls and those for whom we have eternal responsibility.

Chapter 23

Sales Points for the Law of the Fast

One of the most helpful parts of Church work is for us to encourage each other to live those important laws determining our success and happiness. If I had a sufficient power for reasonable argument, I would try to persuade everyone in the world, both in and out of the Church, to live every one of the laws of the gospel. Each of these laws is highly "salable." As an example, suppose we consider some of the sales points connected with one of the least glamorous of these laws: the law of the fast.

Dr. Henry C. Link once wrote, "Nothing puts so much order into human life as to live by a set of sound principles." The most sound of all principles are the principles of the gospel of Jesus Christ. If we lived them as we should, we would be better human beings and far more prosperous in material as well as spiritual things. As leaders we need the power of motivation and the sales ability to get these ideas over to other people. What follows might be thought of as a kind of sales talk on fasting. Sometimes we think of some of these great eternal laws as minor, as having little importance to us personally. This is erroneous thinking. Here are six important reasons why each of us should strictly live the law of the fast.

The first and most important reason is that it is a command of God. What a thrilling quality we could develop in our lives if we would always obey God, if for no other reason than that it is right and he has asked us to do it!

In the Creation, God worked six days and rested one day and he has commanded us to follow this same procedure. It was not intended that we merely rest our arms, our legs, and our backs; we should also rest our digestive systems and give this magnificent physical body a chance to cleanse itself of impurities or waste that it may have accumulated during the month. All through the ages, the prophets have advised the people about the importance of regular periods of fasting. The Master began his own ministry by fasting for forty days and forty nights.

Reason number two: Helping the needy. In the program of the Church, we are asked to set aside a Sunday in each month, usually the first one, as fast Sunday. We are invited to abstain from two meals and give the bishop at least the money thus saved to help provide food, clothing, medicine, etc., to those in need. We go to the house of prayer on this day and there bear our testimonies, express our appreciation, and encourage, uplift, and inspire each other.

If present Church members paid fast offerings on a reasonable basis, an annual sum of over fifty million dollars would be available that could be translated into some fantastic human benefits and in addition would help us to build a substantial reserve for any future emergencies.

The Lord could have said about paying fast offerings what he said about keeping the Word of Wisdom, that it was "adapted to the capacity of the weak and the weakest of all saints, who are or can be called saints." (D&C 89:3.) In view of our many blessings from God, an average payment of thirteen or fifteen cents per meal must be a serious affront to him, and certainly it should cause great embarrassment to those responsible. When this deficiency is called to our attention, it ought to make the nonpayers and the inadequate-payers feel neglectful and repentant. They should immediately take steps to get their actual fasting as well as the payment of their offerings on a proper basis. This would greatly please the Lord. In addition, making the proper payments would help every member of the Church to be more prosperous.

Reason number three: Fasting is one of the finest ways of developing personal discipline and self-control. We hear a lot of talk about the temptations of our day, and many people are falling down before the most trivial sins. The best way to learn self-control is by practicing self-control.

Several polls taken in the last few years indicate that Mohandas K. Gandhi is thought to be one of the greatest men of our time. He is the Indian patriot that helped win India's independence from Britain, and at the time of his death was acknowledged to be the greatest power in India. His followers renamed him the Mahatma, or the great soul. Yet his biographer, Louis Fischer, claims that Gandhi started out on a very low level of self-control. He thought of himself as a coward. He was afraid of the dark. He was afraid of serpents. He was afraid of people. He was afraid of himself. He had a very bad temper.

Realizing the disadvantages that these traits gave him, he deliberately started out to remake himself; and he later called himself a self-remade man. If you would like to have a good phrase to ponder, that is one of the best. Anyone planning to make something worthwhile out of himself must be a self-remade man. There should be an intelligent remodeling job going on all the time. A father once said to his son that he, the father, was a self-made man, but the son thought it was a horrible example of unskilled labor.

Gandhi went on long fasts for discipline. He reasoned that if he could not control his passion for food, he would be hard put to it to handle the more difficult situations in life itself. "How can I control others if I cannot control myself," he asked. Mr. Fischer comments that not since Socrates has the world seen Gandhi's equal for effective self-analysis combined with absolute composure and self-control.

Gandhi's mother believed that eating meat was wrong inasmuch as it necessitated the destruction of other life, so Gandhi took a pledge to his mother that he would remain a vegetarian throughout his life. Many years after his mother had died, when Gandhi became very ill, the doctors tried to persuade him that if he would drink a little beef broth it might save his life. But Gandhi said: "Even for life itself we may not do certain things. There is only one course open to me—to die, but never to break my pledge." Just think what would happen to the Church if every one of us had that kind of integrity and self-control. Since the development of strength in one area quickly extends itself into other areas, by a practice of this kind of self-discipline we could make ourselves stronger than anything that can happen to us.

Reason number four: Fasting is one of the most important health procedures. I have at my desk a great book written on fasting by a man who is not a member of the Church. It is his opinion that primarily there is only one disease. We usually talk of our physical diseases under the headings of heart attacks, cancers, strokes, hardening of the arteries, lumbago, gout, diabetes, arthritis, etc. But this man points out that these are all one and the same, and that they consist primarily of the excess wastes and toxins that accumulate in our bodies.

If I have a boil on my hand, the boil is merely the symptom and there is no particular point in putting liniment on it. The disease is the bad blood underneath. If the blood can be purified, the symptom will disappear by itself. When we get too much cholesterol or too much of an accumulation of harmful fatty substances in our blood, it may cause a heart attack or a stroke. We get hardening of the arteries because the arteries get too heavily lined or clogged with waste. I have never heard of anyone dying of lung cancer from smoking one cigarette. But when we smoke one or two or three packages a day, the system is unable to get rid of the poison fast enough and we get sick.

The man who wrote this book says that we ought to fast one full day every week without fail, and four times a year we ought to fast for an entire week to give our bodies time to throw out the poisons, the waste, and the substances that clog up our blood vessels and our hearts.

On several occasions in the past few years, my eye doctor has put some fluorescent dye in my blood to help him find the leaks in the blood vessels of my eye. Immediately this foreign substance gets into my blood, my body goes to work in throwing these impurities, with their high coloration, out into the urine. After half an hour, the discoloration indicates that the purifying processes of my body are hard at work, and after eight hours the job has been completed and the color is back to normal. If these impurities were put into my blood three times a day with no time provided for the cleansing, I would soon become very sick and would eventually die. Our bodies are the greatest healers. They are the best doctors. They will keep us well if we will just give them a chance, and a fast once a month is a step in that direction.

Reason number five: Fasting is a means of developing great spiritual power. When the apostles asked the Lord why they could not cast the evil spirit out of the young man who was sorely afflicted, he said to them, " . . . this kind goeth not out but by prayer and fasting." (Matthew 17:21.) If by prayer and fasting we can get evil spirits out of other people, we can also get evil out of ourselves.

Reason number six: Everyone needs to be a part of some good charitable causes, and paying fast offerings is one of the best ways. Many of the important things that have happened in our culture have been accomplished through the gifts of charitable people. That is how we got many of our libraries, our hospitals, our universities, our churches, and even the earth itself. Medical research, cultural institutions, musicians and musical organizations, artists and collections of art, museums, and special educational programs are often recipients of charitable contributions. Each of us should have a personal part in supporting some of these worthwhile endeavors. Our giving should not be limited to the Church, even though that should have first call on our charitable donations.

The farmer reserves the best of his crop as seed corn. There are some people who want to take more out of life than they put in, but we will be much happier and much more successful personally if we put back into the community and into life more than we take out.

Now I would like to give you six more reasons why paying fast offerings is one of the finest of our charitable contributions.

1. One hundred cents out of every contributed dollar get to the place where they are intended to go. That is, there is

no overhead in fast offerings. Some of our finest charitable causes have a very high overhead, and that may be exactly as it should be; but there is no overhead in fast offerings.

2. It costs the contributor nothing. Every other contribution comes out of our pocketbook, but fast offerings come out of a grocery bill and does not need to be replaced.

3. If we really practice the law of the fast in combination with Doctrine and Covenants section 89, think how many medical bills we can save. In doing our homework on fasting, we ought to go to the hospital once in a while and find out what it would cost us to spend a month there as a patient; or we could find out how much it costs today to have a stroke or a heart attack or to be laid up for a few years with arthritis or some other disabling disease. Fasting is one of the good health habits which can materially diminish medical bills.

4. Apart from the medical bill situation, fasting and other good habits of health will add years to our lives and make our years more healthy and happy.

5. Think how much we can please Deity by paying a proper fast offering. God gave us a personal insight into his attitude on this when he said through Malachi: "Will a man rob God? Yet ye have robbed me. But ye say, Wherein have we robbed thee? In tithes and offerings. Ye are cursed with a curse: for ye have robbed me, even this whole nation." (Malachi 3:8.) If men were robbing God then by not paying their tithes and offerings, and we are now doing the same thing, we are robbing God now. And we can greatly please God by changing our course.

We can bring about the greatest success by building some solid convictions around these principles which put not only order but happiness and success into our lives. With the right amount of encouragement and leadership, all wards and all stakes and all branches and all missions and all individuals can be a magnificent success by obedience to this important law of the Lord.

The law of the fast can also be a kind of schoolmaster, and if we can learn to live it effectively it will help us to keep every other law better because of the power and faith which will be generated in us as a natural consequence of our living this important law.

Part Five

Leadership Success Ingredients

The Gift of Courage
The Gift of Tongues
The Soliloquy of Success
Success Stories
Some Leadership Ideas
The Convert
Why Not Now?

Chapter 24

The Gift of Courage

Many years ago, the late Paul Speicher wrote a magnificent little book entitled *The Gift of Courage*. In it he asks, "If, as a gift, you could have your heart's desire, if you could have your fondest wish fulfilled, what would it be?"

Then Mr. Speicher affirms that the most wonderful gift is one that only you can give to yourself. It is the gift of courage. Mr Speicher says that greater than intellect, experience, ability, or foresight is that fighting edge that one has when he is not afraid. Therefore, he suggests, "Give yourself the gift of courage, the courage to meet the problems of life each day, for without this gift life slips through our listless fingers and is lost while we sit and wait for fairer days."

In legendary Greek history, Homer tells of the island of the Lotus Eaters. The fruit of the lotus tree caused a state of dreamy self-content and made one forget ambition and home and friends and God. On this enchanted island men lost their purpose in life. Yet the fabled lotus fruit is not more dangerous to human hearts than is discouragement, procrastination, fear, and the stagnation of those lives that lack courage.

Mr. Speicher counsels: "Give yourself the courage to keep on trying." He asks: "When is a man a failure?" Is he a failure when his business falls off, or when he stumbles in his effort? Is he a failure when he makes a mistake or when his goals are not realized? Disheartening as these things may be, they do not make any man a failure. A man is a failure only when he quits trying and contents himself to live on a level less than his best.

Washington met severe adversity at Valley Forge, but he didn't stop. Lincoln fought despair and melancholia all of his life, but he kept on going. Paul the apostle said, "But I keep under my body, and bring it into subjection: lest that by any means, when I have preached to others, I myself should be a castaway." (1 Corinthians 9:27.) And Jesus said, "He that endureth to the end shall be saved." (Matthew 10:22.)

We need to give ourselves the courage that strengthened the heart of Columbus and held him steadfast while he sailed into unknown seas, the courage that, through the dark days and stormy nights, enabled him to greet his fear-stricken sailors with the cry of faith and say: "Sail on! Sail on! Sail on and on!"

Give yourself the courage to utilize your full potential. I remember the story of the lion cub lost in a flock of sheep. As he grew up, he ran and played with the sheep and behaved like a sheep and believed that he was a sheep. One day, on the distant skyline there appeared the silhouette of a great lion. His head was thrown back, his tail was lashing about him. With a great roar, the lion on the hillside sent his voice echoing across the fields of the valley below. The lion playing with the sheep stopped his playing. Something stirred within him. Like was calling to like. Then he knew that he was not a sheep but a lion, and with an answering roar that sent the timid sheep scattering before him the lion with the sheep ran to join the lion on the mountainside.

Sometimes we go through life with the lion sleeping within us, never realizing that our lot is not in the meadows with the sheep but on the mountainside with the lions.

Give yourself the courage to dream of the man or woman you may become. This God-given ability to dream great dreams was not given us to mock us. The holy scriptures point the way for the most magnificent of all accomplishments, which is a life of devotion and service to our eternal Heavenly Father.

To reach the most tremendous goals, we need to give ourselves the courage of the little boy who used to awaken night after night screaming because of a repeated nightmare in which he met a great tiger. He was so affected by his nightly terror that his parents counseled with a psychologist, who said to the little boy: "The next time you dream about the tiger, say to yourself, 'This nice old tiger hasn't come to hurt me. He wants to be my friend. I am going to walk right up and pat him on the head.' "

The boy agreed, and that night the anxious parents stole into his room. There he lay tossing nervously in his sleep. They saw his face whiten and his breath grow shorter, and they heard a desperate little voice saying through tightly closed lips: "I am not afraid; I know that you want to be my friend. I am going to walk right up and pat you on the head." Then the little boy smiled in his sleep, and the parents knew that the tiger would never again send him screaming from his bed. Give yourself the courage to meet the tigers of life.

Almost every one of our problems is a blessing in disguise sent to develop our strength. If we listen closely we can hear the calm, clear voice of the Master saying, "Be of good cheer; it is I; be not afraid." (Matthew 14:27.) May God help us to give ourselves this magnificent gift of courage.

Chapter 25

The Gift
of Tongues

The most astounding of all of God's inventions is a great human being. On the sixth day of that long-ago Creation, God fashioned us in his own likeness, gave us his own abilities in embryonic form, and headed us toward our divine destiny. These gifts were bestowed on a kind of lend-lease arrangement, however, and their permanent possession depends upon the extent to which we develop and use them.

When these gifts are a little unusual, we are more impressed with them. Some of the more unusual gifts are mentioned in the seventh Article of Faith: "We believe in the gift of tongues, prophecy, revelation, visions, healing, interpretation of tongues, etc." This gift of tongues, in all of its aspects, is one of our most valuable gifts. In one of its applications it makes our finest expression possible and is the foundation of our most meaningful communication. This is one of the gifts that is capable of the greatest expansion and makes us eligible for almost any capability and excellence.

The human intellect sits enthroned in all of man's powers, yet it manifests itself primarily through our voices. On a few occasions we have had some miraculous manifestations of this gift. For example, the scripture tells of an interesting event that happened on the day of Pentecost. The record says: "And they were all filled with the Holy Ghost, and began to speak with other tongues, as the Spirit gave them utterance. And there were dwelling at Jerusalem Jews, devout men, out of every nation under heaven. Now when this was noised abroad, the multitude came together, and were confounded, because that every man heard them speak in his own language." (Acts 2:4-6.) In addition to its usefulness, this manifestation was probably given as a miraculous sign to strengthen the faith of these new believers.

It appears that manifestations of divine power of this magnitude have been displayed only infrequently. Another of these rare occurrences took place at the wedding feast at Cana when Jesus turned water into wine. (Other people have accomplished the same practical result on a much larger scale by planting a vineyard and squeezing out the grape juice.) When Jesus began his ministry, he did many miraculous things; then, when he returned to his native city of Nazareth, the people asked him to repeat these miracles to satisfy their curiosity. Jesus said to them: "Ye will surely say unto me . . . whatsoever we have heard done in Capernaum, do also here in thy country. And he said, verily I say unto you . . . many widows were in Israel in the days of Elias, when the heaven was shut up three years and six months, when great famine was throughout all the land; but unto none of them was Elias sent, save unto Sarepta, a city of Sidon, unto a woman that was a widow. And many lepers were in Israel in the time of Eliseus the prophet; and none of them was cleansed, saving Naaman the Syrian." (Luke 4:23-27.) These words suggest it was not the divine intention to heal every leper by a miracle nor to feed every hungry person by some miraculous process, nor to do away with the growing of grapes in favor of the miracle of turning water into wine. In other words, such miraculous events were not intended as a common thing for daily use.

Similarly, this particular use of the gift of tongues, where one man speaks in many languages on the same occasion, is a rare event. We have made some practical modern developments, however, that are reminiscent of this great gift and are in daily use. Not long ago I heard over the radio a Russian leader speak in his own language. In the background there were a great number of interpreters translating what he said, so that Russians, Americans, and people of many other nations around the world clearly heard what he said in their respective tongues. This is also a process used by the United Nations—each man speaks in his own tongue and his auditors hear in their own language.

It is one of the prophetic promises of the latter days that every man should have the privilege of hearing the gospel of Jesus Christ preached in his own tongue. In carrying out this instruction, the Church has set up language-training schools at which new missionaries study the language of the people to whom they are being sent. It would do no good if the missionary didn't learn this new language thoroughly enough that he could speak clearly and effectively and be understood by the potential convert.

A "gift of tongues" has some common and daily uses in that with a little extra effort every person may learn to use his own language or the language of another nation with miraculous effectiveness and great benefit for those to whom he is sent and for himself. With a greater knowledge of word meanings and a clear enunciation, one can greatly multiply the power of his ideas. He can add a little color, some good illustrations energized by some stimulating emotion to give his tongue greater power.

Demosthenes, who became the greatest orator in the world, started out with such a serious speech impediment that very few could understand him even in his *own* tongue. But to overcome his deficiency and improve the gifts of his own personal power, he went down to the seashore and shouted to the waves. Demosthenes' version of the gift of tongues is one that all of us may use with wonderful effect.

This law of success, which involves practicing our desired gift, also works wonders in other fields. Most of our great gifts are given to us only as potentialities which we ourselves may develop to our heart's content. Whether one is given the gift of faith or of tongues or of athletics, he must help to bring about, by practice, whatever excellence he obtains. That is, the Lord does not usually send his gifts to us in their finished states. It is one of his primary laws of success that we learn to do by doing.

The one gift that we need to develop more than perhaps any other is this great gift of tongues, or proficiency in our own language. Language enables us to communicate ideas, arouse ambitions, establish ideals and bring conversion to other people. Such miracles as occurred at Pentecost do not take place frequently. But in any event, what good would it do me to have the ability to speak in all languages if I couldn't even put my message across in my own language? There are many men and women who cannot communicate effectively with their own spouses or help their children to understand those important ideas that parents are obligated to teach them.

In a missionary meeting, I listened to some missionaries who were giving the missionary discussions in my own language. These lessons are calculated to make the principles of the gospel crystal clear to those investigating. I sat on the third row, but I could not even hear what the missionary was saying. At least I could not hear enough of his words to enable me to intelligently follow him. He had very poor enunciation, and the fact that he was not very sure of his material so hindered him that his voice lacked conviction, power, enthusiasm, color, and interest. The lack of clarity and expression in his speech severely impeded the comprehension of his listeners. I was reminded of what we might call the withdrawal of the gift of tongues which the people experienced at the Tower of Babel. Because of the sins of the people, the Lord confounded their language. Thereafter they could not understand one another's speech and were scattered abroad and left off their building of the tower. We sometimes do just about that same thing to our own gift of tongues. That is, we speak so poorly that our listeners may understand only a fraction of what we say.

We frequently lose part of the blessing of our gift of speech because we fail to enunciate clearly. We slur our words or jumble our speech, or we fail to put enough expression into our language for it to be interesting to others. In sacrament meetings, classrooms, and leadership meetings we are frequently guilty, to some degree, of this mumbo-jumbo, so that a large part of our finest meanings are lost to the people in attendance. Certainly the Lord did not command us to hold these important meetings with the idea in mind that the people attending should miss a large portion of their benefits. When a listener misses even one word, it may cause him to lose the whole point of a discussion; and when he can hear only half of the words, any meaning becomes obscure and the listener's interest frequently dies.

I attended a religious convention at which over two thousand people were present. Two of the speakers spoke loudly enough and clearly enough for everyone to hear without any sense of straining or effort. Their language had interest and effective punctuation and was meaningful in its expression.

The other speakers I heard and understood only in part. For different reasons, these speakers put their listeners under a serious handicap. If I were going to estimate, I would say that one speaker was heard only 25 percent, another might have been heard 50 percent, and another 75 percent, and this only with great effort and strain which listeners ordinarily would not make. These three speakers probably gave their audience a sense of frustration more than anything else; for if you take out even one-fourth of a speaker's words, what is left is comparatively worthless, even if heard perfectly.

Suppose you cross out 25 percent of the words in a chapter of a book and see what it does to the total meaning. For example, read the following version of the Twenty-third Psalm with every fourth word blotted out. "The Lord is _____ shepherd; I shall _____ want. He maketh _____ to lie down _____ green pastures: He _____ me beside the _____ waters. He restoreth _____ soul: He leadeth _____ in the paths _____ righteousness for his _____ sake. Yea, though _____ walk through the _____ of the shadow _____ death, I will _____ no evil: for _____ art with me; _____ rod and thy _____ they comfort me. _____ preparest a table _____ me in the _____ of mine enemies: _____ anointest my head _____ oil; my cup runneth _____. Surely goodness and _____ shall follow me _____ the days of _____ life: and I _____ dwell in the _____ of the Lord _____ ever.

Now suppose that the other 75 percent of the words were also jumbled and run together. Even this would not be so bad because the Twenty-third Psalm is familiar to everyone. The problem is compounded when you try to put over something that is unknown to the listeners and that has in it a variety of inaudible and jumbled words.

Anyone who is interested in effective leadership or conversion or in making sales or in promoting good public relations or in doing almost any other thing, ought to convince himself of the need for effective speech and then work a lot harder than most of us do on this great and godly gift of tongues. We ought to learn to speak loudly enough and clearly enough and interestingly enough to be fully heard and clearly understood, and logically and convincingly enough to be believed and followed. Our words must hold listener interest. In his discussion of the gift of tongues Paul makes some points that we ought to understand. For example, he said: "Except ye utter by the tongue words easy to be understood, how shall it be known what is spoken? For ye shall speak into the air. There are, . . . so many kinds of voices in the world. . . . Therefore if I know not the meaning of the voice, I shall be unto him that speaketh a barbarian, and he that speaketh shall be a barbarian unto me. . . . If I pray in an unknown tongue, my spirit prayeth, but my understanding is unfruitful. . . . How shall he that occupieth the room of the unlearned say Amen . . . seeing he understandeth not what thou sayest? . . . I had rather speak five words with my understanding, . . . than ten thousand words in an unknown tongue. . . . Tongues are for a sign, not to them that believe but to them that believe not." (1 Corinthians 14:9-22.)

The seventh Article of Faith mentions the gift of tongues, prophecy, revelation, visions, healing, and the interpretation of tongues. It may be that the broad gift of tongues is by far the most important one for us to work on. Only infrequently do we experience miraculous prophecies, revelations, visions, and healings, but we use this great gift of tongues every day. We have four written scriptural volumes of prophecies, revelations, visions, and healings, all of which came through someone else. But we can't hope to get others to understand the messages they contain if we do not develop an intelligent gift of tongues in ourselves. We should use this gift effectively enough that we will not need an interpreter to make our message understood nor a motivator to see that it is practiced. Through this great gift we ourselves will be able to help them find the meaning, the spirit, the rhythm, and the music of the word of the Lord without confusion or discord.

Certainly one of our most fantastic gifts is the gift of tongues: not only the power to speak in an unknown language, but the ability to speak clearly and enthusiastically and convincingly in the language we use daily, and may learn to be complete masters of.

Chapter 26

The Soliloquy of Success

One of the greatest nonscriptural authors who ever lived was William Shakespeare. During his career, he wrote thirty-seven plays. He peopled these plays with a thousand characters, each of which is the personification of some personality trait. Shakespeare looked with keen insight into human lives. He understood better than most men do those personality traits, mental powers and motivating emotions which make our lives what they are. In his plays he created some miniature worlds into which each of us may go to see our own potential successes and failures reflected.

On one occasion, Daniel Starck got together a group of a hundred literary critics who, after careful deliberation, presented their opinion that Shakespeare's *Hamlet* was the greatest nonscriptural work that had ever been written. In *Hamlet* and in all of his other writings, Shakespeare expressed some great philosophies for life as well as giving some very helpful success formulas which are still applicable. And we may use a great many of them to help bring about our own temporal and eternal success.

Any success is determined substantially by whether or not the candidate himself can firmly make up his mind about what his objectives will be. When young Hamlet was faced with a very serious problem, he gave his famous soliloquy on the question, "To be or not to be." To Hamlet as to all of us, a course of action is not always completely clear; so in his dilemma Hamlet made up a kind of mental balance sheet of pros and cons to help him make up his mind. He said:

> To be, or not to be,—that is the question:—
> Whether 'tis nobler in the mind to suffer
> The slings and arrows of outrageous fortune,
> Or to take arms against a sea of troubles,
> And by opposing end them?

That is still our problem.

Someone has said that the three main subheadings for our general success are: *to know, to do, to be.* They are closely related, and they are endless in their possibilities. Anyone who aspires to success ought to sit down and write his soliloquy under these headings. That is, a person who expects to excel must *know* the fundamental laws of the particular discipline involved and how his relations with others may be effectively promoted.

We can learn a great deal by studying what has been written on a subject by others who have been oustandingly effective in that area. Therefore, to *know* we ought *always* to keep some success books available and become thoroughly familiar with them. There is another way that we can know things, and that is by thinking about them. Someone has said that if you want to hatch out something, just set your mind on it. That is how Thomas A. Edison lighted our world. That is how Brigham Young became a great colonizer and Church leader. God has given us a tremendous instrument called a brain which is tuned in to the Divine and has fantastic capabilities.

Next let us consider number two, *to do.* The scripture says that we will be judged according to our works. The great call of the Lord was not merely for hearers or talkers or thinkers; it was for doers.

If one becomes irresponsible in his assigned task, a hundred people may lose their blessings as a consequence. Our reason indicates that it is a hundred times worse for a hundred people to lose their blessings than for one person to lose his blessing. The worst part of this situation is that it is probably the most widespread sin of our day. We have too many promisers and not enough genuine performers. There are too many people who accept Church assignments who do not perform at the top of their ability.

There are too many who say, "I go, Sir," and go not. There are too many who accept the honor of Church assignments who do not fully accept the responsibility. There are too many leaders who don't lead. There are too many who assume the title of saviors upon Mount Zion who aren't actually saving anyone, not even themselves. There are too many who serve out of their weakness and not out of their might.

There are many who make the covenants of service and have responsibility officially laid upon them but who do not magnify their callings and may thereby come under the condemnation pronounced by Jesus upon the unprofitable servant. Each of us ought to make up our minds what we personally are going to do about it. We get great pleasure from the thought of saving a human soul by our efforts, but how irreparable is our loss if through our neglect a soul is lost! So each of us might ask himself the question, Will I do it or won't I do it on a 100 percent basis?

We come to the third subheading, *to be*. Life writes what we are in letters of light that everyone can see. One of the greatest choices in life is the choice of being—the choice of being genuine, the choice of being true blue. There is no pleasure in being a phony. The obligation to be genuine servants of the Lord applies to all our Church leadership positions. What would you think of an army where only the general could be trusted? Is there any good reason why the elders quorum president should not be just as faithful as the President of the Church?

What kind of an irrigation system would we have if only the canals were capable of carrying water; if the individual head ditches and furrows that lead to the plants were filled with weeds and debris and had so many cross gullies that they could not properly do their job? What would be the use of an electrical wiring system where one group of wires insisted on short-circuiting the current from the power plant so that it could never arrive to turn the factory wheels?

For one to waste his own strength is one thing, but to

short-circuit the entire organization is something else. One negligent player can sometimes lose the game for the whole team. Of course, the general and the watermaster and the electrician all have responsibility for seeing to it that each part of the equipment and each person under their direction functions properly. If the farmer allows the furrows to default, even for one irrigation turn, the entire crop may be lost.

A leader who doesn't lead is misleading, and a coach who can't guarantee excellence in each of his players is doing everyone a disservice. One of the greatest powers in the world is the power of leadership. Someone expressed this idea well when he said, "He that can get ten men to work is greater than he that doeth the work of ten men." If a man can do the work of ten men, he is just a good worker. But if he can get ten men to work at the full limit of their possibility, he is building men into the image of God. And that is our greatest possible challenge.

Every good farmer has a shovel, and it is his job to see that an ample amount of water gets to the end of every row each time he has a water turn. Each leader has a similar responsibility in the organization that he leads.

So we come back to our primary soliloquy of success, wherein we ask ourselves, "To do or not to do." Will we or won't we? If we answer that question with a strong affirmative, it is a comparatively simple matter to develop the knowledge, the attitudes, the skills, the habits and the personality traits that will make our leadership what it ought to be. There will be no delinquent players; no wires will be short-circuiting the whole system. Those that lead the soldiers on the field of battle will be as faithful as those who make the plans behind the lines. The programs of the Church will be applied in the right places, just as the sugar beet on the end of the row will be as well watered as his brothers and sisters who were favored by being closer to the supply source. Then all three of the dimensions of our success will be strengthened almost automatically.

Chapter 27

Success Stories

At the leadership session of each quarterly stake conference held in a certain year, two people were assigned to tell a three-minute success story. That is, each was asked to describe some segment of his or someone else's success which might be made negotiable in the lives of the other leaders in attendance.

Man is a natural collector by divine instinct. Small boys collect things like marbles, chalk, a fishing rod, and a chicken's foot. Girls fill hope chests with beautiful things. Businessmen collect real estate, stocks and bonds, and insurance policies. Some misguided people collect a tobacco habit, lung cancer, dope addiction, and even disease.

The instinct to hoard good things was intended for our good and goes through all nature. The squirrel hoards acorns, the bee stores up honey, the winter hibernation of the bear is supported by his excess of summer's fat. When God created man in his own image, he generously endowed him with this hoarding instinct. We preserve food in the growing season to carry us over until the next spring. We carry over the great literature of the past to motivate our present accomplishment. We have a natural instinct to acquire which is supported and increased by our natural inclination to produce and to save.

James Barrie once said that memory enables us to have roses in December. Jesus said that we should lay up for ourselves treasures in heaven. Since I attended those success meetings at quarterly stake conferences, I have stored away in my literary treasurehouse some seventy-two success stories. This hoarding place is like a stockroom containing the spare parts for success, and I may slip one of these little segments of accomplishment into my personal machinery to help me to reach any desired future goal.

Success story number one: At the assassination of Julius Caesar, the Roman world was divided into two great war camps, one led by the conspirators under Brutus and the other led by Octavius Caesar and Mark Antony, the friend of Julius Caesar. During the long, hard war that followed, Mark Antony distinguished himself as one of the greatest generals in the world.

Success has much in common with itself wherever we find it, and if we can discover its causes we can reproduce it in our own success pattern. Here are some of the things that were said of Mark Antony. Armed with his convincing speech, the power of his logic, the courage of his leadership, and his own self-discipline in the field, he swept everything before him. He took upon himself the hardest tasks with the most wondrous good cheer. He often lived for weeks on a diet of insects and the bark of trees. He won the unquestioned loyalty of his men, the acclaim of the people, and the support of Octavius. Opposed by his dedication and industry, the enemy generals one by one were defeated; and finally, when the war was won, Mark Antony stood at the pinnacle of success.

But when the need for struggle had passed, Mark Antony became idle. Now, inactivity is one of the most serious mistakes anyone can make. When we tie up an arm in a sling, the muscles begin to atrophy. The mole didn't use his eyes, and nature took away his eyesight. We become inactive in the Church, and we lose our faith. Mark Antony made the serious mistake of condoning idleness in himself. He went to Egypt, fell in love with the bewitching Queen Cleopatra, and became a victim of the soft luxury, perfumed elegance, and immorality of the Egyptian court. His mind became clouded by the fumes of wine, and as he abandoned his better self his great personality began to disintegrate. Then Mark Antony lost the loyalty of his men, the acclaim of the people, and the support of Octavius.

Finally a guard of Roman soldiers arrived to take Mark Antony into custody and bring him back to Rome in chains. It didn't require an army to take Mark Antony now, just a handful of the most ordinary soldiers was all that was necessary. Antony avoided arrest by thrusting a dagger into his own heart. As he lay dying, he recounted to Cleopatra that there had been no power in the world sufficient to overthrow him except his own power. He said, "Only Antony could conquer Antony."

As he lay dying, contemplating the arrival of the Roman soldiers and the pitiful disgrace that he had brought upon his family, the great country he had served, and the friends he had disappointed, Mark Antony made to Cleopatra his last speech, which William Haines Little has put into verse:

> Let not Caesar's servile minions
> Mock the lion thus laid low.
> 'Twas no foeman's arm that felled him,
> 'Twas his own hand struck the blow.
>
> He who pillowed on thy bosom
> Turned aside from glory's way,
> When made drunk with thy caresses
> Madly threw a world away.

Mark Antony had held in his own hands the control of a large portion of the world, and there had been no one with enough power to take it away from him except himself. Only Antony could conquer Antony.

Every one of us has within his reach a world far more valuable than that which belonged to Mark Antony. There is no power in the world which can stand between us and the celestial kingdom except ourselves. Yet by a few misdeeds we can throw away the greatest value in the universe with the reckless abandon of a drunken Mark Antony.

Success story number two comes from John Bunyan's great book, *The Pilgrim's Progress.* You may remember the man with the muckrake who had spent his entire lifetime raking to himself the chaff and dust of the earth. There was an angel standing over his head with a celestial crown in his hand offering to exchange the crown for the muckrake. But this man had trained himself to look in no direction but down, so he disregarded the offer of the angel as he continued to rake to himself the chaff and muck of the earth. There is an angel standing over our heads with a celestial crown in his hand offering to confer it upon us if we can just look up to God in righteousness and obedience.

The beast was made to walk on four feet, and thus his vision is cast upon the ground. But man was created upright in the image of his Maker, that he might look up to God. We should sing frequently that great song which says:

> Look up, my soul, be not cast down;
> Keep not thine eyes upon the ground.
> Break off the shackles of the earth.
> Receive, my soul, the Spirit's birth.

In making the most profitable exchange for our muckrakes, we might say with the poet:

> I raised my eyes to yonder heights
> And longed for lifting wings
> To bear me to their sunlit crests
> As on my spirit sings.
>
> And though my feet must keep the path
> That winds along the valley floor,
> Yet after every upward glance
> I'm stronger than before.

Success story number three is one of the great stories of all time. It was taken from Grecian mythology and has to do with Pygmalion and Galatea. Pygmalion was a sculptor from Cyprus; and, like all great artists, Pygmalion loved his work. The day came when Pygmalion would create the great masterpiece of his life. In deathless ivory he would carve the statue of a beautiful woman to show the human form and human personality at its best. Week after week and month after month he labored. Finally the statue was completed. But so great was the devotion and love that Pygmalion had lavished upon his work that the gods decreed that the statue should have the power to move and breathe and live. As the statue stepped down off the pedestal, Pygmalion called her name Galatea. Pygmalion then married the woman he had created. This story is far more than an interesting myth, for the story of Pygmalion is the story of every man who is ever born into the world. For the great God of creation has decreed that whenever a man falls in love with his work, his work shall live.

Success story number four is centered in Sir Walter Scott's protrayal in *Ivanhoe* of the attributes of Richard the Lionhearted, England's king in the latter part of the twelfth century. Richard joined a crusade to go to the Holy Land to dispossess the Turks of the Holy Sepulchre. The expedition was unsuccessful; and Richard was captured and confined in a foreign prison. During his absence from home, traitors had taken over the government; and when Richard finally effected his escape and returned to England it was necessary for reasons of his own personal security that he come disguised in plain, unmarked armor.

Back in England, he quietly gathered around him a few of his faithful followers with the idea of putting England back into the hands of its rightful rulers. When this little group had been assembled, one of the first things Richard did was to attack the castle at Torquilstone. Torquilstone was a stronghold of the enemy in which the wounded Ivanhoe, the faithful follower and friend of Richard, was imprisoned.

Ivanhoe heard the noises of the assault which was beginning outside the castle. Because of his wounds and loss of blood, he was unable to raise himself from his couch, so he asked his nurse, Rebecca, to stand by the window and tell him what was taking place. The first thing he wanted to know was who the leader was. That is the first thing anyone wants to know about any enterprise. He asked Rebecca to describe for

him the insignia or marks of identification on the armor of
the leader, so that he would know who the leader was and
what the chances were for rescue.

Rebecca reported back that the leader fought in plain,
unmarked armor and had no insignia or marks of identification. Ivanhoe said, "Then tell me how he fights and I will
know who he is." Everyone has a set of traits which are about
as characteristic as his fingerprints; and if you can know what
someone does, you will have a pretty good idea who he is.

Rebecca tried to describe this great warrior clad in plain,
unmarked armor, as he swung his ponderous axe with
thunderous blows, assaulting the castle stronghold almost
singlehandedly. "Stones and beams are hurled down from the
castle walls upon him," she said, "but he regards them no
more than if they were thistledown or feathers." She
continued, "He fights as if there were twenty men's strength
in his single arm." "It is fearful yet magnificent," she went on,
"to behold how the arm and heart of one man can triumph
over hundreds."

Now, I suppose that Richard's arm wasn't any stronger
than any other warrior's arm, but that is not where strength
comes from. Rebecca had said, "the arm and heart of one
man." Richard was fighting with his heart. He was fighting
for England. When someone begins to put his heart into what
he is doing, things really begin to happen. Ivanhoe didn't
know who this man was. He knew that Richard fought like
this; but to him no one fought like the king, and he believed
Richard to be a prisoner in an Austrian dungeon. "I thought
there was but one man in England who might do such deeds,"
he said to Rebecca. Then he paid a tribute to this unknown
leader, not knowing who this man was but knowing the
qualities that characterize greatness. "I swear by the honor of
my house I would endure ten years of captivity to fight a
single day by that great man's side in such a quarrel as this."
Captivity would have been the greatest punishment to which
Ivanhoe could have been subjected, yet he said that he would
gladly languish ten years in a dungeon cell for the privilege of
fighting by the side and under the banner of a great man in a
great cause.

As Church leaders and members we have a great cause, the greatest cause of all. The only question that remains to be answered is how we will fight. In our own day, the Lord has said to us, "O ye that embark in the service of God, see that ye serve him with all your heart, might, mind and strength, that ye may stand blameless before God at the last day." (D&C 4:2.)

A friend of mine once asked me to come to the hospital to give blood for a transfusion, and as I sat there on the cot watching the blood run out of my arm I asked the nurse how many blood donations I could safely make in the course of a year. She said it would be perfectly all right to give four. That is, if it were necessary, I could save the lives of four people every year by a transfusion of my blood. I thought of some of the great people along life's way who had given me some transfusions, some transfusions of faith and some of courage and industry.

Let me now give you a transfusion from the testimony of the great Prophet of the last dispensation. He said:

"And now, after the many testimonies which have been given of him, this is the testimony, last of all, which we give of him: That he lives!

"For we saw him, even on the right hand of God; and we heard the voice bearing record that he is the Only Begotten of the Father—

"That by him, and through him, and of him, the worlds are and were created, and the inhabitants thereof are begotten sons and daughters unto God." (D&C 76:22-24.)

May God help us to make this testimony a vital power in our own success program.

Chapter 28

Some
Leadership Ideas

A young man came to see me who had successfully completed a foreign mission for the Church. He had been a very dedicated, ambitious young man, but when he came home, he got into some bad company and fell victim to that syndrome of sin of which Alexander Pope wrote:

> Vice is a monster of so frightful mien,
> As to be hated needs but to be seen;
> Yet seen too oft, familiar with her face,
> We first endure, then pity, then embrace.

That is, this young man had begun doing things that were contrary to his faith. In our conversation he said, "For some reason I don't feel the way I used to about some of the doctrines of the Church."

I replied: "Of course you don't. Doubt, apathy and disbelief are a perfectly natural consequence of improper activities."

We all know that faith cannot survive without appropriate works. When one discontinues the works, the faith dies—it always dies. There is no such thing as preserved faith. You can't keep faith in isolation or in cold storage. Nothing is truer than the old saying, "Actions speak louder than words." Action also has power to change our character and our success and our eternal exaltation.

If you want to learn how to get up on time in the morning, you don't just think about it, or wish you could get up, or exercise your faith. The way you learn how to get up on time in the morning is to get up on time without allowing any wavering or exceptions. When you allow exceptions, you are not building but destroying.

For many years President Heber J. Grant went around the Church reciting this statement by Ralph Waldo Emerson: "That which we persist in doing becomes easy. Not that the nature of the thing has changed, but that our power to do has increased." Over and over again, he stamped that idea into the minds of my generation, until many thousands of people of that day could not only say it by heart, but had made the idea a part of their character and practice.

This thought may work in the negative as well as the positive direction.

The drunken Rip Van Winkle, in Washington Irving's story, destroyed himself by his excuses and by allowing too many exceptions. When he wanted a drink he would try to make it all right with himself by saying, "I won't count this one." *He* may not have counted it and the *court* may not have counted it, but in his nervous system and in his mind and his personality every violation was being counted, and it was modifying his total personality. And every drink would be there to vote against his future temperance efforts.

Here are some great statements about the power of doing:

Disraeli said, "Genius is the power to make continuous effort."

Elbert Hubbard said, "The secret of success is constancy of purpose."

Leonardo da Vinci said, "Thou, Oh God, doth sell us all good things at the price of labor."

There is an old axiom which says, "What wouldst thou have, quoth God, pay for it and take it."

All too frequently we destroy ourselves by our inactivity without knowing it. We alibi and excuse ourselves. We make professions of virtues and abilities which are denied and refused growth by our activities. God will judge us by our works. Our health will judge us by our works, our personalities will judge us by our works, and our character will always take the testimony of our works over that of our promises and our professions. Jesus pointed out that the path to eternal life is a straight and narrow one. And when we start doing things that come outside the narrow path our beliefs will be changed accordingly, and we will soon begin saying to ourselves, "I don't feel as I used to feel about the doctrines of the gospel." No one feels the same about a law when he is violating it as when he is living it.

Remember, Mr. Emerson said, "Do the thing and you shall have the power." Jesus said, "If any man will do [God's] will he shall know of the doctrine." It can be very helpful to study the principles of the gospel, yet it is pretty difficult for a drunkard or a dope addict to get enthusiastic about the Word of Wisdom. You can find out the truth of any doctrine merely by living it. That is, if you would like to know whether or not the law of tithing is true, just live the law of tithing and you will know. If you would like a strong assurance of the Word of Wisdom, just live those principles that you desire to believe in.

Don't make the mistake of thinking that you can continue to believe in something when you don't practice it. Don't make the mistake of believing that you can maintain strong arm muscles when you take away from them the exercise by which the muscles were built up. Likewise, when we don't practice our faith, life takes the faith away. When we don't use these great God-given abilities of mind and spirit, the abilities themselves are repossessed. We are not awarded abilities primarily on the basis of our wants or our needs. We are awarded abilities on the basis of what we do to earn them. Our only protection against mediocrity and failure is success. We need to live by every word that proceedeth forth from the mouth of God.

The apostle Paul said, "Take unto you the whole armor of God." If we leave any part of ourselves unprotected, we are in danger. Among the greatest words in our language are *discipline, self-control, faith,* and *works.* We need more coordination between our deeds and our creeds. In other words, "Do the thing and you shall have the power." Dig the ditch and you shall get the muscles. Pay tithing and you shall know that it is a true principle. Practice the laws of God and you will greatly increase your faith.

In 1967, Elder Neal Maxwell wrote a very interesting and constructive book under the title *A More Excellent Way*. This title was taken from a statement made by the apostle Paul to the Corinthians: "Yet shew I unto you a more excellent way." (1 Corinthians 12:31.) This more excellent way concept is an idea most people would readily agree to for other people. But many of us actually do not do much about improving our own procedures. When we allow ourselves to drift or be blown about like so many weathercocks, we will never achieve excellence in our labors.

When we get deep enough into the ruts of inferiority, it sometimes becomes difficult to free ourselves. It is so easy to do the things we have always done in the way we have always done them. Yet one of the most important success procedures that we can develop is to form the attitudes and habits of improvement. The apostle Paul said, "When I was a child, I spake as a child, I understood as a child, I thought as a child: but when I became a man, I put away childish things." (1 Corinthians 13:11.) One of the most important pressures for each of us should be to grow up.

Before we have gone very far in our lives we ought to understand that order is better than confusion, that law is better than anarchy, that good is better than bad, that success is better than failure, that heaven is better than hell. One of the greatest opportunities is to find not just one more excellent way but a great number of more excellent ways to lift our lives to where they ought to be.

Suppose that each one of us were to write a book on his own life entitled *The More Excellent Way*. In preparing the manuscript we would need to do a little analyzing and appraising. We would need to find more excellent ways of self-control, decision-making, and effective motivation in our various fields of interest.

It was said of Joan of Arc that she could turn a mob of cowards into an army of patriots. She was able to organize their efforts and focus attention on the proper objectives. That is great leadership.

A very successful man was once being interviewed about his success. He said that he had always been successful. He said that he was successful even when he was a small boy. He told his questioners that when he and his friends used to hunt birds' eggs he could always find more eggs than any of the other boys. When they asked for an explanation, he said that he thought it was because he always looked in more bushes. This boy learned one of the laws of success very early in life.

I once heard a great Bible scholar give a series of interesting lectures on the literature of the Bible. For the first assignment he said to the class, "Find your Bibles." They didn't need to brush the dust off them or open them or do any study in them, but just locate them. We should similarly do a little research in an attempt to find our abilities.

As an athlete drills for skill, so should a home teacher, and so should everyone else who wants to be effective. Great faith is wonderful, but it is lifeless without works. A testimony is a great thing, but if it is not translated into effectiveness it profits us nothing.

There is an unfortunate group of people who have been called life's half-believers. Their faith is so weak that it can't support whole-souled conviction. There are some who just partly know their business, and instead of their knowledge possessing power it is weak, sterile, and filled with doubts. They themselves may pass from this world without ever having accomplished the purpose of their lives. This reminds me of an important letter sent out which came back stamped "returned unopened." The great good that it might have done was completely wasted because it was not used.

Thomas Carlyle once said that a man's religion is the most important thing about him. That is what he believes in and thinks about and works at and fights for and lives by. Religion is how we save our souls and bring about our eternal exaltation. And in religion or in life, success is not just the big thing, it is the only thing.

A philanthropist once went out into the parks of New York City and interviewed two thousand tramps. Two thousand human derelicts were asked what had caused the tragic waste of human resources in their lives. He reported that they all told him a different story, but they all ended the same. Each one closed his account by saying, "But I did the best I could." That is the chief tragedy in the world. We lull ourselves into a destructive sleep by taking credit for much more effort than we really expend.

Some time ago a man recounted his version of his failure. He said he had a friend whose father was a pusher. He meant that the father was continually stimulating and motivating his son to do better. He said, "The reason I haven't done very well is that my father was not a pusher." It didn't occur to him that God had given to him a great power to push himself, a power called initiative, and that by far the most effective power is self-motivation.

A group of young boys once decided to scare the women in the neighborhood who were meeting for a literary lesson in one of the homes. They dressed themselves up in devil suits with horns and tails and pitchforks and rushed into the room where the ladies were meeting. All of those attending screamed and ran except one woman, and she retained her seat and seemed perfectly calm and collected. The head devil brandished his pitchfork and said to her, "Lady aren't you afraid of the devil?" And she said, "Oh no, Mr. Devil, I have been on your side all of the time."

The greatest help that Satan has is a slothful, uncommitted set of leaders posing as doing the Lord's work. And if we want to succeed, we had first better be sure whose side we are on and how closely we are following those eternal success laws with which we should be intimately familiar.

A minister was once asked how many working members he had in his congregation. He replied, "Fifty, twenty-five working for me and twenty-five working against me." Each of us should make sure that we are on the success side of the proposition where we can intervene in behalf of righteousness, with an influence that is highly contagious.

In the stirring song, "Stouthearted Men," are the words "A heart can inspire other hearts with its fire." It continues:

Give me some men who are stouthearted men
Who will fight for the right they adore.
Start me with ten who are stouthearted men,
And I'll soon give you ten thousand more.

Even one man can, if he will, change the morale of a whole community.

A stake Aaronic Priesthood leader was once asked how many boys he had under his direction. He didn't know. He was then asked what percentage of them qualified for the minimum award standards, and he said, "About the same as last year." He was then asked what percentage qualified last year, but he didn't know. The records indicated that fifty boys had been lost during the year. But this was a fact that no one, including the leader himself, had discovered or seemed concerned about.

The leader was asked what occupation he was in, and he said, "I am a cattleman and have purebred Herefords." He was asked how many Herefords he had, and he knew the answer immediately without looking it up or asking anybody. He was asked, "Suppose the man who looks after these valuable animals lost fifty of them during the year but he himself didn't even know that they were gone? How would you feel about such an employee?" He thought such irresponsibility would be intolerable. Then he was asked if he thought the Lord didn't think that a boy was about as valuable as a purebred Hereford.

There are many leaders who go over to the enemy because they don't keep as good a score and as close a checkup on those being led as they would if they were responsible for animals.

Ralph Waldo Emerson is given credit for being a very wise man, but the other day I discovered something that even Ralph Waldo Emerson didn't know. A calf got out of the barn and it was Emerson's job to get the calf back into the barn. But Emerson didn't know how to get a calf into the barn. How *do* you get a calf into the barn? The best way he knew was to get the calf headed in the right direction and then put his hands on the calf's rear bumper and push the calf into the barn. But for some reason, calves don't like to go into barns by this method. The calf stiffened its legs, making it necessary for Mr. Emerson to plow four furrows toward the barn if he were to succeed.

After half an hour of the most difficult effort, Emerson had made no progress. Then an Irish servant girl came along and saw his predicament. She offered the calf her finger and, with her finger in the calf's mouth, she walked into the barn and the calf walked in with her. She closed the barn door, and the entire job was completed. Her success required only a few seconds, whereas one of the greatest thinkers that America has ever produced had worked at it unsuccessfully for half an hour without making any progress. As Emerson was mopping his perspiring brow and trying to get the calf's hair off his hands and cleanse himself of the bovine smell, he contemplated this wonder of know-how. He was heard to say, "I like people who can do things." We should keep in mind that the Lord also likes people who can do things.

In American slave days a little Negro girl had been placed on the auction block. A prospective purchaser approached and said to her, "If I buy you and give you a good home and treat you kindly and feed you well, will you promise me that you will be honest?" This little slave girl replied, "I will promise you that I will be honest whether or not you buy me and treat me kindly and feed me well."

Chapter 29

The Convert

One of the first laws of leadership success says that a person must be a convert before he can be a leader. That is also one of the first laws of religious success. Lip-service might well be as serious a blasphemy as profanity. God has heaped some of his greatest condemnation upon those who draw near to him with their lips while their hearts are far from him. Before we can *make* converts we ought to *be* converts.

Someone has described our most serious religious problem as that of being mere "Bible Christians." That is when Christianity is primarily in the Bible rather than in people. It has been pointed out that it is not very important how many times we go through college unless the college somehow goes through us. Certainly great benefits accrue when a person gets into the Church, but the really great things begin to happen only when the Church gets into the person.

A survey made some time ago indicated that over 95 percent of all the people questioned said that they believed in God. But there would be far less than that number who were his real disciples or who were genuine converts to his doctrines. It was Mohandas K. Gandhi who said that for every honest man there were 999 people who believed in honesty. Everyone believes in honesty, but we may remember poor old Diogenes who went around Athens with a lighted lantern in the middle of the daytime trying to find just one honest man. If you were to ask me if I believe in honesty, I would be a little offended. I would feel that you ought to know that I believed in honesty. But let me tell you what I did some time ago:

As our family was driving through Arizona we stopped at a service station, and while the car was being serviced one of the children said, "Could we have some soda pop?" I went over to the vending machine, put in one dime, and got out one bottle. I put in another dime and I got out a second bottle. I put in a third dime and I got out a third bottle. At that point, the gadget didn't lock, and I got out the fourth bottle free. In all, I got four bottles for thirty cents. As I was going over to the car to make the delivery, I thought, "They charge too much for this stuff, anyway." But I have a little mental watchman on duty in my brain who started to make a fuss. "Look, Sterling," he said, "if you're going to be a crook, you had better get more than ten cents out of it." I don't know just what I would have done if the soda pop had cost a quarter, but at any rate I went back and put the other dime into the machine.

Now, how can the Lord tell whether or not I believe in honesty—by what I say about it or by what I do while I am over at the vending machine where no one can see me except myself? By the same token, how are you going to know whether or not I believe the gospel is true—by what I say in testimony meeting or by the way I carry out my Church assignments?

I heard about one man who said that he just couldn't rest until he had borne his testimony; and then after he had done so he leaned back and went sound asleep. He said that he was thrilled clear down to his toes; but when he moved his leg a little bit he discovered that it was just that his foot had gone to sleep.

Some time ago I heard a man tell the story of Balboa discovering the Pacific Ocean. You may remember that in the year 1513 the great Spanish explorer made his way to the Pacific Coast. He climbed to the top of a high mountain, and when he looked over the other side he "discovered" the

Pacific Ocean. The man telling this story said, "I stood exactly where Balboa stood and I don't see how he could have helped but discover it." Anyone standing on the top of a high mountain, looking into the face of the biggest ocean in the world, is bound to discover something.

How much credit do you think I am entitled to because I *know* that the gospel is true? Satan *also* knows that the gospel is true, but his testimony acts as his condemnation because he does nothing positive about it. Actually, I don't know how I could help knowing the gospel is true. I was brought up in a good home. I had good parents. I went to church. I can read a little bit and I can understand some of the things that I read. I can read the gospel. I can understand the word of the Lord and I believe every part of the word of the Lord. How could I help but know that the gospel is true?

It doesn't seem to me that I am entitled to very much credit merely because I know something that I almost couldn't help knowing. But the thing that is very important is that I do something about what I know.

The apostle James gave us a great line for our philosophy of life when he said, "Therefore to him that knoweth to do good, and doeth it not, to him it is sin." (James 4:17.) That is another way of saying that we are guilty of all the good that we do not do. Most of us will not stumble in our lives over the capital sins. It is usually the little, pleasant, "unimportant" sins that make us miss the boat and lose our opportunities. It is so very easy for one to forget his duty or fail to be whole-souled in the testimony of Jesus.

May God help us to become real converts so that we can get pleasure out of being judged according to our works.

Chapter 30

Why Not Now?

One of the serious downfalls in our society, and one of our individual weaknesses that causes many of our problems, comes because of a natural time lag in our nature. Many of our accomplishments are destroyed because we have a damaging tendency for postponement. Without effort in the other direction, we become natural procrastinators, and as a consequence we lose many of the important benefits that were intended for us.

A Sunday School teacher once said to the members of her class, "Will you all raise your hands if you want to go to heaven." They all raised their hands except one boy. The teacher said to him, "Bill, wouldn't you like to go to heaven sometime?" "Oh, sure, sometime," the boy replied, "but I thought you were getting up a group to go tonight."

Everyone wants to do well—sometime. Everyone wants to be well regarded by his friends, his family, and God. Everyone wants to do well in his business. Everyone wants to be effective in his Church leadership and in his personal affairs. The big problem comes in learning to do it effectively and now. We need a greater sense of urgency to get us started toward our objective. To help us correct this destructive habit of procrastination, we might adopt as a part of our natural success program this important phrase: "Why not now?"

We ought to be able to get home teaching done on time.

We ought to be able to make converts and motivate those who are inactive. We ought to learn to eliminate our time lag so that to think would be to act, to resolve would be to do, and to plan would be to accomplish. Inasmuch as everyone wants to do well sometime, why not now? Anyone who hears many of the life stories of other people is impressed with the great harm that is caused by our natural inclination for either a permanent or a temporary postponement.

Those who work with explosives represent this idea with their descriptive phrase *time lag*. That is, they can regulate a series of explosions to take place at any stated period after the impulse has been given. While that may be a very great convenience to powder men, it is disastrous to leadership and all forms of spiritual accomplishment. In human postponement, which is usually unscheduled, it is frequently true that if action is delayed for too long after the impulse is given, the force of the explosion fizzles out and the possible power is lost.

A minister who performs some marriage ceremonies said that for twenty years he had read the service out of his book. He had come to so depend on the book that, though he had repeated the service many times, the service had actually never become a part of him. As he began to get older he began to have some serious trouble with his eyesight, so he decided to memorize the marriage service. One day he sat down to get the ceremony out of the book and into him. In an hour he had it perfectly mastered. When the service came out of his heart instead of out of the book, the quality of his service was greatly improved. Then *he* was performing this important ordinance instead of having the book perform it. He wondered why he had postponed his memorizing for twenty years and lost many benefits during that long period. This one memorization time-lag had appreciably reduced his performance in that one area, but when he included all similar areas he found the total loss to be substantial.

People do this same kind of thing in many ways. There are written philosophies and doctrines intended to inspire and uplift us, and occasionally we get them out and read them to ourselves. Sometimes the book is misplaced, or we forget to read it, and we lose the benefit because the ideas and doctrines still belong primarily to the book and not to us. We would save a lot of time by memorizing these philosophies and these inspiring poems and these uplifting scriptures that we depend upon, instead of having to look them up every time or be compelled to think of them only as the disjointed fragments that our memories are capable of reproducing. Even if we try to piece together what we can remember, we find that the fragments have lost much of the punch that would have been possible if we had full and masterful possession of the whole. If we used our power to memorize, it would not be possible for failing eyesight or old age to wipe us out mentally and bring us spiritual bankruptcy.

When we run an idea through the brain it makes a mental pathway. As the idea is rerun, the pathway becomes deeper and broader so that it channels our thoughts more easily. By memorization, we can make these pathways more effective so that they can give our lives a fine tone, more quality, and greater pleasure.

We should be very careful that the wrong things never become too securely established in our minds. The religious leader referred to above had for some time used a particular phrase in his marriage discussion that he later decided to leave out. For the ten years since he decided to make the change, he has been unable to get this phrase completely out of his mind. Rather, it always seems to be lurking nearby trying to get back into the performance while the marriage service is being conducted. It is always very difficult to forget those things that have once been firmly established in our lives. Of course, it is far more serious when the particular ideas that refuse to be dropped from our memories are evil and insist on leading us in a wrong direction.

Some thirty-four centuries ago from Mount Sinai, the Lord said, "Thou shalt not take the name of the Lord thy God in vain." There are some people, however, who, in an attempt to make themselves impressive or to relieve their anger, violate this law and make profanity a prominent part of their speech. It frequently becomes almost impossible for them to clean up their language and to control their tongue. They may find themselves in the ridiculous position of continually saying things they don't want to say and doing things they don't want to do. Our profane tongues are always wanting to be heard, and our evil inclinations are always wanting to perform. No one of us will want to be profane or immoral or dishonest as he lies on his deathbed or stands before God. All of us would like to change our lives so that they stand for the most worthwhile things. Because this is true, why shouldn't we make the change now while the change is easy? Why not get the profanity out today? Why not do a lot of deathbed repentance while we are still in our youth? Why not form habits of always doing the right things at the right time?

Someone said, "Now is the time for all good men to come to the aid of the party." There is no profit in waiting until the election has been lost before taking action. With this same kind of idea in mind, an ancient American prophet said, "Now is the time for men to prepare to meet God."

We remember the story of the antediluvians. Noah tried for 120 years to get them to change their evil ways. Their refusal brought on the Flood, and Peter indicates that they spent at least the next 2,300 years in the spirit prison house, until the time when, while his body lay in the tomb, Jesus organized his forces for ministry among them. In doing this, Jesus offered them a second chance to repent. Their reformation of life which could have been accomplished in a few months, had it been done at the proper time, later required hundreds of years.

Someone has said that there are two times in the life of every drunkard: one, when he *could* quit drinking if he would, and the other, when he *would* quit if he could. It is much easier to conquer any bad habit, including sloth, lethargy, and depression, if the evil is taken in time. Delays are always dangerous as well as being very expensive. Procrastination is not only the thief of time; it also enslaves us, destroys our success, and relegates us to lesser activities. An important principle of progress and leadership is to develop in ourselves and in those under our direction the ability to take appropriate action at the proper time.

I know a man who had a severe heart attack. The doctors

told him that he would immediately have to take off fifty pounds of excess weight. Thus he had to risk the dangers of a crash diet and an upset equilibrium because of earlier procrastination. This man had known for many years that the additional burden of fat would cause him trouble. How much better off he would have been if he had solved this problem by keeping his weight down in the first place! It would not have worn out his heart, robbed him of his health, and caused all of the related problems. He didn't even think seriously about taking off the excess weight until after the damage had been done. There are a lot more of us who are going to take off some weight sometime, but we are not quite ready yet. This is probably the most discouraging story of our lives. We only lock the barn door after the horse has gone. We wait to take action until it is too late, and then we sing that mournful dirge expressed in the words of Whittier,

> Of all sad words of tongue and pen,
> The saddest are these: It might have been.

So we might say to ourselves over and over again, "Why not now?" Why not begin keeping the Ten Commandments today? Why not live by the rules of success this week? Why not do the home teaching when it should be done instead of making a crash performance at the end of each month? Why not sit down with those under our charge and teach them the art of timeliness in discharging our responsibilities?

In 1853, John Ruskin wrote in his journal, "Today I promised God that from this time forward I would conduct myself as though I believed every sentence in the Bible to be true." To live right is the most profitable and pleasant of all possible activities. But the journey of a thousand miles still begins with one step. We must get started sometime.

Why not now?

Part Six

Planning and Evaluation

Chapter 31

Your Master's Thesis

One of the common educational practices in institutions of higher learning is to require candidates for advanced degrees to write a dissertation on a subject of the candidate's special interest. Alternatively it may be written on a subject that he would like to learn a lot more about. In any event, if he is to receive a master's degree he must write a master's thesis or its equivalent.

The dictionary says that a thesis is a dissertation embodying the results of one's own research. It involves some proposition or affirmation that can be proven by the investigation, experimentation, and reasoning of the person conducting the study. In his thesis, a successful candidate should be able to maintain the position taken by his argument, his industry, and his example.

When an undergraduate begins his university work, he may depend upon the lectures of the professors or the material in the text books which he studies. But as he climbs the educational ladder he is supposed to learn to discover new knowledge, to think problems out for himself, and to make a contribution to others by his own research and reporting. Not only is the research important, but he must be able to report it so that others can understand and believe it. They will, therefore, be able to take advantage of whatever information he may have developed. As any student in or out of the university climbs the educational ladder, he is supposed to become more and more capable of individual thinking, original investigation, and self-directed study, so that he does not have to depend as completely upon the kind of rote learning of facts and theories that he may have used during his earlier years.

Many people have done all the work required for an advanced degree except for the investigation on which a thesis or a dissertation can be based and the actual writing of it. On the other hand, many people write an entire book in which they record the discoveries made while preparing for their dissertation. There was one man who spent ten years in prying and probing for facts and ideas for his Ph.D. dissertation.

Writing a thesis or a dissertation is also a good way for us to promote our own leadership or our success in life itself. To write a thesis on any subject not only requires that we think the idea through but that we put it in written form so that others may benefit from it. An architect would not be worth much if he didn't know how to make his ideas negotiable to the building contractor and others. By the time we get our ideas down on paper, many of our problems should have solved themselves.

Someone was once asked what he thought about a certain subject and he replied, "I don't know; I haven't spoken on it yet." Before we are able to speak intelligently on any subject, we must have done our homework and made those decisions that underlie every success. The teacher always learns more than the student, and we always enjoy the meeting more when we ourselves are on the program. The spectators in the grandstands never get as much out of watching a contest as the players who do the winning down on the field. And those leaders who learn to make the investigation and depend upon themselves for the decisions will far outdistance those who depend on hearsay for their leadership abilities. Suppose we identified those ingredients that went into a successful sacrament meeting and then wrote a master's thesis on each one. Think how our competency would be increased. Not only should we write the thesis in such a situation, but we should develop the skill to see that our findings are carried out each week in our actual performance.

A number of years ago, the General Electric Corporation decided to conduct a laboratory investigation to discover the possibilities for human development. They had already done a great deal of research in order to be able to build better appliances and gadgets, but now they wanted to discover how to develop better men to make and use the gadgets. They selected some of their most successful researchers and allotted a million dollars and four years of time for their use in this project.

In writing their report, the researchers had as their number one pronouncement the assertion that "all development is self-development." It is pretty difficult for someone to develop anyone except himself. That is, no one can do our thinking for us, and no one can develop our ambition for us, and no one can be enthusiastic for us. On the other hand, we can accomplish miracles when we ourselves have a powerful desire to reach those goals which are all-important to us. We also develop great ability when we are willing to do our homework and put our dissertations down in such a way as to pass the graduation committee with flying colors.

Any thoughtful person would learn a hundred times more by the processes involved in writing a master's thesis than an equally intelligent person could by merely reading a master's thesis written by someone else. If, therefore, the processes involved in writing are so much more productive than mere reading, certainly we should write more.

I attended a meeting of a bishopric that was having many leadership problems in their ward. The problems all centered around the fact that the leaders didn't do their homework. None of them had ever written a scholarly leadership thesis or given any kind of a creditable oral dissertation. The bishopric was particularly anxious to increase the percentage of their people who attended sacrament meeting. The problem was that they didn't know how to do the job. And what was even more serious, they didn't seem to know how to go about finding out.

There are some people who don't learn very much by

listening to others, and I was impressed in this case, as in many others, that the best way for one to learn how to solve his problems is to do the kind of research and reporting on which a masterly dissertation could be made on paper. But the leaders involved didn't seem to know what their problems were. If you can find out why people do not come to sacrament meeting, the solution becomes more or less self-evident. This law holds true in almost every field.

A salesman once asked his sales manager, "Will you tell me how to get out of my sales slump?" The sales manager responded, "I will be glad to tell you how to get out of your slump if you will just tell me how you got into it." If a person doesn't know how he got into a situation, he may have a lot of problems getting out. We often don't know how we get into trouble because we try so hard to justify whatever we do that we have difficulty recognizing any of the wrongs in ourselves that are causing our failures.

I have asked a great many salesmen why their sales were lower than other salesmen in comparable circumstances, and most of them say, "I don't know." Many marriage partners that are having problems actually claim that they don't know what the difficulty is. Many Church leaders don't know why their young people are being married out of the temple, or what they can do to change the situation. But before anyone can know how to solve their problems, they *must* know what the problem is.

A doctor who could not make an accurate written diagnosis or at least a good mental evaluation of his patient would not be very helpful. Suppose that I am a doctor and you are a group of sick people who want me to get you out of the hospital. And suppose that I gave all of you a series of treatments for fallen arches only to discover at some later date that you had all died of cancer. This comparison is only slightly more ridiculous than to use the sacrament meeting to scold sacrament meeting absentees. How would any scholar get a degree if he merely wrote after each question on an exam that he did not know the answer? In everything we do we must find the right answers (the best answers) to our problems.

Of course there are other ways to get a master's rating without going to college. The dictionary describes a master as one who has gained great skill or proficiency or excellence in some particular field. It gives examples such as a "master builder," a "master mechanic," a "master orator." A "master" is one who is eminently skilled in something such as an occupation, art, or science. A master is also someone qualified to teach others. Such a person may be a farmer, an educator, a businessman, or a bishop.

Among the great titles by which Jesus was identified is that of *Master*. Under the direction of the Father, he was the Creator of worlds without number. This must have required a lot of investigation and study, and some good discussions with associates and subordinates. In determining a faultless plan for our exaltation, a lot of master's theses could have been written. Before Jesus could become the Master of other men, he must have gained mastery over himself. Only by self-mastery can one become a master of procedures and accomplishments. When Jesus said to some unschooled fishermen, "Follow me, and I will make you fishers of men," he certainly had in mind the development of their faith, their courage, their righteousness, and their leadership abilities.

One of the best ways to develop effective leadership is by the kind of research, industry, investigation, inspiration, and follow-through that goes into completing a masterful master's thesis. When we develop a master's ability, any accomplishment is placed within our easy reach.

Suppose we were asked to help the bishopric I mentioned earlier solve the problems involved in attracting a greater sacrament meeting attendance. It is a very simple matter to find out why people don't do things. All we need to do is uncover the facts and then write up our dissertation. The researches of one ward indicated that several ward members hadn't gone on missions merely because they had never been asked, and some hadn't had their children baptized for the same reason. Some were not coming to their meetings because they were not only uninvited but had actually been made to feel unwelcome. Some hadn't paid any ward maintenance and consequently had a subconscious feeling that they didn't have any right to attend. Some had feelings of guilt and inferiority. Some felt uneasy in the company of Church members. Some felt apprehensive about what the reaction of others would be if they attended church. Many needed a good sales talk to convince them that to attend sacrament meeting was much more in their personal interest than to spend the Sabbath day in work or in recreation. All of these sacrament meeting absentees needed a stronger feeling of belonging. They needed to be needed. They needed to be wanted. They needed someone to go with them. They needed friendship.

Before writing their dissertations on sacrament meeting attendance, one bishopric held a planning meeting and figured out thirty different procedures by which people could be motivated to come. Some of these procedures were: more friendliness, more interesting meetings, more effective recruiting, greater order and reverence, a higher morale, more attractive physical and spiritual environment. Because these are all good subjects for a thesis, in wards having this problem the individual members of the bishopric and the other ward leaders could be assigned to do some further investigation on these subjects. They could discover the details that would enable them to put their plans down in a complete and workable master's thesis.

The purpose of such an investigation is not just to find the facts. The one doing the research should also interpret the facts to discover solutions for the problems. The need then is to develop the attitudes, skills, procedures, and habits by which the desired accomplishment can be brought about. A common weakness in most of us is our tendency to try to cover up our own incompetence by alibis, excuses, vagueness, silence, misrepresentation, and inactivity. There is a great advantage in requiring ourselves to put the details of our program down on paper. There the faults show up more clearly so that they can be more easily criticized and effectiveness is more readily brought about. It is important to develop our success skills into solid success habits.

One of the greatest powers in the world is the power of habit. It is stronger than discipline or willpower. And we can build a habit in a month or so if we allow no exceptions. But when we do good work one day and poor work the next day we are slipping backward as fast as we are moving forward. We must eliminate all weakness, as it always leads toward failure. Our great opportunities allow us to develop those important attitudes and techniques involved in success.

We need to become more competent in our faith, more thorough in our investigation, more convincing in our convictions, and more consistent in our follow-through. Only when we get success into our bloodsteam will we be entitled to a master's degree in that greatest of all enterprises which is the primary business of God himself.

Chapter 32

Problem Solvers

One of the most important things that anyone ever needs to learn about success or leadership or accomplishment or happiness is that usually problems do not solve themselves. Sometimes, when difficulties are waging war against us, we feel that if we just sit still the problem will go away by itself, or that some miracle will happen at the last minute so that we can live happily ever after. If we could each discover and assimilate the great truth that problems don't usually disappear automatically, we would be a long way on our way to success.

When it is discovered that a sick person has live cancer cells in his body, the best doctor is the one who knows that if the cancer cells are not destroyed the patient will be destroyed by the cancer. Certainly the doctor does not expect the cancer cells to disappear automatically.

On the other hand, one of the most hopeful facts in our lives is that with the right kind of understanding, resource-fulness, and courage, the unfavorable circumstances which threaten to block our progress and destroy our happiness may be changed.

William James, the great Harvard psychologist, once said, "The greatest discovery of my generation is that you can change your circumstances by changing your attitudes of mind." Most people want to change their circumstances but many of them do not want to change themselves.

A good leader is a problem solver. First, he is not only able to help other people solve their problems; he is also able to eliminate those influences in himself which threaten to destroy his success and happiness.

In the process of learning how to use the power of electricity to light our world, Thomas A. Edison made five thousand experiments. Frequently people would say to Mr. Edison, "Tom, have you found it yet?" He would reply, "No, I haven't, but I have discovered some additional ways that will not work." As long as we imagine that problems will solve themselves we will not be very likely to discover a way that will work, so we might begin by listing some of the ways that do not work.

Number one is postponement: While we wait for better times, the cancer that threatens us is increasing its strength and enlarging its territory.

Number two: the apostle James mentions a kind of merely verbal Christianity which usually does not do much good. He said:

"If a brother or sister be naked, and destitute of daily food, and one of you say unto them, Depart in peace, be ye warmed and filled; notwithstanding ye give them not those things which are needful to the body; what doth it profit?

"Even so faith, if it hath not works, is dead, being alone.

"Yea, a man may say, Thou hast faith, and I have works: shew me thy faith without thy works, and I will shew thee my faith by my works." (James 2:15-18.)

If we could understand this one idea our leadership would be on pretty safe grounds. In the final judgment we will be judged according to our works. That is also the way our leadership effectiveness is determined. It is very interesting to think about some of the things we ask for in our prayers which are the very things that the Lord has asked *us* to do. For example, we don't need to ask the Lord to forgive our enemies, as we can do that better ourselves. To begin with, the Lord may not be mad at them. There is another reason why we should forgive our enemies, and that is that we made them ourselves.

We don't need to ask the Lord to make us wise and thoughtful and understanding. All of these endeavors he has turned over to us. In a group of men, I heard one man pray that the Lord would help our wives to understand the love which we have for them. But over and over again the Lord has told us that we ourselves should make that matter clear to them.

A Sunday School teacher might ask the Lord to help her students understand the principles of the gospel, but the major burden still rests on the teacher.

I know a bishop who, in practice, continually rejects and refuses his call to leadership. He takes a kind of subconscious attitude that the Lord has commanded everybody to go to church and to get there on time and be reverent when they get there. When they fail to do those things, he doesn't feel inclined to interfere by giving them the encouragement of his own influence and motivation. If they don't pay their ward maintenance or follow the commands of the Lord, by his attitude, he says, "So what?"

Thus we sometimes make a farce out of priesthood leadership assignments in the church of Christ, instead of seeing that the job gets done. We say in our prayers, "Be ye warmed and filled." We bear our testimonies to those who are in the sheepfold, but we don't spend much time out in the mountains at our job of seeking the ones who are lost.

I think when we write the leadership manual for Church workers, we should have in the first chapter the story of Jack the Giant Killer, who is one of my heroes. The story comes from British folklore.

Jack was a problem solver. Back in the days of King Arthur, out beyond the land's end, was an island called Cornwall Island. On this island lived a giant whose name was Cormoron. Cormoron had a bad habit of occasionally wading across this intervening bit of sea, frightening the people out of their villages, and then loading himself up with their sheep and cattle, which he carried back to his island.

In one of these villages lived a farmer's boy whose name was Jack. On one occasion Jack said to his father, "Why doesn't someone do something about Cormoron?" He complained that Cormoron had destroyed their property and robbed them of their livestock, and yet no one did anything about it.

Jack's father pointed out that Cormoron was a giant, and ordinarily people didn't go around correcting giants. Even King Arthur's knights left Cormoron to do pretty much what he wanted to do.

Jack said that his teacher from Salzburg had taught him that there is a solution to every problem. He believed that there was a solution to Cormoron, and he intended to find it.

A couple of nights later he put his shovel, his ax, and his pick in his boat and rowed out to the island where Cormoron lived. After Cormoron had gone to sleep, Jack dug a deep pit in front of his bedroom cave, and just before the dawn began to break, he blew a loud ˙blast on his horn which incensed Cormoron. The giant came stumbling out of his cave shouting his vengeance on whomever had disturbed his sleep. Then he did what Jack had foreseen he would do. He fell into the hole.

When Jack got the giant down where he could handle him, he gave him a good thump on the head with his ax, hard enough that this forever solved the problem of Cormoron.

When the people in the next county heard that Jack had killed the giant, they sent for him to come and do a little work on their giant. When he arrived, he discovered an interesting thing—their giant had two heads. Now you don't kill a giant with two heads the same way you kill a giant with one head, so Jack had to sit down and figure out the solution all over again. Then he went around killing giants.

Some of these giants had eyes in the back of their heads. One had a magic coat that made him invisible. One had a magic cap which enabled him to learn things no one else knew. One had a magic sword that could cut through the strongest iron. One had a pair of magic shoes which gave him extraordinary swiftness.

Jack knew that there was a solution to every problem and that when the right solution was supported with sufficient skill, courage, and industry every problem could be solved. Because of his successes, finally he was given the highly complimentary title of Jack the Giant Killer.

There is a giant killer mentioned also in the Bible. In the fight between the ancient Israelites and the Philistines, young David, son of Jesse, was not old enough to go to the war. His three brothers were fighting for Saul while he stayed home tending the family's sheep. At one point his father sent him to Saul's camp with food for his brothers.

When he arrived, he found the soldiers in a turmoil because they had a problem that no one wanted to solve. Each side had been killing the soldiers of the others for a long time, and then the Philistines came up with the idea of solving their differences by single combat. Goliath was to represent the Philistines.

But none of the Israelite soldiers wanted to fight the giant Goliath. He was nine feet tall and covered over with bronze armor. He had a spear like a weaver's beam.

When David arrived at camp, he went to Saul and said, "I will fight Goliath." Saul dressed him up in his armor and gave him his sword, but David put them off because he knew very little about fighting with armor and swords. And with his sling, he went out to meet Goliath.

As he crossed the creek he picked up four rocks. I don't know why he took four, as he only used one of them. As he approached Goliath he first had a little discussion with the giant, and Goliath said some rather abusive things to him. After they got the conversation all out of the way, David put one of the rocks in his sling. As he ran toward the giant he got a good windup, and just at the right moment let the rock go. That one rock solved the problem. It struck Goliath in the forehead where there was no protective armor. Somebody has said that such a thing had never entered Goliath's head before. Goliath toppled to the ground, and David took Goliath's sword and cut off his head.

The record says that when the Philistines saw their champion was dead they fled. Goliath hadn't expected to get killed; he hadn't wanted to get killed. But David was a problem solver, and he saved Israel from the Philistines.

We have problems to solve. Some are giant problems and some are tiny problems, but we ought to remember that there is a good solution to every one of them. There is a solution to the confusion that sometimes takes place in our meetings. There is a solution to immorality and lack of grooming. There is a solution to the prospective elder problem.

Everything else being equal, the missionary who knows how to have three interesting discussions a day will get more converts than the one who only knows how to have three a week or three a month.

The primary thing to remember is that problems do not ordinarily disappear by themselves. The germs of ignorance, lethargy, sloth, and disinterest cannot be made to disappear merely by saying our prayers or by bearing our testimonies to those who already believe, while we neglect those who are starving for our friendship and testimony.

Chapter 33

The Survey

One of the modern wonders of the world is our American society. Much of the great latter-day knowledge explosion has taken place in our midst, making our science a great collection of miracles. Many of the business procedures that are commonplace to us would have been classified as magic a hundred years ago.

A farmer told me that one year he had grown and harvested three thousand tons of potatoes, and his neighbor had produced five thousand tons of wheat. I was reminded of the parable of the sower who took a little bagful of seed grain and threw it out a handful at a time on a badly prepared seed bed and covered it up with his toe. In contrast to the sower mentioned in the parable of Jesus, my friend did not waste any of his seed grain by throwing it on stony ground or among the thistles or on the hard places. Rather, he had prepared in advance a uniformly acceptable seed bed.

In addition to more advanced science and technology, better business procedures and the ability to produce more wheat, our improved medical procedures have lengthened the human life expectancy from nineteen years in the days of Jesus to seventy-one years in our own day. In the United States in 1886, 120,000 people died of smallpox. But now we haven't had a single death from smallpox in many years. There is a reason why the expectation of life in the United

States has more than doubled since George Washington's day.

One of the most important instruments of modern-day success is a procedure known as the survey. Great merchandising organizations find out what people want and then give it to them. We conduct polls to find out what people are thinking and what they plan to do.

I know a great sales organization that hired a group of outside consultants to study their company and its employees' attitudes and procedures. They wanted to know how the company was regarded by the men who sold its goods. They wanted to know what the salesmen thought of the training they were receiving from their company. They wanted to know how their company rated in the opinion of the public in comparison to their competitors. The salesmen and the customers would more honestly answer the questions of outside surveyors when they knew their identity would be kept a secret. They would not want to answer these same questions honestly to their company officers for fear that their personal success might be placed in jeopardy if they made an unfavorable report. It has been said that everyone lies to the king.

Frequently a company becomes inbred and ingrown by its own selfish interests and prejudices. This phenomenon is like getting so close to the forest that we cannot see the trees. Companies, like individuals, sometimes become victims of these disastrous blind spots and do not see themselves in true perspective. Because we alibi, rationalize, and excuse ourselves, we miss great benefits that might otherwise be ours.

Suppose we could have a group of marriage experts come into our homes and our lives to make a survey of the strengths and weaknesses of our marriage. If an unprejudiced marriage survey team could know the facts as they took place in all the departments of family life, they could make some suggestions which would quickly solve our problems. Isn't it interesting how many perfectly stupid things are done in many of our families which cause so many serious moral, social, financial, and physical troubles? And yet we keep on doing them.

The dictionary says that to survey is to examine a

situation as to its conditions, problems, virtues, and values. It is to ascertain the state of a situation. To survey is to view in detail and to inspect closely. To survey means to view from some high place or vantage point. It is also to make a comprehensive study or a critical examination for a specified purpose. Often, when facts are fully ascertained in this manner, they are put down in reports so that they may be used in making necessary evaluations and corrections. Of course, those who make and prepare a survey must be capable and must operate without prejudice.

Business organizations make market surveys. They compare the qualities of goods. We survey our schools. We ought to make better surveys of our politics and some aspects of our religious leadership. When we are trying to do any particular kind of job, we ourselves are the ones that we usually need to have investigated most thoroughly.

When we allow ourselves to proceed according to our own unchecked rationalizations, excuses, and alibis, we may do more harm to our organization and ourselves than we do good. A person's judgment is no better than his information, and when our information is biased, incorrect and prejudiced our judgment certainly will be of very poor quality.

For example, suppose that antagonistic marriage partners angrily appraise each other through their attitudes of hate and revenge. Everyone around them will be hurt as a consequence. Husbands and wives at their best are supposed to help each other. We may help keep our judgment good however, by having an occasional appraisal done by someone from the outside. Their point of view can be kept clear and unbiased.

What would we learn if we were to have a team of outside efficiency experts make a survey of the effectiveness and righteousness of our personal Church leadership activities? Suppose that a capable, unprejudiced team of investigators from outside of our local group made a detailed analysis of every department in our stake, our ward, and our quorum, and made a full report on our group public relations, our spirituality, our reverence, and our missionary and home teaching effectiveness. Suppose they made a full report on what they thought was wrong with our classes, our family home evenings, and our leadership planning and management. Suppose they made a personal individual investigation of every member who did not come to church and made a complete classification of the reasons for their disaffection and absenteeism.

In another project, suppose we could discover the intimate reasons why so many people married ouside the Church and even outside the temple, what causes such a devastating divorce rate, and why we are unable to motivate our own members to live the great principles of the gospel which we maintain are so extremely valuable to our lives. Instead of having this survey done by outsiders, it would possibly be much more effective if we made it ourselves, since then we would probably develop a more powerful motivation to bring about a proper correction.

It is very significant that some missionaries and some home teachers are several times more effective than others. If we had the real "low-down" on the reasons why, we could greatly increase the performance of everyone. As Church workers and leaders, we sometimes permit ourselves a far higher percentage of ineffectiveness than is desirable. What would you think of a salesman who worked year after year with no sales and no program for improving his presentation or sales procedures? We also need a team of experts to study our individual lives and point out frankly and honestly the places where we are falling down and why.

In the Church, we operate at a great disadvantage because our leaders and our friends are usually so reluctant to tell us the truth about ourselves. The old slogan of the Listerine Company that "even your best friends won't tell you" is one of the harsh facts that we ought to keep in mind. When the vision is distorted by prejudice and sloth, a person frequently becomes an unprofitable servant without actually knowing it. Then, to protect the organization, we release such a leader instead of building his capability. The purpose of the Church is to get us into the celestial kingdom, and those who attain the highest qualification are those who are most valiant and most dedicated. It would be a pretty good idea to look up the meaning of those words, *valiant* and *dedicated*, and try to find out if they are proper descriptions of our Church work. We might make our own appraisal of how many of those people under our direction are on schedule for this high blessing. If we reject the idea of a survey and discourage the frank criticism of our leaders on the grounds that it would be embarrassing or that we do not want someone to become knowledgeable of our affairs, we are manifesting an attitude of weakness and toleration for our sins.

Actually, whether we like it or not, surveys of us are continually being made by God himself. As the record says, ". . . every idle word that men shall speak, they shall give account thereof in the day of judgment." (Matthew 12:36.) In his vision of the final judgment, John the Revelator said:

"And I saw the dead, small and great, stand before God; and the books were opened: and another book was opened, which is the book of life: and the dead were judged out of those things which were written in the books, according to their works.

"And the sea gave up the dead which were in it; and death and hell delivered up the dead which were in them; and they were judged every man according to their works." (Revelation 20:12-13.)

This book-keeping is an ongoing official survey that no one can escape. Many people will suffer a long period in hell and be permanently assigned to an inferior degree of glory because they failed to ascertain the facts and upgrade performance while the work was being done.

Before we go very far in any financial undertaking, someone is going to ask about our financial standing. A rating is constantly being made of our public relations. If either of these shows too many weaknesses, our prestige and credit may suffer seriously unless we know the facts and are willing to do something about them. Likewise we must not have unfavorable moral reports circulating about us.

It is very unprofitable to wait until the final judgment, or until our business goes bankrupt, or until our marriage is in ruins, or until our eternal happiness is lost, to find out what our problems are. It is pretty difficult to make improvement when it is too late. We must not fail in our stewardship. We are not appointed to our Church assignment to prove our ineffectiveness and make telestial beings of ourselves or those for whom we carry responsibility. If our personal leadership were compared to a business enterprise, those making the observation might not think of us as a going concern. An expert surveying team may liken our leadership to a business on the verge of bankruptcy, or to a marriage that is in the last throes of deterioration with a divorce in the offing.

Suppose that your own work were going to be the subject of an exhaustive survey by experts. How well do you think they would say you were doing your job, and how much enthusiasm would they say you create in the hearts of those with whom you are associated? Suppose that the Lord himself would go on your home teaching visits with you for the purpose of appraising the quality of your work. How much pleasure would he get out of your presentation of the principles of his gospel?

There are people who feel that the Lord is going to shut his eyes to their weaknesses, that he will not judge them critically no matter what their performance may be. What a shock some of us may get if we are permitted to see what is written in our section of the Lord's book of life! Suppose that we are among those unprofitable members to whom he says, "Thou wicked and slothful servant." Or suppose that, when he comes to cleanse the earth, we are among those on his left hand to whom he will say, "Depart from me, ye cursed, into everlasting fire, prepared for the devil and his angels." (Matthew 25:41.)

A good survey now, on which we are willing to take intelligent, vigorous action, may save us a lot of problems later on. The Lord utterly destroyed the people in the days of Noah and those who lived in Sodom and Gomorrah, while they themselves probably thought there was nothing wrong. Jesus looked forward to our day and made a rather unfavorable comparison for us when he said, "As the days of Noah were, so also shall the coming of the Son of Man be." (Matthew 24:37.) The facts indicate that he is now conducting another survey to determine what will happen and to whom at the time of the glorious Second Coming.

The Lord has great love for us, but he is the God of

justice and righteousness. He is very much opposed to sloth, weakness, sin, and failure. On the basis of the importance of our eternal life and success, what could be more valuable than a vigorous survey of our work? How do we rate in our preparation? How do we rate in our skill of accomplishment? What can we do about our missionary work? We have some who have been placed in authority over us in the Church, who supervise our work. We should encourage them to see to it that our work is well done. At the same time, we are responsible for analyzing and surveying our own work.

May the Lord help us to be effective critics and good managers of ourselves.

Chapter 34

Statistics

Sometimes ideas, like people, get a bad reputation which is not deserved. With a bad reputation, even great thoughts can lose their power to help us. In our Church work the value of statistics has been a victim of this unjustified downgrading process.

In a Church leadership meeting, one speaker said, "I am going to give you some statistics." He apologized for what he was about to do. Among other things, he said that statistics were dry and uninteresting. He ventured the opinion that by the time he had finished his discussion everyone would be asleep. His statement proved to be fairly accurate, but he falsely laid the blame on the statistics. Any interest that may or may not be in the statistics is largely determined by the speaker. We ourselves are the most important subject of statistics. And the statistics that are the most tiring to us are those that picture us at our worst.

A man dressed in ludicrous clothing and with an attitude to match said: "Don't judge me by what I look like. Judge me by what I am." So far as I could tell they were very nearly the same. Sometimes we think or say, "Don't judge us by our statistics, judge us by what we are." We say, "Our statistics are terrible but we are wonderful."

Some arguments have been made against statistics by saying that they are out of harmony with the spirit of Church work. Yet one of the fundamental principles of the gospel is that everyone must be rewarded or punished according to what he does. John the Revelator, after viewing a vision of the final judgment, affirms in very strong language that we are going to be judged by our works as recorded in the books that are being kept.

God is by far the greatest statistician. He keeps the most detailed and factual set of records. And it may be a little impractical for us to think we can stand before the judgment seat and object to our statistics. That is rather like saying: "My mind is made up. Don't confuse me with the facts."

Statistics are our best way of representing on paper people, things, and circumstances. In almost every field, statistics are among the most fascinating and the most helpful of all forms of knowledge. By the proper use of statistics we can make ourselves more successful in our businesses, our education, and our Church work. Properly used, statistics can make our Church work more interesting, more spiritual, more pleasant, and more effective.

Sound planning and good follow-through are usually based on an accurate and complete set of goals and records. Probably no single habit so profoundly influences all other habits as does the habit of planning and record-keeping—planning tomorrow's activities today, and doing today what was planned yesterday. It might help us to try and imagine how anyone could effectively promote a good athletic program without statistics. In football, every kick, every pass, every run, every down is measured, timed, and counted. If one team doesn't make its yards in four tries, it loses the ball. It is the statistics that make the game. If the score is six to seven and we are on the one-yard line with one minute to play, everyone is excited. If the score is sixty to nothing, most of the spectators have already gone home. You can even do pushups and leg raises more effectively by counting them.

Statistics are among our greatest motivators. One of the best examples of motivation is found in amateur athletics. Ordinarily a football quarterback operates close to the very limit of his capacity. But if you took away the statistics, you would also take away most of the interest, enthusiasm, desire to play, and will to win.

The motivation in athletics, and in almost every other thing, is based on our God-given success instinct which is a part of our natural equipment. All human beings have also been endowed by their Creator with the possibility for a strong, competitive spirit. If one lacks a strong desire to win and has no appetite for victory, something is wrong.

Karl G. Maeser said, "A laudable ambition to excel is an indispensable requisite to success." God himself has made success the most pleasant of all of our experiences. For a very good reason, God put this instinctive desire to win into our very natures, and we ought to develop it to the limit.

We are better baseball players when our hits, runs, and errors are published. And anyone planning to become a big-league baseball player had better keep track of his batting average. If you bat .350 in the big leagues you may make ten times as much money as a .250 batter. The .350 batter gets on first base three and one-half times out of ten tries, whereas the .250 batter gets on two and one-half times out of ten tries. The difference is only one more success out of ten times at bat.

Actually, the .250 man may hit the ball further and more frequently than the .350 batter. His problem may not be that he doesn't hit the ball often enough or far enough. His poorer showing may be because he can't run fast enough. There are enough photo-finishes at first base to indicate that many who are called out would have been safe if they had been one-half step faster in ninety feet. A .250 batter would not have needed to have been faster three and one-half times out of ten. He was fast enough two and one-half times. All he needed was a little more speed on the extra try.

We all need to see ourselves on paper. You couldn't accurately judge even a Babe Ruth if you didn't see his accomplishments on paper. Most Church members would think quite differently of their Church performance if they saw their tithing and church attendance on paper. Some of the reasons why the accomplishments of athletes are at such high levels is that they have access to more accurate statistics, which provide them with better motivation. As long as we allow ourselves the luxury of indefinite goals and make light of statistics, we may never reach our full spiritual possibility.

In a certain year in one stake there were 117 Aaronic Priesthood boys receiving an individual merit award. The next year only 52 earned an award. That indicates that in one year they had lost 65 of their award winners. And not one of the leaders was even aware of what had happened. They were going out of business and didn't even know it. None of them could even make an intelligent guess as to whether they were going up or down. And what is even more tragic, no one seemed to care very much.

They were like baseball players who didn't believe in statistics, failed to keep score, and had no will to play. Actually, they didn't even know how many boys they had on the roll.

Jesus said that we should leave the ninety and nine and go seeking the one that is lost. But it would give urgency to our quest if a person had a good set of records showing that fifty were now lost instead of one and that most of these had strayed away during his own term as their leader. What hope would there be for a basketball player who didn't believe in statistics and didn't know that he was losing the game?

Some Church leaders may say, in effect, "We are nice people, so don't judge us for what we do." There isn't much demand for merely "nice" people, however. God has said that we are going to be judged by our works. We like to refer to ourselves as saviors upon Mount Zion, but the only way I know of to be a savior is to save someone. How many people have you saved recently?

A sales organization can substantially increase its production merely by publishing the sales records. There are some Church people who argue against making comparative accomplishment reports even between wards, stakes, and quorums on the grounds that a stating of the facts may embarrass some of those with low scores. A little embarrassment is frequently very constructive, however. Embarrassment over his speech defect made Demosthenes the greatest orator in the world. There is a great deal of evidence pointing to the fact that when we bury this God-given competitive instinct and hide the records so that we keep all of our failures as well as our successes a secret even from ourselves, great damage may be done. Some might argue that it embarrasses a criminal to let him know about his crime. A little embarrassment now may save us from a lot of embarrassment later on, however, for how can anyone intelligently govern his life if he doesn't know what the facts are? It has been said that to him who doesn't know where he is going, no wind is favorable.

One of the great laws of life is the law of contrast. The scriptures say that if we didn't know the bitter we couldn't appreciate the sweet. Many people have found that the embarrassment of some temporary failure has produced the joy of a permanent success. How else can we learn that success is better than failure? One of our biggest problems comes from our natural blind spots. And we add to this deficiency by hiding the facts so that we may think we are winning the race when we are not.

Some maintain that it is unfair to make comparisons because of the great differences in abilities, conditions, and experiences between those groups being compared. But these same differences hold in every other field. One basketball team may come from a school having fifty thousand students to choose from, while another school has only one thousand. Sometimes, the Davids kill the Goliaths.

Some people have maintained that the only valid comparison is to compare a person's performance with himself. But that contention may also have some weaknesses. One business organization may be 20 percent ahead of last year, and those involved may reach around and pat themselves on the back without knowing that the entire industry of which they are a part is 50 percent ahead. It is true that, if you compare the members of a sales organization, one may be a new salesman without experience and in a poor territory, competing against veterans in better territories. But many people have raised themselves by looking at those ahead of them.

Many salesmen have received their greatest encouragement from seeing sales leaders doing great volumes of business who did not do as well when they started as the newcomer is now doing. In addition, in many fields the leaders and the beginners are constantly trading places. And anyone can find some doing well in poor territories. There could never be an absolutely fair comparison, but instead of selecting the discouragement in our situations we are at perfect liberty to choose to be inspired by the good.

Many men have developed a fighting spirit by suffering discouragement and defeat. It has been said that no one ever wins in the struggle of life without having an uphill heart.

If you want to effectively practice being a high jumper, lay a bamboo pole across on two measured uprights and jump over it instead of just going out onto the field and jumping up in the air. Progress is very difficult unless we have some accurate measurement of the progress made. "When performance is measured, performance improves. When performance is measured and reported back—the rate of improvement accelerates."

A strong desire to win and a competitive spirit can help us to qualify for success and the celestial kingdom. The greatest sin of any military commander is to lose the battle. And that is also our besetting sin of leadership. There should be more church in business. But we should also be more businesslike in the Church. We work in the greatest of all enterprises, which Jesus referred to as "my Father's business." May we be worthy businessmen with our fingers on the facts.

Chapter 35

The Cause

Aristotle, the great Greek philosopher, once gave us one of the primary secrets of success when he said, "You never know a thing until you know it by its causes." That is, every success has a cause; every failure has a cause; indigestion has a cause; overweight has a cause. If you can find out what causes happiness, you can reproduce the cause. We can bring about our own spiritual, mental, moral, or physical health in any desired degree if we know and follow the specific laws that govern in the areas of our projected accomplishments.

Among the greatest enemies of mankind are two giant sins known as ignorance and sloth. Between these two scissor blades of *not knowing* and *not doing*, we find the causes for most of our failures. We are horrified by the devastations of divorce, yet there are many of those involved who either say they don't know what is causing their problems or are unwilling to admit the truth of their situation to themselves or to make the effort to bring about a correction.

A man who was being divorced against his will after ten years of marriage was asked for a description of their problems. He said, "I didn't even know that we had a problem until thirty days ago when my wife filed for divorce." She said that he had been a continual source of irritation and heartbreak for her for the entire ten years, but he claimed that he was not aware of any problem. Likewise many of us are insensitive to some of those difficulties that are presently destroying not only our success and happiness but our souls as well.

One of the most frequent complaints arising from sick marriages is that the partners can't communicate. They won't discuss their problems, let alone make an effective attempt to solve them. There is little hope for marriage success unless the partners know how to give joint consideration to the *cause* and then do something about the *solution*. There are large numbers of couples who have lived together as husband and wife for thirty years who don't know as much about each other as a marriage counselor or a divorce lawyer can discover in thirty minutes.

There are other serious problems about which many are uninformed. Jesus said, "And this is life eternal, that they might know thee the only true God, and Jesus Christ, whom thou hast sent." (John 17:3.) Despite this affirmation, too many of us know very little about God, and what such people do know is mere hearsay. They don't read the scriptures; they don't understand the principles of the gospel; they don't pray; they don't meditate; and they don't go to church as they should. They don't live in such a way as to entitle themselves to have the Spirit of the Lord or the spirit of leadership. They can't even seem to master that information on which our eternal exaltation is based, although it is so simple that any wayfaring man, though a fool, need not err therein. And they frequently fall down in even their most simple leadership responsibilities. In many wards we can't even get our children baptized on time. Many people are never as fully prepared for missions or for marriage or for life as they should be. What is worse, too often they are unable to identify those things that are holding them back.

A high school football player once wrote to his mother and said, "The enemy found the hole in our line and the hole was me." This young man had made a great discovery. In searching for what is causing our problems, we might find the answer by looking in the mirror.

Isn't it interesting that the thing we know less about than almost anything else in the world is our own individual selves?

If you ask someone to talk to you about science, invention, history, or politics, he will answer you. But if you ask him to sit down and write out an analysis of himself and tell you about his mind and his qualities of soul, you may not get a very good answer. Ask someone where he came from or what his purpose in life is, or to tell you something about his eternal destiny, and he will probably stand silent and uncomprehending before you. Alternatively, try to discover why it is that we do the things that we do while we believe the things that we believe.

There is another area where our lack of information, coupled with our lethargy, causes some very serious problems, and that is in our Church leadership situations. We have too many leadership duties that aren't being done well. We are going through a lot of strenuous motions without reaching the objectives that we aim at. The Lord appointed Peter to be the leader of the Church in his day. And he said to Peter, as a commission to all his leaders, "Feed my sheep." The extent to which we are involved in the sins and weaknesses of the world indicates the unpleasant fact that this job of feeding the flock is not being properly done. Most of us would probably claim that we don't know the particulars about what is holding us back.

Jesus also said that we ought to be friendly with each other. He said, "A new commandment I give unto you, that ye love one another; as I have loved you, that ye also love one another." (John 13:34.) Because the Creator recognized love and friendship as one of our needs, he gave us a natural, instinctive desire to try to satisfy it. That is, everyone hungers for appreciation. We have a natural need to be loved, and everyone wants to feel that his own life is worthwhile. One of the most devastating of all human emotions is the sense of being alone, of being unloved, and of being unimportant. The feeling of not being wanted, of not being worthy, of not being important is causing far too much distress in our civilization and among our Church membership.

We need each other. This means that we should bring everyone into full Church membership and into full Church fellowship and activity. The fact that the Lord has told us to do it is an indication that he thinks that we *can* do it if we will. We might inquire of ourselves why we don't.

Someone was asking for suggestions about how to get people to come to church. To some people this seems like the hardest job in the world. In fact, for some it would be impossible. Yet no one would say that, in our religious leadership, we are functioning on a level of maximum performance in this area.

A man was asked to serve as a bishop in a ward where church attendance was very low. This man was a first-class salesman, and he had discovered that it was never a very profitable procedure to try to stumble into success. He himself had been far more successful in his business when he had selected his prospects carefully and had done an adequate amount of homework so that he was familiar with their wants and needs and personality traits before an approach was made. When one is properly prepared, he can more intelligently touch the buttons of people's interests.

With a great desire to succeed, the new bishopric went to work on their problem. They looked up the names of those who had been inactive in the Church and made a personal call on each one for what, in the bishop's business, would have been called a "fact-finding interview." This is the time when, as a salesman, he would be getting ready to make the sale. Because of this bishopric's intelligent, friendly approach, their people told them frankly many of the reasons why they hadn't been coming to church.

Some of these reasons involved personal problems, almost all of which had an easy, pleasant solution. Some of these reasons were backed up by sins which may not have been uncovered if the person involved had had to make a formal call on the bishop and go through the embarrassment of a confession. Many of these people revealed some offense that had occurred in their earlier experience, the hurt of which had now pretty well vanished. Many of these confessed to the bishopric that they really wanted to be active in the Church and were really waiting for an invitation.

Each night after the calls had been made, the bishopric prepared a card file listing in some detail the attitudes, objectives, and desires of the member. The bishopric tried to uncover any problems where the parents would like to have some assistance with their children. These were all carefully noted on the card.

I am reminded here of an expert life insurance official. His agents used to bring him difficult cases to sell. Facing the prospect, the official would make a kind of modest apology for the situation and then say: "I would be interested in knowing something from you. If you were going to buy such a policy as my friend here is talking to you about, what would be some of the reasons prompting you to make the purchase?" The prospective client might usually say, "I am not going to buy it." The official would respond: "I understand that. But if you *were* going to buy it, what would motivate you to do so?" By this process, the official could get the prospect to open up and talk a little about the situation. This is another of those situations wherein knowledge is power.

In his visits the bishop would say, "We would very much like to have you actively associated with the ward. What changes are there that could be made to make your association with us more pleasant?" Many people would voice some objection that they might have, or might imagine, wherein improvements could be made. The bishop was conscious that if he were running a commercial business he would as far as possible try to please those who patronized him; and that he should also follow that procedure with regard to his ward members. Every one of them is tremendously important. Every one of them who becomes active adds to the ward family. In addition, think of the tremendous value to this inactive member and his family in returning to an observance of the principles of the gospel. With this kind of understanding and effective follow-through on the part of a friendly, enthusiastic leadership, many people could be brought back into Church activity.

We need to understand that many great events swing on little hinges. A shortage of five cents' worth of iodine in one's thyroid gland may make the difference between a great scholar and a helpless idiot. A little love in a person's heart or a little genuine consideration in his attitudes may make the difference between an inactive prospective elder and the most faithful high priest. When we can discover what causes any failure, the solution is usually made self-evident thereby.

The laws of success in any undertaking are just as definite as are the laws of gravity or the laws of electricity or the laws of health. An intelligent leadership that is fully committed and has enough industry and courage can accomplish miracles. But we need plans and convictions to support our projected success. It is possible for sacrament meetings to be made so pleasant and profitable that no one would think of missing them. The spirit of reverence and worship can be powerful magnets. Then there are the matters of our education and our eternal welfare to be considered. God said, "Remember the sabbath day, to keep it holy." What did he mean? What could hold a man away from church if he believed that the eternal exaltation of himself and his family depended on fully doing as the Lord commanded?

The assigned function of the Church is to build happiness, character, and success into the lives of every member. Suppose that the ward were a great and potentially profitable business. It would have a corps of the finest quality salesmen who would teach and train us to take full advantage of our available opportunities.

I do not know the details that brought about the translation of the people in the city of Enoch and caused them to be taken up to God. Yet we can be absolutely certain that before it happened, the people had to find out what their problems were and how to solve them on a united and enthusiastic basis. There must have been a lot of personal coaching, and certainly the people of Enoch must have had great pride in their city, a great love for God, and a great confidence in their leaders before they could bring about such a perfect situation among their members.

Any football team can be a *great* football team if they are willing to understand and train and work. And any Church leader and any Church organization can accomplish wonders by the same processes.

Chapter 36

Planning

The first ingredient in any success is planning. That is the place where every accomplishment begins. One of the most thrilling quotations I know is to the effect that planning is the place where man shows himself most like God. Just try to think of anyone engaged in more God-like work than the planner. He is the thinker. He is the organizer. He is the one who devises strategy and draws the blueprint. He is the one who develops the initiative and builds the roadway of activity on which each accomplishment must travel.

The planner is also the one who guarantees the dependability of the accomplishment. Try to imagine God as he worked out the details of our world with all of its laws, order, and beauty. Then think of the know-how and industry that went into the actual construction.

All military battles are first won in the mind of the general. The architect lays out on paper every detail of the building before construction is started. The effective Church leader is also this kind of man.

Henry Ford once said that the difference between the old Model T and the new Lincoln was planning. With effective planning and an industrious follow-through, any success in or out of the Church may be assured.

When we try to create a happy, constructive family home evening without planning, we are trying to make something out of nothing—something that, if we understand correctly, even God cannot do. Planning and follow-through are like the two blades of a scissors. One is of little value without the other. Likewise no one can make a great home teaching accomplishment out of nothing. We may be sure, too, that we will never get more out of a sacrament meeting than goes into it.

I once heard Dr. Adam S. Bennion say that he had never gone before a Sunday School class to teach a Sunday School lesson without spending an average of eight hours in preparation. No wonder that he was an exciting, inspiring teacher. He was a planner; he did his homework and was particularly mindful of the follow-through.

Oliver Cowdery once tried his hand at translating, and the Lord afterwards said to him: "Behold, you have not understood; you have supposed that I would give it unto you, when you took no thought save it was to ask me. But, behold, I say unto you, that you must study it out in your mind. . . ." (D&C 9:7-8.) The Lord was trying to teach Oliver Cowdery about this great success combination of planning and industry. Jesus came seeking doers. He wanted someone who could see the problem and then solve it; someone who could get the ship into port.

Thomas A. Edison was one of the greatest creators who ever lived upon this earth. He gave his success formula as being 1 percent inspiration and 99 percent perspiration. Someone has said that no one can be *in*spiring who is not *per*spiring.

The first step in planning is to find out what the problem is. I attended a leadership meeting where a bishopric with an excellent record for sacrament meeting attendance presented a demonstration. They reported on a person-to-person survey made to discover why people did not come to sacrament meeting. The major absentee causes were reported as follows:

1. The absentees said they did not feel comfortable among Church people.
2. Because of personal problems, some had feelings of guilt and inferiority, together with a fear of censure.
3. No one had ever made a wholehearted attempt to

make them feel either needed or wanted in the Church.

4. They had made no adequate financial or other kind of contribution and they felt they had no real right to participation.
5. They were not sold enough on the gospel to feel that what they did made very much difference anyway.
6. Some said they would rather work or play on the Sabbath day.
7. A great many were offended because of the irreverence, disorder, people walking in and out of the meetings, etc. They said these things made it impossible for them to enjoy what they felt should be a quiet, sacred, and peaceful service.

When the real, honest, individual causes of sacrament meeting absenteeism became known, the solution was more or less self-evident. In the ward council meeting, the bishopric held a combination planning and get-it-done meeting. Each member present was given a piece of paper on which to write down suggestions, as they were made, for improvement in attendance. This group developed and discussed a list of thirty things which should be done every week. The laws of success governing sacrament meeting attendance are just as definite as those governing gravity or electricity, and follow-through on these thirty things guarantees an excellent attendance at sacrament meetings every week.

Suppose that *you* figure out what these thirty rules are which, if carried out each week, will make all the sacrament meetings successful. If you only discover twenty-nine you are leaving one out, and your success may be reduced accordingly. This must not be allowed, as the Church hath need of every member. (No exceptions.) Therefore, the bishopric made assignments of those things which should be done without fail each and every week. Each one assigned was asked to carry his full share. (Those who can't do this need some special work done with them.)

At another leadership meeting, an elders quorum presidency demonstrated their plans for getting their newly acquired prospective elders on an activity schedule that would qualify them for the celestial kingdom. Again, they began with a personal visit into the homes of those inactive men to find the reason for their spiritual retardation. The presidency made written suggestions to themselves about how to sell their members on the importance of keeping Church standards and attending to their duties. They recognized that when people are fully convinced about the many benefits that come from living the gospel they will gladly make commitments about doing their part, and that with the vigorous, helpful follow-through of good leadership, the job will get done.

This presidency made written, detailed plans about how they could make these people feel wanted, important, needed, and loved. They made equally detailed plans about who would get the message over and how to get action. No leadership failures take place when we properly follow the laws of leadership success.

James G. Harboard was a general in World War I. Before and after his war service, he was the chief executive officer of the Radio Corporation of America. Speaking before a group of national business leaders, he gave his own formula for leadership success. He said that before anyone under his direction undertook any assignment, he must do four things:

1. Make a *written*, detailed statement of objectives.
2. Make a *written* inventory of all available resources. (List all possibilities for reinforcement.)
3. Make a *written* inventory of the resources of the enemy. (List all reasons why the mission may not succeed.)
4. Lastly, prepare a *written* plan explaining exactly how he will use his resources to overcome the resources of the enemy to accomplish the objective.

We clarify our thoughts and make them definite when we think them through and write them down. We also make a deeper impression in our minds when we keep our leadership ideas constantly before us in visual form with a timetable attached. The only proof of our leadership is when we effectively follow through and complete every assignment on schedule.

Part Seven

Improving the
Ward Family

Chapter 37

Father
of the Ward

We have a very interesting word in our language: *father*. It has a great many meanings. George Washington is referred to as the Father of his country. The Mississippi River is called the *Father* of Waters. Satan has been called the father of lies. He is also the father of rebellion and every other evil. Plants and animals have both fathers and mothers. So do ideas and ambitions and attitudes. From just about any point of view, parenthood is one of our biggest single ideas and supplies us with our greatest opportunities. Every parent always brings forth after his own kind.

Father is one of the titles of God himself. In foretelling the birth of the Savior of the world, Isaiah says: "For unto us a child is born, unto us a son is given: and the government shall be upon his shoulder: and his name shall be called Wonderful, Counsellor, The mighty God, The everlasting Father, The Prince of Peace. Of the increase of his government . . . there shall be no end." (Isaiah 9:6-7.) Christ is also called the Redeemer, the Savior, the Son of God, the Propitiator for our sins. What title could ever outrank that of God the *Father*? Next in importance comes that group of twenty-two words laying the basis for our own parenthood: "So God created man in his own image, in the image of God created he him; male and female created he them." (Genesis 1:27.)

Paul said something to the Hebrews on this subject of parenthood. He said: "We have had fathers of our flesh which corrected us, and we gave them reverence: shall we not much rather be in subjection unto the Father of spirits, and live?" (Hebrews 12:9.) Try to think of something more exciting than the fact that the great God of Creation is our literal Father!

But we not only had a Father of our spirits and fathers of our bodies; we also have fathers of our ambitions and of our faith and of our morality and of our enthusiasm and of our success. Perhaps one of the most profitable things any one of us might do would be to sit down and write out a set of job descriptions for this most important office of being a father.

If a good father properly thought out, planned, organized and put in writing a good set of job descriptions, this activity in itself would teach him many things. A thoroughly planned program can teach us how to be better providers, better personal counselors, better motivators, better teachers, better examples, better holders of family home evenings, and better companions. We should eliminate from the plan all possibilities for dissension, misunderstanding, and the causes for rebellion. There should be no evil centered in the father.

A good father is much more than a mere parent. He is also a guardian, a trustee, a godly steward, a coach, an example, and a friend. He should be able to build righteousness, success, and faith in other people. But there are other applicants for this great title of *father* besides the one who is a begetter of literal offspring. The bishop is called the *father* of his ward. This is much more than a figure of speech.

When Alexander the Great was twelve years of age, his father, Philip, the king of Macedonia, arranged for Aristotle, the great Greek philosopher, to become the lad's companion and tutor. Later, Alexander said that Aristotle was his father. What he meant was that, while he had received his body from Philip, Aristotle was the father of his mind.

There are many people who have been adequately supplied with a father for their flesh who need fathers for their minds and fathers for their spirituality and fathers for their success. Alexander said that he was more indebted to Aristotle for knowledge than he was to Philip for life. Therefore, whether our calling is to be the father of a ward, or the father of a nation, or the father of a quorum, or the father of an auxiliary organization, or the father of that group of families on our home teaching beat, it is an all-important office.

Suppose we sit down and make up a set of individual plans as to how we are going to get into the celestial kingdom all those included in our home teaching responsibilities. If we have a good set of plans for them and a good set of job descriptions or specifications for ourselves, with timetables attached and a good executive department to carry them out, we will be well on our way to becoming a great father. Of course, we should keep in mind that the one purpose of our service in the Church is the success of those we serve.

Henry Thoreau once said that no one was ever born to fail. Certainly we were born to succeed. As Church members and leaders we ought to succeed as stewards and as human beings.

We should keep in mind that not all fathers are successful. Satan is the father of lies, the father of evil, the father of indifference, the father of failure. Satan would like nothing better than to see us fail in our leadership role. This we must not do. As stewards of the Lord, we should strive to guarantee the success of those under our direction; that is, guarantee that they will qualify for the celestial kingdom.

One of the most distinguishing characteristics of a great athletic coach is that he will not let his players fail either in their training, their attitudes, or their efforts during the game. That is also one of the marks of effective Church leadership. Under one bishop, 10 percent of the people may come to sacrament meeting, whereas under another bishop 80 percent may do so. What tremendous good fortune it is when one has a good bishop to be the father of his ward, the father of his faith, and the father of his enthusiasm!

Some time ago, I heard a high councilor tell how as a boy he had lived on a farm. It was his job during the sugarbeet harvest to sit up on the beet wagon and drive the horses until the load got so heavy that the horses would not pull the load with him holding the reins. Then his father would take over. With his father holding the reins, the horses could pull a much greater load than with the boy holding the reins. With the father holding the reins, the horses were organized, they had a better spirit, they were more united because of the excellence of their management on the other end of the reins.

The bishop holds the reins on the Sunday School, the Primary, the Relief Society, the priesthood, the home teaching, the welfare work. He is the closest one to the people. He has the greatest prestige. He should have the greatest wisdom, the most industry, the finest diplomacy, the greatest devotion, and the greatest faith. A good father of the ward, like the father of a family, should spend a lot of personal time associating with those who come under his direction. He does the planning. He is the shepherd that knows what to do about lost sheep. He is the leader that instills reverence into the lives of the people.

If the one who holds the reins in the classroom or in sacrament meeting cannot maintain a proper discipline and reverence, the bishop himself may have to shoulder the blame. Children who have not reached the age of responsibility must be directed by their parents, and if parents do not exercise those qualities of properly directing the lives of their children, the Lord has said that "the sin [will] be upon the heads of the parents." (D&C 68:25.) But the sin must also be upon the head of the leader who carries the responsibility for the parents. If the bishop allows distractions or lack of organization or lack of leadership training to cut down our learning procedures or the joys of our worship to a fraction of their possibility, he may have to carry this heavy load of responsibility upon his own shoulders.

But by his instruction, his example, and his personal counseling, a good father of the ward will build order, reverence, self-control, love, and happiness into all of those who are present in his meetings. A good father of the ward gets the greatest amount of personal growth and personal righteousness into his members by helping them to study and take part in righteous activities. A good father is a great giver of inspiration and good ideas, so that every time you meet him you are lifted up. Because the outgo of any life cannot exceed the income, a good father of the ward must have a very large intake of good and some great internal reservoirs, so that the spiritualizing influences may be carried over from one time to another and from one person to another. When a good father has an ample supply of inspiration, answers, and solutions to meet all people in all situations, he will bless many people throughout eternity.

It is also important that a good father of the ward, or one carrying any other great responsibility, should regularly reconsider the importance of his title. It may be that by constant and continued consideration we can add to our callings some new meanings, or develop new powers for increasing the excellence of our performance.

Chapter 38

The Sabbath Day

A large-scale problem in many lives is that we so frequently fail to understand the importance of some of those great ideas that otherwise could make our lives outstandingly successful. In one of the greatest of these success ideas, the Lord has said that we should properly observe and honor the Sabbath day.

We set aside one day each year for Thanksgiving, one day for Easter, and one day for Christmas. These are all fine days which contain great potential for our good. But the Lord himself has set aside one-seventh of all of our days from the beginning to the end of our lives, not as holidays but as holy days.

Someone has said that our civilization would never have survived for even half a century if it had not been for this one day in seven that we call Sunday. This is the Lord's day. This is a kind of heavenly Father's Day. This is the day when we try to live at our best. This is the day when we pay particular attention to the washing of our bodies, put on our best clothes, read our best books, and think our best thoughts. This is the day when we try to reach a pinnacle in our lives.

On Sunday, after we have laid aside the cares that usually concern us on the other days, we go to the house of prayer which has been dedicated to the worship of the Lord. We let our minds reach up and try to understand the things of God and the purposes for which this day was set apart. We also let our hearts reach out to our fellowmen. Above everything else we ought to understand that the Lord knows what he is doing, and by all means we ought to do what he says. The holy scripture points out that the Lord created the earth in six days and rested on the seventh. He sanctified and hallowed this special day, and if we honor it it will sanctify and hallow us.

Some thirty-four centuries ago, the great God of creation again reemphasized the importance of this great idea. He came down onto the top of Mount Sinai in a cloud of fire, and to the accompaniment of the lightnings and thunderings of that holy mountain he said:

"Remember the sabbath day, to keep it holy.

"Six days shalt thou labour, and do all thy work:

"But the seventh day is the sabbath of the Lord thy God: in it thou shalt not do any work, thou, nor thy son, nor thy daughter, thy manservant, nor thy maidservant, nor thy cattle, nor thy stranger that is within thy gates:

"For in six days the Lord made heaven and earth, the sea, and all that in them is, and rested the seventh day: wherefore the Lord blessed the sabbath day, and hallowed it." (Exodus 20:8-11.)

This great idea, this important command, has been emphasized by God over and over again. But generally we have not been very obedient to it. The most important experience of our earth took place when the Son of God came here on a mission centered in bringing about our eternal exaltation. He established his Church upon the earth with the intention that everyone should have the opportunity to belong to it and live its laws. As a part of this program for our eternal benefit, he made a covenant to redeem us from death, to give us a glorious resurrection, and to permit us to live with him and with our families and friends forever if we would only enter into this covenant and live its eternal conditions of righteousness.

While Jesus was eating the Last Supper with the Twelve, just prior to his crucifixion, an interesting event took place as follows:

"And as they were eating, Jesus took bread, and blessed it, and brake it, and gave it to the disciples, and said, Take, eat; this is my body.

"And he took the cup, and gave thanks, and gave it to them, saying, Drink ye all of it;

"For this is my blood of the new testament, which is shed for many for the remission of sins." (Matthew 26:26-28.)

One of his eternal laws is that we are baptized for the remission of our sins, and then we covenant to serve him and keep his commandments. (Mosiah 18:8-12.) In our own day the Lord has spelled out our responsibilities and our rewards relative to the law of the Sabbath in a little more detail than in Exodus. He has said:

"And that thou mayest more fully keep thyself unspotted from the world, thou shalt go to the house of prayer and offer up thy sacraments upon my holy day;

"For verily this is a day appointed unto you to rest from your labors, and to pay thy devotions unto the Most High;

"Nevertheless thy vows shall be offered up in righteousness on all days and at all times;

"But remember that on this, the Lord's day, thou shalt offer thine oblations and thy sacraments unto the Most High, confessing thy sins unto thy brethren, and before the Lord.

"And on this day thou shalt do none other thing, only let thy food be prepared with singleness of heart that thy fasting may be perfect, or, in other words, that thy joy may be full.

"Verily, this is fasting and prayer, or in other words, rejoicing and prayer.

"And inasmuch as ye do these things with thanksgiving, with cheerful hearts and countenances, not with much laughter, for this is sin, but with a glad heart and a cheerful countenance—

"Verily I say, that inasmuch as ye do this, the fulness of the earth is yours, the beasts of the field and the fowls of the air, and that which climbeth upon the trees and walketh upon the earth;

"Yea, and the herb, and the good things which come of the earth, whether for food or for raiment, or for houses, or for barns, or for orchards, or for gardens, or for vineyards;

"Yea, all things which come of the earth, in the season thereof, are made for the benefit and the use of man, both to please the eye, and to gladden the heart;

"Yea, for food and for raiment, for taste and for smell, to strengthen the body and to enliven the soul.

"And it pleaseth God that he hath given all these things unto man; for unto this end were they made to be used, with judgment, not to excess, neither by extortion.

"And in nothing doth man offend God, or against none is his wrath kindled, save those who confess not his hand in all things, and obey not his commandments." (D&C 59:9-21.)

A sacrament is a special spiritual covenant between God and us. The Lord has provided the ordinance of the sacrament, with the solemn covenants which attend it. The Lord has also given us the actual sacramental prayers, which in themselves are covenants. The prayer says:

"O God, the Eternal Father, we ask thee in the name of thy son, Jesus Christ, to bless and sanctify this bread to the souls of all those who partake of it, that they may eat in remembrance of the body of thy Son, and witness unto thee, O God, the Eternal Father, that they are willing to take upon them the name of thy Son, and always remember him and keep his commandments which he has given them; that they may always have his Spirit to be with them. Amen." (D&C 20:77.)

In spite of the spiritual knowledge explosion of our day, many people are still not doing much about our Sabbath day opportunities, and they make all kinds of excuses for *not* keeping the Sabbath day holy and for *not* attending sacrament meeting. Yet this is a time when we are supposed to pay our devotions to the Most High as we attend Sunday School and sacrament meeting, not with much laughter, and certainly not by keeping those sitting near us distracted and disturbed by our irreverence, the noise and confusion of unnecessary movement, uncontrolled children, talking, whispering, and so on. These things keep others from the valuable meditations of deep worship. In our sacrament prayers we ask that we may have the Lord's Spirit to be with us, and this may not be possible when the attention is distracted by irreverence and confusion. Some day offenders will bitterly regret their failures in this important matter of keeping the Sabbath day holy.

On the other hand, what an exciting privilege it ought to be to recovenant weekly to faithfully serve and properly worship and reverence God, and then strictly keep those covenants—with no exceptions permitted! So again, with a little more emphasis, we might say to ourselves and to any we have responsibility for as leaders, "Remember the Sabbath day, to keep it holy."

Chapter 39

Meeting Management

Some time ago a small social group of young married people were invited to visit in the home of one of their member couples. The host and hostess spent a great deal of time preparing to entertain their friends. They wanted to make sure that everything was in readiness, not only inside the house itself but also in the garden, which likewise must show a proper amount of grooming.

Anyone who visits a large number of homes has been impressed with what a home reveals about its occupants. Of course, there are vast differences in the way homes are managed and maintained. Cleanliness, order, efficiency, taste, and general atmosphere can vary greatly between one home and another. And these differences, on both the outside and inside, sometimes have a permanent influence, not only on the residents but on visitors as well. Even in passing homes as one walks down the street, the order and general appearance of each establishment bears a loud testimony about the character of its custodians.

If we extend this experience a little further and visit a number of different sacrament meetings, or attend stake conferences in several stakes, it will be found that substantial differences also exist in the various "homes" of our religious lives. The Lord himself has asked us to hold sacrament meetings and stake conferences. He has set aside these important meeting periods for us to engage in reverent meditation and soul-inspiring worship. This is when we renew the covenants on which our eternal salvation depends, and where we can get the spirit of living life at its best.

Certainly our worship assemblies should be well organized and conducted with dignity. No officer should ever attempt to conduct a meeting without spending ample time in preparation and in getting the spirit of his calling. The audience should feel dignity, order, love, spirituality, and preparation coming from the stand. Because of the great differences that exist in our meetings, it naturally follows that some may be more productive to those who attend and more pleasing to the Lord than others.

The Lord wants all of us to have the greatest experiences in being spiritually instructed and motivated. He wants us to feel each other's love and friendship. Our meetings are also a good place to learn to enjoy the Spirit of the Lord. It is the responsibility of those in charge of Church meetings to see that they are well attended and that they are as profitable as possible to all concerned.

We always invite the Spirit of the Lord to be with us, and we should make certain that he is pleased with what takes place. No one would want to grieve his Spirit by being absent, or cause it to be withdrawn because the meeting was not what it should have been. It might be of great help for us to imagine that the Lord himself is going to be visibly present during the coming stake conference or the coming sacrament meeting. How many ideas could we then think of to make the meeting more pleasing to him?

The following are some of the things that we might consider:

1. *Order.* Alexander Pope once said that "Order is heaven's first law." In an editorial in the *Juvenile Instructor* of April 1, 1886, George Q. Cannon said that obedience must precede order and that order is the result of obedience. They are very close together. And they would include attendance at our meetings. They would also include preparation, reverence, spirituality, punctuality, love, faith, godliness, and dignity in all those who participate.

2. *Cleanliness.* There is an old proverb that cleanliness is next to godliness. The Sabbath is the day when we try to live at our best. On this day we pay particular attention to our personal cleanliness in mind, body, clothing and surroundings generally. Certainly a house dedicated to the worship of God should be spotless, with everything in the best possible good taste and order.

3. *Decoration.* In some stakes and wards, certain members are given the responsibility to see that the meetinghouse itself is at its best. Flowers in season, brought from the gardens of the members and artistically arranged, can provide much added beauty and great personal delight for everyone present.

4. *Ushers and greeters.* Friendly, effective ushering can make an important contribution to the success of a religious assembly. If you were to invite important people to your home, you would want to be there to personally greet them, make them welcome, and minister to their comfort. Some people may sometimes be a little ill-at-ease at church. Someone may be bothered by a feeling of personal guilt or an offense that he has received from someone else. A friendly, interested usher can do much to make these people feel needed and at home. Good ushers can also make it unnecessary for the presiding officer to take up valuable time in the meeting trying to solve the ushering, order and discipline problems from the stand.

5. *Fellowship.* We speak of the importance of fellowship in our religious activities. Our meetings offer an ideal opportunity to practice it, which we too often neglect. It is wonderful to greet people from the pulpit, and we hope to help them get the spirit of friendliness, fellowship, dignity, and worship from the stand, but nothing can take the place of the personal, individual, enthusiastic welcome that one gets when he arrives. Every member of the ward should be involved in fellowshipping, and any group can be given a head start toward success by being known for their outstanding, genuine friendliness. Some of the finest fellowshipping can be done by leaders, ushers, and members after the meeting is over.

6. *Punctuality.* An important part of effective meeting

management can be made by encouraging people to come thirty minutes early. This time can be profitably employed in greeting, meditating, and enjoying the sacred preliminary music. This gives time for the people to be properly seated in a leisurely manner so as. to avoid the crowding, confusion, traffic jams, and the necessity to walk on other people's feet in getting to an unoccupied seat in the middle of the row. Early arrival enables people to be seated in the front of the hall first. Presiding officers should be in their places well in advance of the time to begin.

7. *Personal counseling.* If the meeting runs as smoothly and pleasantly as it should, the presiding officer must have done a lot of personal work in training ushers, greeters, and everyone else in advance. He must anticipate anything that would mar the meeting and solve it in advance.

At a stake conference, the stake president whispered to a guest, "I hope the boys in the rear of the recreation hall won't bother us today." At that time there were no boys in evidence. After the meeting was underway, however, a group of a dozen or more boys showed up in the rear of the recreation hall. They pulled their chairs into two circles and spent the conference time visiting with each other. Not the slightest attempt at correction was made by any usher, bishop, or parent, or by any messenger from the presiding officer. The only reason the presiding officer knew in advance that this might happen was that it had happened in previous stake conferences. Undoubtedly these boys were fine boys who wanted to do what was right, but they destroyed the meeting's value for themselves, and their noise disturbed the people sitting within their sound range. The failure was that they were not properly instructed and supported by their leadership. This fault should have been corrected by some personal coaching many meetings ago.

It would have been very simple for an usher or someone appointed and trained by the stake president to make a temporary correction so that no one in the meeting would be disturbed. Then, in an understanding way, he could have made a contribution to the boys' permanent education afterwards by counseling them how they should proceed in the future. Great leadership should always be able to guarantee the advantages of an effective management to all who attend.

Good meeting management should mean that everyone was fully prepared and well-trained for his particular assignment in advance. This should apply particularly to the presiding officer, who should know the program. He himself should carry a spirit of love, good cheer, and inspiration. No detail of meeting success should be overlooked. Those who are to be on the stand should be seated there well in advance of the meeting. Everyone should be involved in the meeting. And all should be fully trained in their responsibility as greeters, ushers, fellowshippers, teachers, presiding officers, and members, so that the meeting can proceed without any flaw from a half-hour before the meeting starts until a half-hour after it has been completed.

Chapter 40

Creative Silence

There is a psychiatrist in New York City who writes an interesting prescription to cure people of their most serious problems of tension, fear, inferiority, guilt, resentment, and anger. He prescribes that they attend a certain church at least once each Sunday. If they say they do not believe in religion or that they do not like sermons, he asks them to go anyway even if they don't listen to what is said. His idea is that if they will sit quietly once a week and absorb the healing atmosphere and peace of the surroundings, their mental, spiritual, and physical health will be greatly improved.

A church is a place set apart in which to worship God; and the need to commune with him is universal. The Lord said, "For where two or three are gathered together in my name, there am I in the midst of them." (Matthew 18:20. See also D&C 6:32.) As we attend our Church meetings, we should be able to say, as did Jacob at Beth-el, ". . . the Lord is in this place . . ." (Genesis 28:16.)

We are familiar with the power of the atomic bomb. But there are yet greater forms of power in the universe that wait to be discovered. The greatest of these is the power of God. Just before the Lord ascended into heaven, he said to his apostles, "Ye shall receive power after that the Holy Ghost is come upon you." (Acts 1:8.) The New Testament declares, "But as many as received him, to them gave he power to become the sons of God." (John 1:12.) When an individual properly conditions his mind to the Spirit of the Lord, the healing power of the Lord will be with him. We ought to understand our Heavenly Father in his role as the God of power and life.

About Jesus, the scripture says, "In him was life; and the life was the light of men." (John 1:4.) When we go to church in the right spirit and become relaxed in body, clean in mind, and active in spirit, his power of life and light permeates our minds and bodies. It is a thrilling thing to hear a great choir, to see the beauty of a place of worship, but it is even more helpful to feel God's Spirit revitalizing our lives.

We might give some attention to the copper wires that bring electric power into the church building. They are the conductors of energy, light, and heat. We know very little about the actual qualities or origin of electricity, yet its power fills the church, it operates the pipe organ, and it provides power for the air conditioning. By means of thermostatic controls, the heat-flow automatically adjusts itself as needed. Electrical energy operates the loud-speaker system and carries the message of a speaker to the overflow auditoriums and other parts of the building. The entire structure is a network of wires which constitutes a medium through which power flows.

Isn't it a reasonable assumption that, in a building dedicated to God, where hearts are pure and many minds unified in peace and love are concentrated on the same spiritual objective, a reception center is created to draw down power far greater than that of electricity? It is as though we had several hundred spiritual and mental antennas attracting power and intelligence to one location. This power permeates the bodies, minds and spirits of those who have become attuned to this mystic yet real force.

There is no power in the world equal to religion when it comes to satisfying basic human needs. In our church services we listen to the beautiful music of the organ and the choir. We sing the meaningful hymns, running the important messages of the gospel through our hearts. We may also hear sacred gospel principles discussed in a sermon or in a class.

And the Lord and his Spirit will be in our midst. The principles of the gospel are organized, beautified elements of truth and common sense which we should understand and be enthusiastic about. The dictionary indicates one meaning of *enthusiasm* as "God in us."

Every Sunday morning in the particular church I mentioned they have a time of reverent meditation which they call the period for creative silence. In this place of peace and quiet, each one yields himself to the Divine and partakes of the spiritual medicine which is far better than that medicine which can be bought at the drug store. This is a period when the emblems signifying the Savior's suffering and sacrifice might be passed to the assembled worshippers. The doctor who writes prescriptions for church attendance as a curative medicine points out that any devout, practicing Christian can avail himself of a more powerful therapy than is in the hands of any other scientist. The religion of Christ can reach to the very depths of human nature and bring to the surface a maximum of strength, peace, and success.

In their services the Quakers have long periods of silence. They have learned a great deal more than most other people about creative silence. Jesus has promised that if two or three shall meet together in his name, there will he be also. Yet what good does it do for him to be near if we make no contact with him? Sometimes we come to a house of worship loaded with our own cares and problems, and because of the confusion in our own lives or the disorder around us the still small voice is unable to get through to us.

In the Church we excuse our disorder and irreverence in the house of the Lord by saying that we are a very friendly people and are anxious to greet and talk with each other. There are many places, such as in the foyer before and after the church service, where such talk is very proper, but in our worship service it is far more important that we establish contact with God than with each other.

Edwin Markham wrote a poem called "The Place of Peace," from which the following lines are taken:

> At the heart of the cyclone tearing the sky
> And flinging the clouds and the towers by,
> Is a place of central calm;

So here in the roar of mortal things,
I have a place where my spirit sings,
In the hollow of God's palm.

Even the devastating power of a cyclone is generated around a calm center. And in our relations with God we sometimes become involved in a destructive cyclone of our own confusion and unsolved problems, so that we miss the creative silence at the center of our own lives that could give us spirituality and power.

The greatest of all experiences available to human beings is a close contact with God. This may be achieved through righteousness, obedience, and the peaceful reverence of creative silence.

I remember the words of the great apostle Paul in which, speaking of God, he said, "In him we live, and move, and have our being." (Acts 17:28.) Instead of living in him in peace, quiet and worship, we frequently give ourselves over to disorders, tensions, fears, feelings of inferiority, and guilt. During the period of worship we are discussing, and particularly the period of silence, we should allow our bodies to assume a relaxed position so that the tensions, disorder, and ungodliness may go out of us. We are in the world but we should not be of the world and certainly we should not let worldliness, disorder, and confusion get into us at this sacred time.

God who created us has also the power to recreate us. Every time we have a striking new experience we become a new person. We can be born again as many times as we like, and each time we can be born better. When any new ambition or righteous habit penetrates our mind, we become a new person and we are born again. Thus during our period of creative silence we may wish to shut our eyes in order to close out the world and let the Spirit get through. This quiet period is not a time to think about ourselves or our problems any more than to laugh and joke with our neighbors. Our hearts should be centered on God and our minds engaged in creative meditation. There should not be any coughing or shuffling of feet or whispering or walking in and out of the room. Nor is this a time or place for disciplining the young.

Creative silence is not dead silence, for in our worship there should always be a living power surrounding us. This period should be a period of expectancy as though some important miracle were about to happen. When we live and move and have our being in him, it is as though God himself were touching our minds with his strength. And one of his great prophets has said, "Thou wilt keep him in perfect peace, whose mind is stayed on thee." (Isaiah 26:3.)

Scores of people have expressed themselves as to the miraculous benefits that have come to them during this period of silence and cleansing and strengthening and worship. There can be no question that, when this vibrant healing silence encompasses a group of worshippers, actual power is being generated in their lives. It is as though a spiritual monitor walked the aisles carrying a large basket and gathering up the tensions, fears, disorders, inferiorities, sins, and guilt of the worshippers. During this time it is possible for God to touch these same human lives with his righteous purposes and his almighty power. But to achieve this we must give ourselves over to him in spirit and understanding.

Another form of healing power is light, spiritual and intellectual light. It kills the germs of darkness and disorder. We can cast out worry, sin, and guilt by our study and by our industry. We ought to read some good religious books to prime our spiritual pumps. Napoleon Hill wrote a book entitled *Think and Grow Rich*. But we can think and grow spiritual, we can think and grow friendly, we can think and grow powerful. A magnificent religious fertility can occur in us, and we can have a dozen of the greatest impulses ripening in our lives at the same time.

The Church and the gospel provide the atmosphere in which we may turn up the power and the purpose in our souls by our righteous, positive, peaceful, powerful, creative silence. With our help, God has the power to take an ordinary person and make an extraordinary person out of him. Frequently God uses even a period of sleep as a time to get ideas into our minds. Certainly we need a time of quiet. When our minds are jumping from one thing to another and our attention is constantly being distracted, the greatest miracles can pass us by without giving us their blessings.

The Lord has said, "Hear, and your soul shall live." (Isaiah 55:3.) In this context, *hear* may mean a great deal more than merely to listen with the outer ears. It means that we must hear not only what comes through our ears from the outside, but also the still small voice of the Spirit, and we need to hear and understand those godly impulses that arise in our own hearts.

What peace can come in God's holy temple where there is absolute reverence and silence! Think how this peace would be disturbed if the honking of automobiles, the shouting of vendors, or the dissonant sounds of the world were admitted. Certainly constant walking in and out of the room could change the whole personality of this service of worship. If our contact with spiritual power is being continually interrupted and broken, the message does not get through.

The church building is not merely a classroom or a place of recreation. It is also a temple, a place dedicated to the worship of God, where we may receive communications from him. Certainly one should not go grudgingly to church in a spirit of unhappiness, nor should any confusion or disorder be permitted there. All tensions should be erased; all problems should be left behind. God is not the author of confusion but of peace and joy.

Christianity is a religion of happiness, and one good way to attain this condition is by the quiet and sanctity of worship.

Many people have rumpus rooms in their homes. There are also many people who have rumpus rooms in their lives, the spirit of which they carry with them everywhere they go. Sometimes the spirit of the gymnasium or the rumpus room is brought into the sacred areas of the church. We ought to have quiet rooms in our lives where we can regularly practice creative silence. The ancients used to take off their sandals and wash their feet at the door before entering a house. Their rest was more comfortable if their feet had been cleansed and refreshed by washing. We should likewise shed our worldly considerations at the door of the church and dress ourselves in the spirit of worship.

The great apostle Paul said, "For God hath not given us the spirit of fear; but of power, and of love, and of a sound mind." (2 Timothy 1:7.) He has given us also the spirit of peace and calmness within ourselves, if we will, that we may communicate with him in our worship. May God bless us that it may be so.

Chapter 41

Ushers
and Greeters

Two important Church functions that we don't always do very well are ushering and greeting. In these, as well as all other important leadership assignments, both in and out of the Church, it is necessary that particular attention should be paid to the selection, training and supervision of leaders. Because we so readily absorb the attitudes of those around us, a good usher should be enthusiastic about his calling. He should have a substantial appreciation of the privilege of attending church. He should also possess a radiant spirituality and a fine sense of fellowship. Because spiritual traits are contagious, a friendly, spiritual usher can often set the tone for an entire meeting. Inasmuch as a trained man is always more effective than an untrained man, a good usher should be well drilled in the scope and importance of his opportunities. Some suggestions for more profitable ushering are as follows:

Ushers should personally know as many as possible of the people they will meet at church, and know something of their virtues and problems. Ushers should be on a personal, friendly, happy basis with each member of the ward. It can be a great boost to Church activities when ushers do their job with dignity, friendliness, skill, and responsibility over a long enough period of time to acquire excellence in their calling.

Over a period of many years, I observed a really great usher in operation. He used to write down in his usher's notebook the names and addresses and telephone numbers of all newcomers. Not only did he make them welcome, but he arranged a meeting for them with the bishop. While he was an usher, everyone felt that they belonged and were completely welcome. There were no strangers in that ward. What a contrast is presented when ushers are not functioning as they should!

A woman reported that during the previous twelve months she had persuaded her husband, a prospective elder, to go to church with her five different times. On none of these occasions had anyone offered to speak to them, shake hands, or show any other sign of friendship or interest. They probably got there a little late and sat down on the back row. No one spoke to them and they spoke to no one. What a godsend a good usher would have been who would have gotten acquainted with them and then met them after church and introduced them to a few friendly, likable people, including the bishop!

Airlines and other businesses have stewardesses to make people feel at home. Even movie houses have ushers on hand to take their patrons to their seats. Church ushers sometimes congregate near the door and point at vacant seats. If theatre ushers did that they would certainly not be functioning properly in their jobs.

Some members frequently come to a church meeting thirty or more minutes ahead of starting time. This time before the meeting begins can be very profitably used for greetings, introductions and meditations. Ushers should be the first arrivals at church and should be on hand throughout the meeting. The people who arrive early can be given a friendly greeting and be seated in the proper place. Ushers can help people overcome their natural tendency to sit along the aisles or mass in the rear of the hall. They can also eliminate the necessity for latecomers to go all the way down to the front of the chapel or to climb over the feet of those already seated in order to reach the vacant seats in the middle of the row.

By seating people as soon as they come in, the habit of congregating in the aisles can be avoided and those annoying bottlenecks in the entrance halls and in other sections of the building can be eliminated.

With the expert direction of a good usher, people will feel more free to take a seat close to those who are already seated, and thus it will be unnecessary for the presiding officer to waste valuable time doing the ushering from the pulpit. The ushers can also greatly assist with the order of the meeting.

During the early part of a stake conference, the stake president took a great deal of time in bringing the people to order and getting them seated. On five different occasions he announced that there were still some vacant seats in the front of the chapel and some on the stand. Those who were standing in the rear were asked to come forward and take those seats, but they seemed too timid and were reluctant to do as he directed. Because they were unattended by ushers, only three responded to the invitation and many of the best seats remained unoccupied throughout the entire meeting, yet some of the people stood during all of the sessions and others became discouraged and left the building. This need for "pulpit ushering" is very wasteful of time, and often the spirit of the meeting is seriously disrupted by it.

Many people have had their feelings hurt when well-trained, responsible ushers are not available to manage seating arrangements. Valuable worship time and educational opportunities can be saved and the entire spirit of a conference can be greatly improved by effective ushering. Ten minutes lost by each of 1500 people amounts to 250 hours, or over thirty eight-hour days. But a 20 percent reduction in the spirit of the meeting or the learning ability of those present because they can't hear or because they have their attention distracted can be responsible for an even greater loss.

In greeting and ushering, as in so many other important activities, a great deal depends upon the vision and responsibility of those assigned to do the job. This particular assignment contains some of our finest Church opportunities to do good. As in other areas, much depends on leadership. People who do not understand their job, or who are too timid, or untrained, or unenthusiastic are seldom very effective as ushers. This assignment is sometimes used as a "make work" project for those who themselves may be comparatively inactive in the Church or who lack sufficient aggressiveness and friendliness for this particular assignment. When an usher is suffering from some Word of Wisdom violations or from guilt or inferiority complexes, he may so draw within himself that the possible benefit to others is lost. On the other hand, this could be a wonderful opportunity for those who have been inactive, if they are fully instructed, fully trained, fully supervised, and fully responsive. Their tenure in office should be long enough to give them assurance, influence and enthusiastic public relations with all of the ward members.

It frequently happens that at sacrament meetings and stake conferences many young people are loitering in the halls during meeting time, or walking around the grounds, or sitting in their cars. This is sometimes done by the same young people Sunday after Sunday. They feel perfectly safe from supervision and instruction because all of the responsible leaders are in the meetings. Certainly this is one place where some good, friendly, interested ushers can do a lot of good missionary work. They can attract the interest of these young people and help keep them from developing bad habits. They can help them instead to form the good habits of effective churchgoers with fine inclinations toward worship and learning.

An alert, thoughtful usher may also do other things such as helping families sit together. He may encourage those having special problems to take advantage of quiet rooms, such as the Relief Society and other rooms, that have been especially prepared to provide for those needing these accommodations. He may assist those with special needs to find a seat on the aisle or close to an exit.

Obedience is the first law of heaven, and order springs from it. The Lord's house is a house of order, and ushers are his instruments for creating and maintaining that condition.

Chapter 42

Personal Appearance

An important factor in any success is a clean, wholesome personal appearance. One who expects to be a successful salesman, a successful teacher, or a successful anything else should take a bath every morning and wear clean, well-pressed, appropriate clothing. He should be well-shaven and have a proper haircut. Certainly he should not wear ludicrous clothing that would distract the attention of his prospective customers or make his friends ashamed of him. He must not have dirty fingernails, soiled clothing, or bad breath. His shoes should be shined and he should have a happy, helpful, honest attitude about himself, his work, other people, and life in general.

Someone has said that while clothes do not make the man, they do account for about 95 percent of all that one ever sees of him. And what a person is, on the outside, has a great deal of influence over how he responds on the inside. The Lord has made great promises to those who have clean hands and a pure heart. (Psalm 24:3-5.) And in many instances these two qualities go together and depend upon each other.

We are influenced by the appearance of others. Certainly women who dress immodestly can cause various immoral responses in themselves and in others. It has been demonstrated that when people dress in the uniform of rebellion they soon attract others to join their ranks. But when men and women are properly groomed, attractively dressed, spotlessly clean, and wholesome in attitude, they inspire others. The opposite condition also causes exactly the opposite result.

I once watched a parade in which many groups of people were dressed to represent various nations, accomplishments, and ideologies. Those playing Scottish bagpipes were dressed in kilts. The Shriners had on their traditional red hats. Some people were dressed as pilgrims and some as pioneers. Some wore badges representing political candidates. There were clowns with painted faces and ludicrous costumes that matched the frivolous spirit they represented. It is much easier for a person to do foolish things when he has a foolish expression painted on his face and is foolishly dressed.

In the sixties we had an influence born into our society in the form of a great rebellion. Some people became very unhappy with conditions and began to defy time-honored social conventions. They exhibited a strange desire to tear down the "establishment" and destroy the property of others. Instead of helping, some wanted to overthrow the system of government which God himself established. Many felt that they had a right to dictate to and harass legally elected or appointed officers. The great rebellion was staged also against parents and against God. Many large communal camps were established where new styles in living were adopted, based on rebellion. There emerged a "new" morality that makes the grossest kinds of immorality, dope addiction, and other evils acceptable conduct for its adherents. As a kind of uniform or badge of recognition, those involved took to dressing themselves in dirty, offensive clothing, letting their hair and whiskers grow, and allowing their personal appearance to deteriorate about as much as possible. They marched in their own protest parades, carrying placards downgrading the government and shouting obscenities at the police.

Such people represent the worst in our society and their actions tend to pull everyone down by destroying harmony, morality, and unity. They increase taxation and weaken the economy. This terrible sponsorship of ugliness and evil has infected many and has swept over our country like a plague.

In trying to help these young people, the Church has called the attention of everyone to the unchanging standards of conduct that are acceptable to the Lord. Thirty-four hundred years ago from the top of Mount Sinai he gave the Ten Commandments, which contain very definite instructions against immorality, dishonesty, profanity, violation of the Sabbath day, and so on. He has given us the Word of Wisdom, and he has said, "Be ye clean that bear the vessels of the Lord." (D&C 38:42; 133:5.)

The Lord has made it clear that governments were instituted by him for the benefit of men and that he himself established the United States of America on Christian principles under an inspired Constitution. The Church also teaches that high standards of dress and personal appearance are very important. It strongly advocates modesty in dress and suggests that everyone should maintain an attractive personal appearance as befitting our relationship to that great being in whose image we were created. The Church is pleased when those representing it in the mission field are clean and attractive in every good way so as not to give the impression that they represent or have any connection with those representing the worst in life.

This principle of modesty and attractive appearance does not apply only to missionaries. It applies to all good Church leaders and members. Certainly a returned missionary or a member of a bishopric should not have standards below those set for members serving as missionaries. Someone with a bushy moustache and long hair said that he was asked a dozen times a week, "Who are you rebelling against?" When we put on a uniform of rebellion we may naturally expect to be judged by the standards that our appearance suggests to others.

If, during the war with Nazi Germany, an American soldier had gone into battle dressed in a German uniform, waving a Nazi swastika and shouting, "Heil Hitler!" he might well have expected to be treated as a traitor to his country. Everyone is judged by the uniform he wears. Dirt and unsightly hair on the outside can be a sign of something wrong on the inside.

In a Church leadership meeting there was a man all decked out in whiskers, sideburns, moustache and long hair. I didn't know who he was, but I felt very sorry for him because of the kind of attention and pity that he was getting. I thought what a benefit it would be to him if someone with stable character qualities would spend some time with him and help him understand the kind of impression he made on others. This distortion of his personal appearance could prevent him from having a normal, happy association with normal, happy people.

There are some people who claim that an unkempt appearance is merely a style, but it is much more than that. It is also an outward symbol of an inward condition. Some may claim that participating in protest marches or shouting obscenities at the police is merely a style, but the people who do it will soon be a different kind of people.

We have many good styles to choose from. Some might argue that smoking or the "new" morality are merely styles of behavior. But we will be much better off if we put on the uniform of righteousness and act accordingly. In this, as in many other things, people need the personal help and counsel of someone who can help them not to make a spectacle of themselves. If they don't wear the uniform of evil and rebellion it will be easier for them to resist the temptation to adopt the standards of evil and rebellion.

A man joined the Church in a little branch where a comparatively large number of people had allowed themselves some serious deviation in dress and manners. The man soon left the Church with a statement that it was very unpleasant for him to associate and be identified with what he referred to as the "wrong kind of people."

Our appearance is important, both in helping us to become the kind of people we want to be and in representing our Savior as members of his Church on earth. As his ambassadors, we need to adopt and encourage wholesome, clean, and modest clothing, and practice high standards of personal grooming and behavior.

Chapter 43

Beware of Permissiveness

One of the things that I remember best from the first time I heard Shakespeare's play, *Julius Caesar*, was the ghostly voice of the soothsayer chanting the unearthly refrain, "Beware the ides of March." This was the day that had been set by conspirators to murder Caesar.

This little word *beware* might well be chanted in the ears of a great many other people. What a lot of troubles President Nixon could have avoided for himself and for the entire world if he had had a soothsayer chanting in his ear, "Beware of Watergate, beware of wire tapping, beware of improper recordings, beware of untruthfulness, beware of false statements and wrongdoing"!

A little thoughtfulness before our weaknesses are developed and before our evil is committed could save us a great deal of trouble later on. Our highways are marked by a great many caution signs which say, "Dangerous Curves Ahead," "Slippery Pavement," "Deer Crossing," "Road Under Construction," "Beware of Falling Rocks," and so on.

State law will not allow a bus driver to drive without time between trips to sleep, or with any amount of alcohol in his veins. His own mental caution signs say to him: "Beware of drowsiness and drunkenness." The holy scriptures also have some important *bewares*. In substance they say, "Beware of sloth, beware of false pride, beware of false prophets, beware lest men shall deceive you." In one of the most important "bewares" of the scriptures, the Lord said: "And I now give unto you a commandment to beware concerning yourselves, to give diligent heed to the words of eternal life." (D&C 84:43.)

There could not be much argument about the fact that we are our own worst enemies. It is for this reason that this book hoists a beware sign on our leadership. It says, "Beware of permissiveness."

Permissiveness is a situation in which we tolerate unworthy standards and make them allowable or even acceptable to ourselves. Permissiveness has at its center a philosophy which encourages people to endlessly "do their own thing." That is, doing endlessly what one wants to do, whether it is right or wrong; permitting experiences for other reasons than that they are right or good. It is a serious sin and also a manifestation of very bad judgment to continue to do those things which are not in our best interests. This idea of permissiveness is in direct opposition to the philosophy of the gospel, which says that we should always do the right thing, that we should keep our feet securely on the straight and narrow way instead of following the path of least resistance or the one that offers us some merely temporary advantage and has danger and unpleasantness at its end.

Permissiveness is characteristic of a leadership which does not adequately lead or which leads in the wrong direction. I attended a ward sacrament meeting where the eight deacons who were passing the sacrament sat restlessly on the front row. In full view of the bishopric, they kicked and pushed and annoyed each other during the entire meeting. Not one attempt was made by anyone to restore order. The bishop seemed to have the attitude that if these boys wanted to do their own thing by violating the sacredness of this holy ordinance in which they were the chief participants, he would not attempt to influence them to a higher level of conduct. I was disturbed by the disorder and I am sure a great many other people were, but I could not help feeling sorry for these boys because of their misfortune in growing up under the direction of a bishop who had this kind of attitude toward his job.

It would be such an easy thing for a fine bishop to get

these young men into an intimate meeting and talk to them about the sacredness of their high calling of being the Lord's ministers in distributing the sacred emblems of his atonement to other worshippers. They could be reminded how pleased the Lord would be if they had a proper understanding and reverence for the holy sacrifice he made for us when he redeemed us from death. Often, because young men have not been properly trained, they do not understand how badly they are being cheated by their own misconduct. And as members of the Church, bearing the Aaronic Priesthood, and presided over by a high priest who should have their welfare in his heart, they have an inherent right to expect the bishop to train them in the formation of good habits and good attitudes toward the Church and an exercise of reverence and order in the house of the Lord.

What a tragedy it is for young boys full of life and energy to be leaderless in such important spiritual affairs! They are forming habits that will continue to influence them as long as they live. For the bishop to be so completely passive is, to them, actually a confirmation of the acceptableness of their misbehavior. Some of these boys may also have this kind of disadvantage in their homes if their parents do not take the time to teach them righteousness and the tremendous profitability of good behavior, so that they are left to be harmfully and irresponsibly free to do their own thing, not knowing the disastrous results of the consequences of every evil activity.

What a simple thing it would be for a good bishop to build character and manliness and reverence and faith into these young men under his direction!

Many surveys have been made indicating the qualities that young people want in their parents and in their Church leaders. Some of these are righteousness, good judgment, firmness, and a kind of expert ability to produce champions in those being led. They want to believe wholeheartedly in the integrity and capability of those to whom they look for success. They want to feel a great love for their organization and an inspiring confidence in their leaders whom they would like to resemble.

A tremendous enemy of a high morale and the qualities of excellence and success is permissiveness in our leadership. What kind of a football team would one have or what kind of a marriage or a business organization would result if everyone worked individually according to his own rules and always did his own thing whether it be wrong or right or helpful or destructive? Suppose we consider some hypothetical examples of what we might call permissive leadership, and then see to it that nothing resembling it is ever allowed to get into our own affairs.

Bishop A has a large percentage of tardiness at his meetings. The bishop himself sets the example; he is not punctual. Time schedules are not very important to him. Meetings start late. He himself is frequently not on time. Over the years his ward members have formed the habit of arriving at church when they feel like it, and they know that a great many others will also be tardy. People also feel at perfect liberty to leave the meeting before it is finished. What a simple thing it would be for an orderly bishop to train an orderly congregation, and give his group the appearance of the highest level of uniformity and the greatest standards of excellence!

It is unlikely that a disorderly leader will ever produce orderly followers who have pride in their organization, their leadership, and themselves. A bishop with good, orderly, personal habits could get his people together and discuss the situation. People would be able to see the value of observing and teaching promptness and punctuality in all the things they did. Not everyone would be perfect in this matter at first. It would require a little training. There could be some friendly, helpful personal interviews with those who needed special help. Many people would be delighted to come fifteen minutes ahead of time and enjoy a few minutes of friendship and hear an inspiring preliminary period of sacred music. If everyone else was punctual and happy, with a pleasant leadership, no one would want to break this harmony by doing his own thing.

A Sunday School class taught by Sunday School teacher B was unbelievably chaotic, and the reasons were easy to see.

Certainly she did not have the spirit of teaching. She did not have the spirit of the gospel. She did not have the spirit of friendliness and personal interest in the children under her direction. As soon as the class began she put her nose in the book and tried to read the lesson, but it seemed as though this was her first time over it. Many of the words in the lesson she could not pronounce. It appeared that she was almost completely unfamiliar with the material. Naturally the children were not interested, and they were doing their own thing while she was trying to do hers. The fact that no one was listening seemed to make no difference to her as she went steadily on. Any one of these young children could have told this teacher how to improve her lesson.

Such a statement as the one made above may seem to some to be critical or negative. A leader sometimes contributes to a problem when he shuts his eyes and closes his ears and does not, in love and kindness, try to remedy a bad situation.

The bishop of ward X does not know how to get his people to come to sacrament meeting. He takes the attitude that it is their business. Someone once questioned him about it and he said, "I can't force them to come if they don't want to." He could, however, make them want to come if he would provide a better atmosphere and more interesting meetings, and would exhibit more encouragement, love and friendship for his ward members. It has been said, "You can lead a horse to water but you can't make him drink." But there are several ways of making a horse thirsty; then he will want to drink by himself.

The President of the Church has made many appeals that we should be the most reverent people in the world. And that is what every good Latter-day Saint would like to see happen. But the meetings which we hold do not always convey that impression. Suppose that you were appointed by the Lord or by the President of the Church to write up a set of suggestions, the implementation of which would convince everybody who attended our meetings that we were the most reverent people in the world. If you felt perfectly competent in this assignment and unafraid of being called critical, what would you say? That is, what are the things that we are doing that we should not do, and what are the things that we are presently not doing that we should do?

Anyone who conscientiously made such a study and who had the leadership to get his ideas accepted would probably discover that he had added a large number of names to the list of those eligible for the celestial kingdom. High morale and expert leadership usually go up together.

Chapter 44

Sacrament Meeting Ingredients

The following is a list of some of the ingredients which should be included in the planning and conduct of a sacrament meeting. A good planner and manager should be completely familiar with each item.

1. Good meeting management. (See chapter 39.)

2. There should be something provided for those who come. Bishop Marvin O. Ashton used to say that when we invite someone to church we should always make sure there is plenty of hay in the manger.

3. The physical facilities, air conditioning, sound system, temperature controls, cleanliness, decorations, etc., should all be well provided for.

4. The meeting should have a decided spiritual tone and atmosphere. It should be such a meeting that the Spirit of the Lord and the spirit of happiness would attend. It should also be the kind of place where the people would delight to come.

5. The music should be appropriate and of high quality. Every ward ought to have a well-trained choir, as well as a membership well trained in their understanding of and ability to sing and enjoy our great hymns.

6. There should be effectively prepared speakers. A good sacrament service should not be devoted primarily to travelogues or entertainment. Much training should be given to help prepare speakers to give an inspiring, stimulating

message to the members. Dr. Adam S. Bennion used to say that in every sacrament meeting there should be better music and more of it, and better speaking and less of it.

If speakers are assigned two minutes ahead of time to give a ten-minute talk, they get a total of twelve minutes of development. If they are assigned three months in advance to make a ten-minute talk, they may get three months and ten minutes of development. A good speech instructor could do much to help members of the ward make an effective preparation as speakers.

7. One of the greatest success factors is timeliness. There should be proper prelude and postlude music. Meetings should begin and close on time. Speakers should not use the time allotted to others. Leaders should be in their places well in advance of starting time.

8. Punctuality plus—some wards and some individuals form a very bad habit of tardiness. In a well-ordered church meeting, people ought to be in their places well in advance of the time when the meeting is scheduled to begin. Members should be trained to arrive at sacrament meeting early enough to enjoy the beauty of the surroundings, and the fellowship of the members, and to get the spirit of the meeting and of the prelude music.

9. Friendly professional greeters. (See chapter 41.)

10. Involve all members in fellowshipping in a substantial way.

11. Reverence for God and a feeling of sensitivity for the welfare of others.

12. Individual coaching—some members will need individual help outside of meeting time in preparing talks and maintaining order. Some will need personal coaching about their grooming and individual appearance. An effective counselor can do much in assisting ward members in their personal affairs. (See chapter 42.)

13. All home teachers should regularly attend sacrament meeting and be involved before and after the meeting with the families for whom they have responsibility. It might also be very helpful during the home teaching visit to have a discussion and follow-up on the lessons taught in sacrament meeting.

14. Home teachers should see to it that the members of their teaching families, as well as their personal families, are present and made to feel welcome and that they are an important part of the sacrament meeting.

15. Every member should be personally involved in the meeting in some specific way. Every member of the ward is very important to the ward's success.

16. As part of ward management it should be arranged that every family of the ward pays an appropriate amount of ward maintenance so that he will get the full benefit of that great principle: "Where your treasure is, there will your heart be also." (Luke 12:34.)

17. Every family should subscribe to and read the Church magazines. This can help every individual to get the spirit of worship for the sacrament meeting itself.

18. There should be an effective, authoritative follow-up by the home teachers on the absenteeism of their family members to let them know that they were missed and to see that any curable cause for the absenteeism is corrected so that it does not become a habit.

19. Every ward should see to it that they have a good set of sacrament meeting statistics. All the members should understand that their ward is a "going concern" in all of the best meaning of that term.

20. High morale—members should all be made to feel proud of the ward. It should be the kind of place where they would love to take their out-of-town friends as a means of helping them to become enthusiastic about the Church. The ward, its officers, and its members constitute the ward's showcase and represent The Church of Jesus Christ of Latter-day Saints. (See chapter 21.)

21. Physical environment—expert attention should be paid to the appearance of the grounds and buildings, as well as to flowers, decorations, and the atmosphere in the meeting-house itself.

22. Personal appearance of members—the Church has established standards which they advise missionaries and students at the Church schools to maintain. It is much more important that these high standards should be maintained in the temples and in the ward meetinghouse, which has also

been dedicated to the worship of God. Certainly the highest standards of appearance and conduct should be maintained by bishoprics, quorums and auxiliary leaders, music leaders, ushers, teachers, and those who supervise, administer, and pass the sacrament, as well as all others. Everyone has blind spots so far as he himself is concerned, and a little personal, private, friendly counseling could accomplish wonders in improving the personal appearance of members and the esprit de corps that comes as a consequence. (See chapter 42.)

23. Everyone should be able to clearly hear the program. Frequently people complain that they cannot hear or cannot understand the speaker. He may not use the microphone or he may have a very quiet voice or may not enunciate distinctly. Much of the good of the meeting depends on being able to clearly hear what is said without straining or irritation. A good bishop should be the members' guarantee that everyone will clearly hear and understand what is said by each and every speaker.

24. Ward bulletin—some wards send out a weekly letter to their members. This letter can be a kind of ward promotion and educational letter.

25. The members should be fully persuaded of the purpose of the sacrament meeting and the importance of their individual attendance each week.

26. There should be dignity, order, thorough preparation, and good meeting organization behind the pulpit. Probably the biggest reason why family home night or home teaching or marriage fails is lack of preparation. It is important that a speaker or a Sunday School teacher be thoroughly prepared, not only with his materials but with his attitudes and his spirit. The one conducting the meeting should also be prepared. He should not mumble his words or be asleep on his feet. His attitude of love and spirituality and enthusiasm should carry a message that goes even beyond his words. (See chapter 39.)

27. The bishop should probably make a regular survey as to why all absentees, including prospective elders, are not coming to sacrament meeting. A doctor frequently makes a postmortem examination to determine why an operation was

unsuccessful. A good salesman frequently makes a post-mortem examination of lost sales. A good lawyer should consider every legal case as to why it was won or lost. Certainly the bishop should know the reasons for the success or failure of a sacrament meeting and what should be done about it. (See chapter 36.)

28. A good bishop should make a mental survey after each sacrament meeting as to how it could have been improved. No good bishop should ever "turn off his hearing aid" so that he hears only what is pleasant to hear.

29. Every sacrament meeting should have a reverent, inspiring sacrament service conducted by Aaronic Priesthood members who are well dressed, well mannered, and well prepared in every other way.

30. (To be filled in by the reader.)

Suppose you now go over the above list and see which items in your opinion should be modified and which others could be added.

Now, here are some things not to do:

1. Don't scold from the pulpit. A church meeting is not a good place to "get after" those who are not present. Counseling should usually be done on a personal, private basis.

2. Don't collect funds or sell Church magazines from the pulpit.

3. It should not be necessary to do ushering from the pulpit.

4. Don't advertise failure or defects over the pulpit.

Part Eight

Problems
and Pitfalls

Eyes That See Not
Feelings of Inadequacy
Failure's Big Four

Chapter 45

Eyes That See Not

The greatest invention ever made in heaven or in earth occurred on that important sixth day of creation when God made his greatest masterpiece—man.

Not only did God create the spirit of man in the likeness of God, but he also fashioned a physical body to match. As a part of this godly invention, God gave us potentially magnificent brains, miraculous personalities, and matchless spirits. He gave us the marvelous gift of vision which may reach out across the world or look up to the stars. He gave us a wonderful sense of hearing which may bring back to us all of the symphonies and harmonies of the universe. He ordained our divine destiny; and, according to the laws of heredity, the offspring of God may eventually hope to become like their eternal heavenly parents.

God has given each one of us many potential abilities and gifts, and we profane God's magnificence when they are not fully developed and used. We should not only seek the best gifts, but seek to develop them to their maximum of usefulness. We sometimes allow our abilities to deteriorate and permit our gifts to lapse. This neglect may cause the godly mechanism itself to malfunction and bring difficulties to us and to all of those around us.

Probably our most serious malfunctions take place because we fail either to hear or to see effectively. Often we fail to hear and see our own shortcomings. Then, even when our conscience begins to bother us, we insist upon maintaining our self-esteem by turning our conscience off so that we can no longer hear its troubling admonitions. One of the most serious weaknesses of leadership is that we train ourselves to ignore the difficult things we should do which are in the best interests of those being led. We permit the grossest kind of leadership malfunctions because real leadership would require that we take some action which would necessitate too much planning and effort. Every leader should remember the story of Kitty Genovese of New York City. This woman had neighbors who allowed her to lose her life to a murderer merely because they did not want to get involved. Involvement would have meant effort and courage, which they were not willing to give.

Every leadership situation calls for skill, courage, and industry. If we are to be worthy of our office, we must be able to apply these elements in the right places in the necessary volume and intensity. As a kind of prototype of a hearing and seeing leader, I envision the director of a great symphony orchestra standing to instruct and coordinate the efforts of the players of eighty-five musical instruments. The maestro knows that the effect produced by the total orchestra will be determined by the individual successes of its members. He also knows that the discordant performance of one player can destroy the inspiration and harmony of the entire orchestra. He knows that the secret of the orchestra's success rests entirely in his leadership. I can visualize eighty-five individual communication lines going from the leader out through his ears to keep him in contact with each individual musician so that there is not one instrument in the entire orchestra that he does not hear, and there is not one mistake that is not carried immediately to the directing center of his mind. Then, by his instruction and inspiration, the destructive discord may be changed into constructive inspiration.

Some time ago during a great symphony concert participated in by some celebrated artists, and listened to by a large group of music lovers, a disturbance arose in the rear of the hall. The leader continued as long as he could, dreading the embarrassment that would come to everyone if he stopped the orchestra while the source of distraction was removed. But his finely tuned mind could not function while the discord prevailed, so he stopped the symphony and suffered all of the embarrassment which came to him because he was forced to ask that the discord be removed. Each one of the thousands of people present suffered because of one who was insensitive to the welfare of those around him. Because of him, the inspirational balance of the leader could not be regained during the entire remaining period of the concert.

There are many leaders in spiritual, political, educational, and business affairs who, instead of making the correction, merely tune out the discord. They become as an orchestra leader would be if he trained himself to tolerate as much discord as could come from a multitude of participants. For the sake of comparison, suppose that the orchestra leader should close his ears to all the mistakes of his players. It would then not be possible for him to correct them, and he would be in the same position as the artist who closes his eyes to the imperfections in his painting, or one who aspired to religious success but who closes his eyes to the many sins and weaknesses to which he is liable. In each case a potentially inspiring achievement would be smothered by problems.

On one occasion before a challenger got into the prize fight ring with Jack Dempsey, his friend said to him, "While you are in the ring with Dempsey, be sure to keep your eyes open." His friend asked why. "Simply because," he replied, "no one should ever run the risk involved of getting into the fight ring with Jack Dempsey with his eyes shut." Likewise, no Church, political, business, or other leader will ever do very well who has eyes that don't see and ears that don't hear the things that could seriously jeopardize the best interests of those being led.

There are some would-be sales managers who allow their salesmen to develop devastating weaknesses which the sales manager should know in advance will lead the salesmen to failure and the loss of their jobs. A Church leader who has eyes that see not or ears that hear not or a heart that fails to understand may permit the loss of someone's eternal life, when his duty is to perfect that person's life.

There are employers and other leaders who close their eyes to dishonesty and immorality among those under their direction, and they allow these sinful blotches to grow until the picture is spoiled by a contagion which could have been stopped if it had been treated in time. We know the story of the rotten apple in the barrel, of which there are many spiritual and moral parallels. But if the correction cannot be made, the apple should be taken out of the barrel so that it does not jeopardize the welfare of those near it.

There are some leaders who close both their eyes and their ears to the discords of irreverence and confusion in their membership because they lack the courage and the skill necessary for inspiring, constructive leadership. Some leaders seem to feel that if they keep their eyes and ears closed, the discord will go away by itself. In many cases, this is like assuming that the rotten apple in the barrel will stop its devastating contagion merely if no one notices it.

A great Church leader has said that if we fail in our leadership responsibility it is as though we ourselves are guilty of the damage caused.

President McKay was performing the function of a great orchestra leader when he used to say at general conferences that he was glad to welcome everyone to general conference but that, when they came, it would be appreciated if they would remain throughout the meeting and not disrupt the attention of others by leaving before the end of the meeting.

In one stake, the stake clerk counted 276 moving violations during one stake conference.

At the rededication ceremony of the Arizona Temple, President Kimball said, "You are now in a dedicated building and all unnecessary conversation should be eliminated. If any communication is necessary, see that you do it in whispers." In going through the Salt Lake Temple with a group of people who were fully aware of their responsibility for reverence and silence, the one in charge said in the very beginning of the meeting, as he does in every similar meeting, "We would like to remind you that this building has been dedicated to the worship of God and there should be no whispering."

Those who come to sacrament meeting likewise come to a dedicated building where reverence and peace and quiet should prevail. One cannot show respect and reverence in the house of the Lord without building up respect and reverence to the Lord himself in one's own soul. What a thrilling thing it is to go to the house of the Lord with reverent, sensitive co-worshippers who have their minds tuned to the worship of God! It is unfortunate when our minds are drawn off the wave length of his Spirit by the distractions around us or within us.

The Presidency of the Church has written numerous appeals to stake and ward leaders requesting that reverence be maintained in all of our Church meetings. This instruction has been and is being disregarded in many instances.

A similar attitude prevailed in the mind of King Saul, who completely disregarded the direction of the Lord. The prophet Samuel said to him, "Behold, to obey is better than sacrifice, and to hearken than the fat of rams." (1 Samuel 15:22.) In reproving Saul, Samuel said, "Because thou hast rejected the word of the Lord, he hath also rejected thee from being king." (1 Samuel 15:23.) We have no evidence that the Lord has changed his procedure in regard to those who fail to follow his direction.

The ostrich has been maligned by some who have accused it of burying its head in the sand when danger threatens, hoping that the danger would go away if the ostrich didn't see it. Actually, this would give the predator his greatest opportunity. I have checked this accusation out with those who are supposed to know, and they have said that no ostrich ever does this. But in a little different way, many human beings actually do. As has been said, all that is necessary for evil to prosper is for good men to do nothing. All that a Sunday School teacher or a bishop or a stake president or even a Solomon has to do to liquidate that part of the work of the Lord for which he is responsible is to close his eyes so that he sees not and stop his ears so that he hears not those dangers that threaten to destroy our souls. Richard Moreland put this idea in verse when he wrote:

It was such a little, little sin
And such a great big day,
That I thought the hours would swallow it
Or the wind blow it away.

But the hours passed so quickly
And the wind died out somehow,
And the sin that was a weakling once
Is a hungry giant now.

The way to stop a herd of stampeding buffalo is not by standing in their pathway and defying their progress. Nor is it a good idea to attempt to train people by issuing ultimatums about their sins. But there is a way to stop sins and produce order and exaltation in human lives, and that is by developing a keen distinction between right and wrong, between reverence and irreverence, between religion and irreligion. We need to develop the characteristics of the orchestra leader who has his eyes and ears open and is able to transform the discords of his players into the most inspiring harmonies. When we turn off our seeing and hearing or hide our heads in the sand, Satan has his greatest opportunity to put us in conflict with ourselves and reduce the excellence in our lives to mediocrity.

All around us, however, we still see many people who are highly insensitive to their own conduct. And if they are not helped, the evil may increase and flourish more abundantly in them. Their disease may infect others. What every good orchestra needs is a great leader who knows his job and who can tell the difference between harmony and discord and who can produce the one and eliminate the other in the activity of his players.

To the extent that Church leaders have the abilities to do these things, we may develop a membership with a greatly improved spirituality and success. The First Presidency once wrote a letter addressed to the members of the Church, the first sentence of which was "We earnestly call upon members of the Church everywhere to clean up and beautify their homes, surroundings, farms and places of business." They have also given a great many instructions that we should clean up our lives so that we can act and lead with greater effectiveness. This is also the primary message of the scriptures.

We can build great spiritual excellence and every other success by hearing and following the approved program of the Church.

Chapter 46

Feelings
of Inadequacy

Over the years as I have interviewed people to fill Church assignments, they have frequently expressed the feeling that they thought they were worthy of the assignment, but then they have added, "I feel so inadequate." Some time ago, I looked up this word to make sure that I understood what it meant. The dictionary says that one who is inadequate is one who is insufficient and lacks the necessary power of adaptation. He is deficient in those qualities necessary for success. One of the disadvantages under which most of us labor is the inadequacy of our thought and our speech.

Verbally we sometimes express a feeling of false modesty; or we say things we do not mean merely to make conversation. Sometimes, by this inaccurate speech, we help produce the very inadequacy we talk about. That is, we sell ourselves on what we tell ourselves. Many of us become inadequate because we hold thoughts of inadequacy in our minds. On the other hand, if we actually feel inadequate we are fostering a serious fault. If we live with an inferiority complex long enough, it makes itself permanent. A psychiatrist once said to a mental patient, "I think you have an inferiority complex." The patient said, "I don't have an inferiority complex, I'm just inferior."

The members of a medical association were told at an annual convention that ten million people in America were in serious need of treatment for depression.

A wrong attitude which we do nothing about and a habit of being satisfied with poor work can foster a condition of inadequacy, and when we overdo a sense of false modesty, we frequently intensify that condition in ourselves. To cultivate or even to tolerate feelings of inadequacy is a very serious fault which quickly grows into a bad habit that is very difficult to change.

Walter D. Wintle expressed this idea in verse when he wrote:

> If you think you are beaten, you are;
> If you think you dare not, you don't.
> If you'd like to win but you think you can't,
> It's almost a cinch you won't.
>
> If you think you'll lose, you're lost,
> For out of the world, we find,
> Success begins with a fellow's will—
> It's all in the state of mind.
>
> If you think you're outclassed, you are;
> You've got to think high to rise;
> You've got to be sure of yourself before
> You can ever win a prize.
>
> Life's battles don't always go
> To a stronger or faster man;
> But soon or late the man who wins
> Is the one who thinks he can.

During a stake conference I attended it was announced that a certain man had been released from a stake position which he had held for ten years. Then the president called on him to say a few words. The man began by saying, "I'm just as frightened to stand up before you today as I was when I stood up here ten years ago to accept this position." Then, for the next ten minutes, he breathed out over fifteen hundred people the most negative, depreciating, belittling kind of speech that one could imagine. In substance, he said, "I'm just as frightened and just as ignorant and just as sinful and just as depressed and just as worthless as I was ten years ago." And everyone knew that he was telling the truth.

We have no business being just as frightened or just as

ignorant or just as unprepared as we were ten years ago. There are ways to overcome fear. There are ways to overcome ignorance. There are ways to overcome depression. We need to know what they are. The consciousness of a high skill is one of the greatest motive factors in life, and we can build a strong habit of actual accomplishment around every ambition.

If I were selecting someone for a Church appointment, I would want to know at least three things about him.

First, is he worthy? Sometimes we develop some secret sins that never get up to the surface of our lives and yet they disqualify us for Church leadership responsibilities. If this candidate had any dishonesties or disloyalties or immoralities or any other thing that would make him unworthy, I would like to know what they were.

Second, I would like to be assured that he had no questions about the doctrines of the Church, either as to his belief in them or his practice of them. Sometimes we get an idea crossways in our minds that we can't get satisfactorily resolved and it remains there to fester and become infected and inflamed and finally malignant. We sometimes let ourselves think that we believe in something when we don't practice it. That is, we may say we believe in paying tithing but we don't actually pay an honest tithe, or we think we believe in the Word of Wisdom, but we don't live it fully. If someone had any questions about the doctrines of the Church, either as to a belief or a practice, I would want to know what they were.

Third, I would want to know if he was able and willing and would do what his assignment required. And this is probably the biggest problem we ever have in the Church or in any other leadership situation. Many people accept the honor of the assignment without the responsibility. They think it's a great idea but they don't do it.

We are reminded of the vine dresser, in the parable of Jesus, who had two sons; one was disobedient and the other was irresponsible. When the vine dresser said to these two sons, "Go and work in the vineyard," one said, "I won't go." The other said, "I go, sir," and did not go.

Jesus did not use up all of the possibilities of this situation, and someone has finished the parable by adding two other possibilities, as follows: The vine dresser's third son said, "I go, sir," and he went and he stayed until the job was done and he did it the best way it could be done. But the fourth son of the vine dresser is the one who will probably someday own the vineyard. He went to his father and said, "The vineyard needs some attention, and if you would like me to I will go and take care of it. Then he went; he stayed with the job; and he got it done in the best possible way. The fourth son had initiative. Someone has said that the world reserves its highest rewards for but one quality, and that is initiative.

Apparently the Lord also regards initiative highly. He said: "For behold, it is not meet that I should command in all things; for he that is compelled in all things, the same is a slothful and not a wise servant; wherefore he receiveth no reward. Verily I say, men should be anxiously engaged in a good cause, and do many things of their own free will, and bring to pass much righteousness.

"And inasmuch as men do good they shall in nowise lose their reward.

"But he that doeth not anything until he is commanded, and receiveth a commandment with doubtful heart, and keepeth it with slothfulness, the same is damned." (D&C 58:26-29.)

I'm not sure what all of that means to us except I think it takes a pretty dim view of any Church worker who has to be reminded two or three times a month to get his job done. I think it also has something to do with the one who does his job in a minimal way.

This feeling of inadequacy that we complain about, if tolerated, adds to our insufficiency and ineffectiveness. We ought to have some good procedures for building up our strength, as it is pretty difficult to think of ourselves as something that we are not, or at least are not aspiring to become. We ought to study the lives of men who have been adequate and effective. Suppose we had been given the job of Winston Churchill or George Washington or Abraham

Lincoln. We probably would have said, "I feel so completely inadequate."

We sometimes feel inadequate even for the pleasant little jobs wherein all we have to do is go out and preach the gospel to nonmembers, or fellowship prospective elders, or give encouragement to someone who is afraid to come to Church.

One thing the great champions do not say is, "I feel so completely inadequate." When Mr. Churchill was made the Prime Minister of Great Britain, he rejoiced at the opportunity of taking upon himself the most difficult and the most dangerous task. He talked about blood, sweat, and tears, which he offered to give gladly and enthusiastically to his countrymen. He had not thought of failure; he knew that under his leadership the nation would be saved. That is the way we ought to feel, and in order for us to have that feeling of adequacy it must be deserved.

Some time ago I read an article in the *Reader's Digest* about someone who put a block of silver next to a block of gold and left it there for two years. When these metals were taken apart, there were little flecks of silver found in the gold and little flecks of gold found in the silver. The molecular action in these metals had thrown little particles of each metal across the boundaries to be embedded in the other. There isn't any place where this principle works as well as in human beings. We are sending out radiations of ourselves to settle in all of those around us.

We must not spend our lives with this devastating feeling of inadequacy. We can build self-confidence and we can build adequacy by deserving them. Most people wait until they are called to a teaching or leadership position before they begin to get themselves prepared. We ought to become good teachers whether or not we are ever called to do formal teaching. We should do our homework on leadership before we are ever called to lead. We should always be great human beings and keep a long way ahead of every assignment.

Chapter 47

Failure's Big Four

The Lord himself has indicated that every member of the Church should be a missionary. This calling and appointment has been reaffirmed by each President of the Church. Each missionary should make sure that he is not only a missionary, but a good missionary.

It has been suggested that when we contemplate any success, we ought to see it in all of its parts. The title of this chapter has been listed negatively, as negative motivation is often stronger than positive.

As far as I know, there are four fundamental places where we might fail in our missionary work. These are:

Inadequate numbers and quality of investigators
Insufficient exposure
Ineffective presentation
Indifferent missionary.

Suppose we take these four missionary success problems, one at a time, and see how they can best be solved.

Inadequate numbers and quality of investigators: Issuing the missionary call to his apostles anciently, the Lord said, "Go ye therefore and teach all nations, baptizing them in the name of the Father, and of the Son, and of the Holy Ghost." (Matthew 28:19.) In the present dispensation he has given us the call in similar terms.

Before we can teach we must be able to find someone who is willing to listen. We may be sure that investigators will not present themselves to us in sufficient numbers to suit our purposes without our aid. We can be just as sure that no third party on his own initiative will automatically keep us supplied with investigators.

The term *investigators* may not be the best way to describe the people we are looking for. Many of those who will soon be members of the Church are not presently investigating the Church. A salesman thinks of his future customers as prospects. But whatever name we may use for future members, they are people who have a high possibility of becoming members of the Church in the near future who are presently unaware of that fact. It is suggested that we figure out how many new investigators we need each week and then work out a program for getting them with a few to spare. The Church already has an excellent program, but if those appointed do not find investigators for us, we should be prepared to find them for ourselves so that the program will not fail.

One very good way is to select some proven techniques and set up some definite standards of work. If we have definite hours of planning and definite hours of working and we allow no exceptions in our planned programs, we will soon be well on our way toward success.

Some people are better qualified to be investigators or prospective members than others. We know the kind of people we are looking for. I think of everyone as a kind of thermometer. One person may be 32 degrees below zero as far as his interest in joining the Church is concerned. Others may be about 210 degrees Fahrenheit. Two hundred twelve degrees is the point where water boils and investigators are baptized.

There are many ways to find investigators. Examples are:

Recommendations from personal centers of influence.
Observation.
Change of circumstances in the one involved.

It is suggested that you make a list of the methods you can use for effectively finding investigators; and then, under each heading, work out some good procedure for getting and qualifying these names for an interview.

Insufficient exposure: A salesman asked for help in developing his sales ability. He was asked what he conceived his problem to be. In the discussion that followed, the idea came out that he didn't have any time in his schedule to have sales interviews. He was all bogged down in an elaborate program for study, making service calls, doing public relations and handling office detail, and he didn't have any time to make calls. Good salesmen understand that sales come out of interviews. Similarly, converts come out of discussions. Some would-be missionaries fill their time with unimportant things and don't have time left for actual discussions. On the other hand, there are some people who know how to get good, solid appointments which can be used to make the presentation.

A large group of full-time missionaries indicated that while some of them gave as many as six to eight discussions in a single day, the average discussions given by the entire group was three per week per pair of missionaries. This would total 312 discussions during a two-year (104-week) mission by two missionaries. A very large percentage of these discussions are first discussions, the visits then being terminated so that the contact never gets beyond that stage. Of a total of 156 interviews per missionary during the entire course of his mission, only about twenty-two of these go beyond the first discussion. If a pair of missionaries could learn how to give three discussions per day instead of three per week, and if they could make the first discussion so interesting that the investigator would want to continue with the other discussions, the number of converts obtained would not be merely six times as many; it would be a much greater number than that. Under these improved circumstances, both exposure and effectiveness would be multiplied.

A good missionary should learn as early as possible how to effectively organize his time and his efforts so that he can keep himself occupied with an investigator for the greatest possible period, engaged in an effective discussion.

As faith without works soon dies, so faith with works grows by leaps and bounds. But if a person is going to be an effective missionary, he must have lots of investigators and he must have a lot of good, solid, interesting discussions with them.

Ineffective presentation: An effective proselyting message must be marked by interesting content, good continuity and good presentation. The missionary should know his subject matter backwards and forwards and upside down. He must be able to present it with skill and enthusiasm. He should have a strong conviction of its truth, a reassuring self-confidence about his ability to deliver it effectively, a genuine friendliness for the investigator, and a great joy in giving his message.

I listened to a series of full-time missionaries present their discussions. I sat on the third row, but for the most part I couldn't even hear the discussion. The missionary was so bound up in remembering the words that the presentation was very indistinct and lacked expression or conviction.

Like many other people, some missionaries do not enunciate clearly, and the full impact of their message therefore does not get over. What the missionary says should not only be true, but it should be well organized, interestingly given, and easily understood. If the missionary does not speak loudly enough or clearly enough or interestingly enough, the contact cannot hear without straining and without losing many of the words and much of the meaning and interest. The missionary should so thoroughly master the discussion that he can give it with apparent ease, great conviction, and obvious delight.

It might be helpful for some of us to do as Demosthenes did and practice giving our message to the waves; or we might go somewhere alone, where we could cast off our inhibitions and practice letting ourselves go so that we could become more natural and more forceful in our discussion with an investigator. Reading aloud with proper expression and clarity can be helpful. We should do a lot of memorizing and then do a lot of drilling for the feeling of ease. We should study the presentation of successful actors, lawyers, teachers, etc. The presentation of almost all highly capable people seems, to those observing, to be effortless. That is, the expert actor, teacher, salesman, doctor, and football player appear to be performing almost effortlessly.

Indifferent missionary: An important key to missionary success is found in the missionary himself. You can't deliver a great message without being a great messenger. Some people have been concerned that investigators are converted to the missionary instead of to the Church. It has never seemed to me, however, that this is a serious problem, as the convert must in any case have confidence in and love for the messenger before he wholeheartedly accepts the message.

Even the *authority* to make converts does not help us much without the *ability* to make converts. It has been pointed out that no one ever failed in any kind of human relations because too many people liked him. It is so much better if they are impressed with his integrity and his ability. A great sales organization analyzed a hundred of its worst salesmen failures to try to find out what caused their failure. They discovered that 37 percent failed because of discouragement. An additional 37 percent of the salesmen lost out because of lack of industry, and 12 percent more failed because they would not follow instructions. These are all spiritual problems that can develop indifferent, ineffective missionaries. We need to get more of ourselves on the job.

Edward Everett Hale once said that the best education is to be perpetually thrilled by life. We need to get excited about what we are doing. And if we can just eliminate the possibilities of failure in the four areas discussed in this chapter we will likely be highly successful in our greatest enterprise. Then, when we have developed the positive dimensions of success in our own program, we will be great missionaries with lots of good investigators. We will have the ability to give many good solid discussions. We will have the skill for making the presentation itself effective. And all of this will come from an enthusiastic, convincing, pleasant, hard-working, good-looking missionary. We will also be outstanding leaders in other fields.

To find total volume, you multiply the dimensions. Multiply the four factors: adequate investigators, sufficient exposure, effective presentation, and an enthusiastic missionary, and you get missionary success.

Part Nine

Stewardship

The Power of Example
Responsibility
The Dust from Our Feet

Chapter 48

The Power of Example

It is a natural God-given law that as soon as anyone understands and accepts the message of the gospel he is given the responsibility of being its messenger. When we were born into this world of opportunities and privileges, it automatically became our responsibility to do our full share in helping to bring these opportunities and privileges about. That is, if we expect to participate in the beauties and advantages of our world, we must also share in those responsibilities on which these blessings depend. And when we become partakers of the benefits of the gospel, we also have the obligation to share them with others. Therefore it becomes one of our greatest responsibilities to learn how to effectively share the gospel's blessings.

The work of the Lord also offers us our greatest opportunity to promote our own personal interests. The Lord has said that if we should labor all our life in bringing but one soul unto him, great shall be our joy with that soul in the kingdom of our Father. He indicated that because our joy would be great with one soul brought unto him, it would be correspondingly greater still if we bring many souls unto him. (See D&C 18:15-16.) When we stand before God in the final judgment, every one of us will want to have the credit for having brought many souls unto him. We will want to have a lot of marks on the credit side of God's ledger and we will not want to have any on the debit side.

There are at least two good ways that we may improve our effectiveness as messengers. One is to know the principles of the gospel and be able to effectively transmit the message. The other is to be an inspiring personal example of righteousness and effectiveness. Thomas Carlyle once said, "We reform others when we walk uprightly." One of the greatest powers in the world is the convincing force of example. That example, of course, may go in either direction. It may be either good or bad.

Basically we do and say the things that we see other people do and hear them say. Example is the way we learn to walk, the way we learn to talk. That is the way we acquire our mannerisms. It is also the reason we dress as we do. Example determines the way we wear our hair and develop our other success procedures and techniques. If I had seen you eat your breakfast this morning in the United States I would probably have discovered that you operate with a fork in your right hand. But I was in Australia some time ago, and I noticed that people there eat with the fork in the left hand. If they had been born in China, however, they may not have eaten with a fork at all. Example is still largely the source of our manners, our morals, our convictions, and our attitudes.

The great apostle Paul once wrote to his young disciple Timothy and said, "Let no man despise thy youth; but be thou an example of the believers, in word, in conversation, in charity, in spirit, in faith, in purity." (1 Timothy 4:12.)

The apostle did not exhaust all the possibilities of the situation in this one short statement. We need to get some good examples in all the fields of industry, good judgment, and exemplary conduct. It is possible for us to drive more people away from the Church by our bad example than we bring in by our preaching. Someone has said:

I'd rather see a sermon than hear one any day;
I'd rather one should walk with me than merely tell the way.
The eye's a better pupil and more willing than the ear,
Fine counsel is confusing, but example's always clear.
And best of all the preachers are the men who live their
    creeds,

For to see good put in action is what everybody needs.
I soon can learn to do it if you'll let me see it done;
I can watch your hands in action, but your tongue too fast
may run.
And the lecture you deliver may be very wise and true,
But I'd rather get my lessons by observing what you do;
For I might misunderstand you and the high advice you give,
But there's no misunderstanding how you act and how you
live.

When we seek mastery over an idea, it is a pretty good procedure to get its contrasts so that we can understand it in both its positive and its negative sides.

We bear our testimonies to each other in our meetings, but we frequently act as though our testimony were a top-drawer military secret as far as our neighbors are concerned. We frequently quote the fact that the Church is growing very rapidly throughout the world. We should also be interested in the quality of that growth. Some time ago a book was published entitled *Meet The Mormons*, in which was described the growth and some of the accomplishments of individuals and groups in South America, the Orient, and other places. But the Mormons that the people we work with want to meet are their neighbors and business associates.

If we actually had an intimate acquaintance with all the Mormons in our own stake, we might find that some of us are not an attractive advertisement for the Church. This not only has an influence on our own salvation, but our bad example is the stumbling block which may cause many other people to lose the way despite our testimonies or our knowledge of the gospel.

I talked with a friend in California who said: "A member of your church is trying to get me to join your church. But why doesn't he pay me that five dollars that he has owed me for six months?" It is pretty difficult to persuade someone to believe a message when he believes the messenger to be immoral or dishonest.

If all Latter-day Saints fully lived the principles of the gospel and were good examples of righteousness and faith, we would have great numbers of people who would want to join the Church. There are many people who believe that the gospel of Jesus Christ is true. They believe in Joseph Smith, they believe in the Book of Mormon. But they say, "Why does my neighbor who is a member of your church do the kinds of things that he does?"

The thing the world wants to know is what kind of a neighbor a Mormon makes and how he behaves in sacrament meeting and how he pays his debts and how he treats his family. Our challenge is to conduct our services and our lives so that every nonmember will want to come to our ward for friendship and inspiration and quiet and peace and well-prepared sermons, and for associations with intelligent, pleasant, successful, devoted, and fully righteous disciples of the Master.

Chapter 49

Responsibility

God has given us a great many wonderful blessings: his own form as well as his own potential. He has given us many outright gifts. But he has also given us a large number of the most worthwhile potentialities, with the added privilege that we may develop them to our heart's content. In making us heirs of a divine destiny, he has put into our hands many unalienable rights. In addition to life, liberty, and the pursuit of happiness, we have been provided with all the raw materials necessary for developing the most godly characters. This may be supplemented by a wonderful variety of useful abilities and satisfying virtues.

One of God's greatest gifts to us is the gift of a language. Language is a unique gift. Man, of all God's creations, enjoys the exclusive use of this wonderful ability for communication. No other form of life has been equipped with a similar talent. Language gives us the ability to formulate ideas and think thoughts. We can sing and laugh and meditate and write and plan and dream and act and grow. God also equipped us with some wonderful abilities for imagination and ambition. And one of the finest of our abilities is to be able to transform our greatest ideas and our most satisfying ideals into virtues, character traits and accomplishments so that they become an actual part of us. That is, we may take words such as *faith, repentance, obedience, beauty, love* and *opportunity*, with all of their wealth of pleasure and meaning, and transfer them from our language into us.

One of the most profitable places to start this transformation is with that inspiring, exciting word *responsibility*. This is one of the great treasures, even in the language of God himself.

To have a sense of responsibility indicates that we can be absolutely depended upon, not only by others but also by ourselves and by God. By divine right, each of us is a free moral agent, capable of making his own choices on his own power and materializing his own ambitions. One who is responsible is fully accountable and is willing and able to deal effectively with consequences.

What a thrill goes with the contemplation of one who can be depended upon to be morally, financially and socially responsible! And this great trait of responsibility shines all the brighter when it is contrasted with some of its antonyms. The opposites of responsibility are all failure words such as *unaccountable, irresponsible* and *untrustworthy*. Certainly one of the greatest privileges of our lives is to completely eliminate from ourselves these low-meaning words and translate the greatest words into genuine traits of character and qualities of personality.

The apostle John recounts one part of creation when he says:

"In the beginning was the Word, and the Word was with God, and the Word was God. The same was in the beginning with God. All things were made by him; and without him was not anything made that was made. In him was life: and the life was the light of men. . . .

"And the Word was made flesh, and dwelt among us. (And we beheld his glory, the glory as of the only begotten of the Father,) full of grace and truth." (John 1:1-4, 14.)

I am not sure that I comprehend all that is here involved. Nor do I understand why the Savior is also called the Word. I do know that God referred to him as "the word of my power," and that he created this earth, and that he speaks the word of God to us. He is the embodiment of great words. How awful it would be to think of God without a language!

What could he be without the use of words and meanings? He has given us the ability to make his greatest words into flesh—our flesh.

Suppose that we work on this important word *responsibility* to make sure that our flesh will always carry the full amount of its significance and that under all circumstances we can always be trusted and depended upon. To develop this ability to its maximum, it might be helpful to think about men who have had this quality of responsibility developed most productively.

Everyone engaged in the work of the world should be responsible. Certainly those called to carry on the work of the Lord should be responsible. No one can allow any degree of irresponsibility in himself without causing serious losses to others and paying a terrible price himself. I am not very concerned that I will ever become a son of perdition or a murderer or an adulterer or a non-tithepayer or a dope addict or a liquor drinker. It is so easy, however, to allow just enough irresponsibility into our lives and our programs to make us fall down in our duty. The most important assignment that has ever been given to anyone is to carry some of the responsibility for the great enterprise in which God himself spends his entire time.

I attended a quarterly conference in a stake where 27 percent of all of the home teachers did no home teaching at all, either good or bad, during the entire month. Sixty-nine percent of the Latter-day Saint parents did not hold their family home evenings. At the conference we held four special leadership training meetings—one with the stake presidency on Saturday at 2:00 P.M., and the other three at 4:00 P.M. and 7:00 P.M. on Saturday and at 8:00 A.M. on Sunday morning. These meetings were attended by other top stake and ward leaders, including the stake presidency, members of the high council, all bishoprics and clerks, and all Melchizedek Priesthood officers. At every one of these meetings, 100 percent of the members of the stake presidency were present. All of the bishops were also present at every meeting. The high council fell down a little, however, and quite a number of bishops' counselors were absent. The leaders of the various elders quorums had a very low percentage of attendance. How can they succeed in their assignment if they do not even attend their meetings? Why shouldn't the presidents of the elders quorums be just as responsible as the stake presidency and the bishops?

In this stake there were 441 elders, 217 of whom had not attended a single meeting during the preceding month. They also had 311 prospective elders. These men were members of The Church of Jesus Christ of Latter-day Saints, but none of the members of this group had been ordained to the Melchizedek Priesthood because of a lack of interest, of activity, or of worthiness. These statistics were in contradiction to the promise inherent in accepting a call that they would all magnify their callings.

The purpose of leaders is to lead. That is the reason for their assignment. But many of these men were not magnifying their calling. They did not even attend the meetings which had been planned to help them promote the program of the Church for both themselves and their members. Almost every stake always has 100 percent of the members of the presidency in attendance. And if the members of the stake presidency can always be depended upon, why not the members of the elders quorum presidencies? And what effect does their weakness have upon their members? No nation could ever hope for a very effective army if only the top officers were faithful. It would greatly improve an army's fighting power if the captains, sergeants, and privates could also be depended upon.

Sometimes we go through the motions of accepting Church appointments without really accepting them. We accept the honor but not the responsibility. We promise to be faithful with our lips when our hearts and our industry are not parties to the agreement. Speaking of some sectarian leaders, the Lord said that they had limited themselves to "a form of godliness," but "they deny the power thereof." (See Joseph Smith 2:19.) We may frequently do about the same thing.

Sometimes we commit this very serious sin of irresponsibility because we just don't make up our minds not to be irresponsible. We should never accept any assignment in the work of the Lord or anywhere else unless we are willing to give it everything we've got. Otherwise we are misleading others and are molding deformity into ourselves.

When Socrates expressed his determination never to desert a responsibility, he was showing himself to be a wise man. He was being responsible. Jesus gave an inspired expression to this same idea when he said that we should serve God with our minds, our emotions, our determination, and our physical strength.

How does one serve God with his heart? That means with his devotion, his love, and his obedience. How does one serve God with his might? That is by the use of his determination, his willpower and his courage. How does one serve God with his mind? To do this, one needs to make a firm, solid decision on every point. A person can serve God with his mind by having a positive mental attitude and an ambition to do his studying, thinking, and planning. How does one serve God with his strength? That is done by using our physical activity in actually doing the job, and by using our resources in the follow-through to actually get the job done. We need to know our business and energetically follow it to success.

The scriptures as well as our logic are filled with reasons for success, and we may be absolutely certain that God will not approve of any fraction of irresponsibility that we allow to get into our Church work. Those who are fully determined in the work of the kingdom are the ones who will qualify for the celestial glory. Industry and responsibility are two of the component parts of being valiant, and valiance is one qualification for a celestial inheritance. (See D&C 76:79.)

On the night of Benedict Arnold's betrayal of his country, colonial headquarters was in a state of great confusion and uncertainty. No one knew just how far the betrayal had gone. General George Washington needed someone who was dependable, loyal, and courageous to stand guard during the balance of that long, awful night. In selecting the father of Daniel Webster for that assignment, he said, "Captain Webster, I can trust you."

What commendation could be greater than that? What

would give us more joy than to hear God say to us, "My son, I can trust you."

We pray, "Give us this day our daily bread." As leaders we need also to ask, "Help us to be responsible."

Chapter 50

The Dust
from Our Feet

It is likely that none of us will ever fully realize the tremendous privilege it is to live a mortal probation upon this earth, but this privilege carries some responsibilities that are actually frightening.

The Lord has referred to this period as our second estate. It connects our long antemortal existence in God's presence with our eternal lives when, as we hope, we return to his presence. It is not only an all-important connecting link, but it determines and conditions forever everything that will come after it.

This life is the time when we determine whether we will live forever with God himself and other celestial beings in the highest heaven, whether we will suffer in regret and torment with the most evil associates in the lowest hell, or whether we will exist in a situation somewhere between those two extremes. Thus this life presents us with the most fantastic opportunities that could possibly be conceived even by an infinite mind, and at the same time we have hanging over our heads an awful degradation if we totally fail.

We have not arrived at this situation without the means of helping ourselves. We brought with us from our antemortal estate a directing conscience. Our first mortal ancestors ate the fruit from the tree of the knowledge of good and evil, and we have inherited a fundamental, instinctive knowledge of what is right and wrong which will either exalt or condemn us.

In the antemortal council in heaven, Lucifer, a brilliant son of the morning, rebelled against God and drew away one-third of all the hosts of heaven after him. Now the time is near at hand when he will be forever segregated and confined in hell with his companions in evil. But some others of those who were present in the council of heaven have loved Satan more than God in this life, and they will share his dreadful fate.

In our antemortal lives we walked by sight. We have all seen God. He is our father. We lived with him. But in this life we are supposed to learn to walk a little way by faith. Mortality is a period when we are tested and proven and tried. To enable us to know the right, God has given us an important set of directions in the holy scriptures telling us exactly what we should and should not do. But our world furnishes us with a long sad history in which we have disregarded the word of the Lord. Some have defied him, some have disobeyed him, some have scoffed at him, some have disbelieved in him, and some have ignored him.

In the meridian of time, the Son of God organized his Church and placed in it inspired men to help us solve our problems. Just before his ascension into heaven from the Mount of Olives, he gave his final commission to those members of the Twelve who stood at his feet. He directed them to carry his message to everyone upon the earth. He said, "He that believeth and is baptized shall be saved; but he that believeth not shall be damned." (Mark 16:16.)

In this divine commandment there are two great factors involved. One is the command to carry the message to every nation, kindred, tongue, and people. The other is that everyone is obligated to hear and believe the message and obey the commandments. There are some who imagine that they come into this life foolishly and irresponsibly free to do as they choose. They feel that they may disobey, or disbelieve, or listen not at all, or do according to their own whim. This is a serious mistake.

The Lord said to the Twelve: "And whosoever shall not

receive you, nor hear your words, when ye depart out of that house or city, shake off the dust of your feet [against them]. Verily I say unto you, It shall be more tolerable for the land of Sodom and Gomorrha in the day of judgment, than for that city." (Matthew 10:14-15.) Both Mark and Luke say approximately the same thing as Matthew, that the messengers of the Lord should shake off the dust of their feet as a testimony against those who refuse to hear the message.

In our own dispensation the Lord has given similar instructions:

"He that receiveth you not, go away from him alone by yourselves, and cleanse your feet even with water, pure water, whether in heat or in cold, and bear testimony of it unto your Father which is in heaven, and return not again unto that man.

"And in whatsoever village or city ye enter, do likewise.

"Nevertheless, search diligently and spare not; and wo unto that house, or that village or city that rejecteth you, or your words, or your testimony concerning me.

"For I, the Almighty, have laid my hands upon the nations, to scourge them for their wickedness.

"And plagues shall go forth, and they shall not be taken from the earth until I have completed my work, which shall be cut short in righteousness." (D&C 84:92-94, 96-97.)

To ceremoniously shake the dust from one's feet as a testimony against another was understood by the Jews to symbolize cessation of fellowship and a renunciation by the messenger of all responsibility for consequences that might follow. By the Lord's instructions to his apostles it became an ordinance of accusation and testimony, as cited above. Again, the Lord has similarly directed his authorized servants in our day to so testify against those who willfully and maliciously oppose the truth when authoritatively presented.

"And in whatsoever place ye shall enter, and they receive you not in my name, ye shall leave a cursing instead of a blessing, by casting off the dust of your feet against them as a testimony, and cleansing your feet by the wayside." (D&C 24:15.)

This ceremony of relieving oneself of the responsibility

might be considered similar to that employed by Pilate when he was asked to judge the Son of God himself, even though he could not truly absolve himself of blame. He gave his judgment by saying, "I find no fault in this man." (Luke 23:4.) But the Jews clamored for the Savior's death, so Pilate took a basin of water "and washed his hands before the multitude, saying, I am innocent of the blood of this just person: see ye to it." (Matthew 27:24.) Thus we commonly use the phrase, "I wash my hands of it," meaning, "I will accept no further responsibility for it."

The responsibility of testifying before the Lord by this accusing symbol is so great that the means may be employed only under unusual and extreme conditions as the Spirit of the Lord may direct. But this has been a responsibility of a qualified messenger since the beginning, and it has some frightening overtones not only for the one who hears the message but for the one who speaks it.

Having been a salesman, I know that there are some sales talks that are so weak and illogical that it would be difficult for one to be converted by them even if he wanted to be. Under some circumstances, then, the curse might recoil and light on the head of him who set it in motion. In the days of Moses, the Lord said to the children of Israel: "Behold, I set before you this day a blessing and a curse; a blessing, if ye obey the commandments of the Lord your God, which I command you this day: and a curse, if ye will not obey the commandments of the Lord your God, but turn aside out of the way which I command you this day, to go after other gods, which ye have not known." (Deuteronomy 11:26-28.)

The awesome responsibility does not apply merely to those who are supposed to hear. It also applies with equal or even greater severity to those who are supposed to testify. Several hundred years before the coming of the Savior, God said to the prophet Ezekiel:

"So thou, O son of man, I have set thee a watchman unto the house of Israel; therefore thou shalt hear the word at my mouth, and warn them from me.

"When I say unto the wicked, O wicked man, thou shalt surely die; if thou dost not speak to warn the wicked from his way, that wicked man shall die in his iniquity, but his blood will I require at thine hand.

"Nevertheless, if thou warn the wicked of his way to turn from it; if he do not turn from his way, he shall die in his iniquity; but thou hast delivered thy soul." (Ezekiel 33:7-9.)

This drastic idea concerning the responsibility of leadership certainly agrees with the direction given by the Lord to the people who lived in ancient America over five hundred years before the coming of Christ. About this the prophet Jacob said:

"For I, Jacob, and my brother Joseph had been consecrated priests and teachers of this people, by the hand of Nephi.

"And we did magnify our office unto the Lord, taking upon us the responsibility, answering the sins of the people upon our heads if we did not teach them the word of God *with all diligence*; wherefore, by laboring with our might their blood might not come upon our garments; otherwise their blood would come upon our garments, and we would not be found spotless at the last day." (Jacob 1:18-19. Italics added.)

It should be stimulating to those of us who are called to serve as the Lord's ministers to know of the tremendous importance of this message. The eternal life of both the messenger and the hearer depends upon it. Certainly if one will not hear, a very unpleasant consequence is bound to follow. But there is another important part of this proposition, one which might be summed up in Jeremiah's words to King Zedekiah: "Obey, I beseech thee, the voice of the Lord . . . and thy soul shall live." (Jeremiah 38:20.)

It is likely that all missionary work comes under one of these two headings: Number one, we must understand the tremendous importance of the great message of righteousness which we bear. The gospel has been restored to the earth in our day with all the information and power necessary to get people into the celestial kingdom. Number two, important as the message is, it demands a great messenger. It is pretty difficult for anyone to believe the message when he doesn't have confidence in and affection for the messenger. It is very hard for the messenger to deliver a message that he himself doesn't understand very well or isn't a master of or doesn't have perfect convictions about. It would be a bit ridiculous for a person to go around shaking off the dust of his feet against those people to whom he had made a very weak and unconvincing presentation.

If this is a divine procedure (to shake off the dust of our feet against nonmembers of the Church who do not accept the message), it seems as though it would be even more valid to shake off the dust of our feet against the inactive members of the Church, those who are visited every month by the home teachers yet continue month after month to ignore the commandments. I think, however, before I shook off the dust of my feet against nonmembers or members, I would first like to hear a recording of my missionary discussions or my home teaching lessons to see if I thought they would hold up before the Lord as valid reasons for conversion or as capable of arousing real activity. If a recording were made of my home teaching discussions or my family home evening teachings, would I be willing to have someone else condemned because of the presentation I had made? Alternatively, if the situation were reversed and I were on trial for my eternal exaltation, would I think it fair that I should be condemned by a message with no more power than my own?

There are serious consequences for us as we stamp off the dust of our feet against those who have not followed our teachings. Certainly the Lord is serious about the importance of our teaching, and I am sure he doesn't want to have us play games with him or with the souls of his other children. They must be effectively warned, however, and be prepared to suffer the consequences of disobedience.

This places a tremendous responsibility upon the messenger to make the message clear and convincing and enthusiastic. With the conversions that will result, a smaller number of people will be required to suffer. But one of the greatest regrets that I can conceive would be that, because of my weakness and my inability to make an effective presentation, others would suffer eternally.

The second Article of Faith says, "We believe that men will be punished for their own sins, and not for Adam's transgression." Every day I pray to God that no one will be punished because I have shaken off the dust of my feet against someone whom I did not give a proper chance to hear the message.

Part Ten

A Summary
of Success

Getting and Giving

Chapter 51

Getting and Giving

There are a great many purposes that must be served and a great many things that we should get if we are to make our lives successful. It is very important that we get an education, that we get married, that we get a job, that we build in ourselves a basic godly character with a powerful supporting ambition. Our mortality is a time when we are added upon with these beautiful, wonderful bodies of flesh and bones without which we could never have a fullness of joy either here or hereafter. This is also a place where we organize a family and rear our children in righteousness and teach them those fundamental laws leading to success and happiness. We must acquire the talents and the inspiration to effectively carry forward our share of the work of the world as well as that part of the work of the Lord that we are given to do.

Solomon said, "Wisdom is the principal thing; therefore get wisdom: and with all thy getting get understanding." (Proverbs 4:7.) With all our getting, we should also get faith and ambition and self-control. We ought to build good attitudes, develop effective personality traits, acquire useful skills, and develop good habits. A good life must have some effective social, mental, and spiritual abilities. A man must be able to provide for the material needs of himself and his family with some left over to provide for those who are unable to take care of themselves.

On several occasions during our human history the Lord has instituted the united order, wherein everyone works to the limit of his ability to supply the needs of other members of the order. It seems that this has never worked very well for long periods, partly because of the tendency on the part of some to let the ambitious and the industrious carry too much of the load. Our more usual system of individual enterprise has advantages in that, under some circumstances, it fosters greater personal initiative. But regardless of what system we employ in our getting, we need another important set of procedures for giving, and these may be equally as important.

The Psalmist wrote, "It is a good thing to give thanks unto the Lord." (Psalm 92:1.) This is true for many reasons. The more we understand the important benefits we have received from God, the greater our own lives will be. As we recount our blessings, we increase them. As we express our gratitude, we grow better. It is also good to give thanks to our parents and our wives and our children and our employer and our friends. And as it is good to give thanks to others, so it is also good to give them information and encouragement and a helping hand. It is good to pay our tithing and our fast offerings. One of the important areas where a great human being may distinguish himself is as a giver of good things. We can give people enthusiasm and self-confidence and faith. The greatest power in the world is the power of example, and by what we do we can give people happiness and righteousness and other virtues which can lead them to the celestial kingdom.

As I walked down the street on one occasion, I met a friend of mine. We shook hands and joked and visited and laughed. He had a friendly, genial sparkle in his eye, and we had a fine background of friendship. I put my arm around him and expressed to him my appreciation and commendation. I suppose this interview lasted for a total of a minute and a half, but when I went on down the street, I thought, "My, how much better I feel." It seemed to me as though I was now standing ten feet tall. He had brightened my day and made life itself seem more worthwhile. I had actually absorbed part of my friend.

In thinking about what my friend had given me, I

thought of some of the things that other people have to give. Think what a great parent can give. Think what a faithful bishop can give. Think of the magnificent gifts in the possession of a good Scoutmaster or a resourceful home teacher or an enthusiastic missionary. Each great human being who is a capable getter should also be a generous and effective giver. Each of us has a magnificent fortune to share with others which has a magic quality. With each gift we give, the remaining total is increased. We learn to do by doing, and as a missionary exercises his testimony for the benefit of others his testimony itself increases. And so does his virtue, and his knowledge and his ambition. This means that, with every good deed done, a profit is made available to everyone involved.

Jesus said, "It is more blessed to give than to receive." If a parent makes a child happy at Christmas time, who gets the most benefit, the giver or the receiver? When we send out a benefit, it always comes back to us multiplied. When we plant our seeds in good earth, we always get them back, some thirtyfold, some sixtyfold, and some a hundredfold.

Someone has said that only that which we give we keep. That which we keep we lose. I know a twelve-year-old deacon who, out of his earnings as a newspaper boy, gave $150 to help build the Los Angeles Temple. It will always be true, even during the Millennium, that this deacon has an investment in the great function served by this house of the Lord. If he had kept the money it probably would have been spent and thus lost to him. Likewise when a returned missionary hoards the scriptures he has learned and doesn't continue to share his message with others, the message, the scriptures, and even his testimony may eventually be lost to him.

Many years ago I heard a successful businessman say that everyone has an obligation every time he meets any other person to give him something. Everyone you meet during the day should be better off because of you. Every time an idea goes through our minds or an emotion goes through our hearts or a feeling of admiration lifts up our souls, we are modified forever.

Oliver Wendell Holmes once said that a mind once

stretched by a new idea never returns to its original dimensions. The thought itself may pass beyond our ability to recall, but because of its passage, we ourselves will never be the same.

John D. Rockefeller, the world's first billionaire, formed this philosophy of giving: Every morning as he began the day, he filled his pockets full of brand new silver dimes; and everybody that he met during the day received from him a ten-cent silver coin. The dimes were accumulated by his great ability as an organizer and a thinker. His wonderful energy, resourcefulness and industry created a great industrial empire that not only produced millions of dollars to pay taxes, establish philanthropies, and do good by way of direct gifts, but also furnished employment for many thousands and helped to develop valuable United States resources. Rockefeller became a symbol that motivated the imagination and the industry of the entire world.

Someone has said that the only real gifts are those wherein we give of ourselves and that all other things are mere apologies for gifts. Mr. Rockefeller was born with a certain amount of time and energy at his disposal to be expended as he desired. He transformed his energy into many great accomplishments, some of which were represented by material things and a great deal more by those qualities of ambition, labor and enthusiasm by which wealth is always produced. He transformed his life's energy and his allotment of time into those things that could be made negotiable.

Somebody said that wealth is preserved labor. It is stored up accomplishment, it is industry made negotiable, it is material prosperity which can be transferred to someone else. It represents benefits that may be passed on and negotiated by others living in distant places and other ages.

John D. Rockefeller was a getter but he was also a giver. He became a symbol of success. Everyone who wants to give must first learn to get. A great teacher must get before she gives. A successful home teacher should be loaded with ideas and spirituality and good deeds, and he must have his spiritual pockets full of things that are transferable and negotiable in other lives.

Think how dreadful it would be to have a Scoutmaster who had nothing to give to the members of his troop. Or think what a tragedy for parents to go to their family home evening session empty-handed, with nothing to give either in their pockets or in the kitchen or in their minds or in their hearts. The most serious kind of poverty is that devastating condition of the spirit.

Someone wrote a great poem in which he said that everyone ought to leave the world richer than he found it, whether by an improved poppy, a perfected poem, or a rescued soul. We should also leave each day better than we found it. And each person we meet should be left richer than he was before we came along.

I know of a very popular man who always gets along well with his grandchildren. On one occasion, in explaining his success, he said he thought it was because he always had a bag full of peppermints in his pockets when he went to see his grandchildren. But he also had some peppermints in his mind and some peppermints in his heart and some peppermints in his enthusiasm. God also has a pocketful of peppermints.

It is said that, in becoming a millionaire, Andrew Carnegie made thirty-eight other men millionaires. No one can do well without pulling others up with him, and no one can go broke or become morally bankrupt without dragging others down.

Some time ago I heard a successful businessman tell of the large number of people who sent him messages saying, "I merely want to have some of your time." This businessman was a great philanthropist. He gave a great deal of money away. He also gave a lot of his time in some kind of service. But these people wanted him to endorse or assist them in some kind of impractical enterprise, and they felt that his time spent in talking about these schemes was of no consequence.

I don't know exactly, but I imagine that fifteen minutes of his time would have been worth several hundred dollars in cash. In one way, that would not be true of everyone, but in another way it is. Time is all that we have; and we can save or lose our souls, depending upon how we spend our time. From that point of view, everybody's time may be worth more than a thousand dollars a minute. What a tragic waste if as a Church leader or other worker I use the valuable time of the families that I visit in idle conversation about the weather or politics or other trivia that I know very little about and that gets them nowhere! On the other hand, think how profitable a resourceful Church leader or other worker could make this period by always having available for giving some great scriptural truth, some stimulating experience, some uplifting philosophy, some well-prepared enthusiasm, or even the excitement of a little humor.

We are all familiar with the analogy of the two seas in Palestine, the Sea of Galilee and the Dead Sea. The first is fresh, the home of fish, its waters surrounded by the green of grass and trees and by the nests of birds, its banks the playground of children. Above the other sea the air is heavy; no fish dwell in its waters, humans avoid it if at all possible, and neither bird nor beast nor man will drink there. The difference is not in the soil nor the countryside. The river Jordan supplies them both, but the Sea of Galilee does not keep the water it receives. It gives it all out again. The Dead Sea is dead because it hoards every drop it gets.

All good Church workers and all great human beings and all those who hope to be successful in life must be getters. But we must also be givers. We have a great obligation to give something to everyone we meet on every occasion, and it should be something greater than a dime.

Index